T0328553

JFK: Assassination Rehearsal

JFK: Assassination Rehearsal

Nick M. Nero

Introduction by Dr. James H. Fetzer

The never-before-told story
of the rehearsal for the assassination of JFK
at the Doral Country Club in Miami, and
the connection between the Bay of Pigs, the assassinations of JFK,
MLK, and RFK, Chappaquiddick and Watergate

Algora Publishing
New York

Library of Congress Cataloging-in-Publication Data —

Nero, Nick M.
  JFK: assassination rehearsal / Nick M. Nero ; introduction by Dr. James H. Fetzer.
    pages cm
  Includes bibliographical references and index.
    ISBN 978-1-62894-081-7 (soft cover: alk. paper) — ISBN 978-1-62894-082-4
(hard cover: alk. paper) — ISBN 978-1-62894-083-1 (ebook) 1. Kennedy, John F. (John
Fitzgerald), 1917-1963—Assassination. 2. Conspiracies—United States—History—20th
century. I. Title.
  E842.9.N418 2014
  973.922092—dc23
                              2014025368

Front Cover: Image: JFK (Wikimedia Commons)

Printed in the United States

Acknowledgments

I need and wish to thank the following individuals for their help, encouragement, faith, love and friendship.

Rosemary Nero, my wife
Patrick Hennelly, my friend
Kristina Nero Rodriguez, my niece
Patti Fazzino, my cousin
David Whittaker, my friend
Liz Wilmes, my friend
Lora Nigro, my cousin
David Luhrssen, my friend
Patricia Barker Foster, my friend
Kevin Rutkowski, my cousin-in-law

Table of Contents

Foreword

In the aftermath of November 22, 1963, American consciousness began to shift, often in perilous ways. The immediate, shocked reaction to the assassination of John F. Kennedy is not surprising. He was a popular president who embodied a new spirit in U.S. politics and in American life, and his murder seemed an affront to the nation's hopes for a better future. But Presidential assassinations had occurred before and, with the exception of Abraham Lincoln's death at the end of the Civil War, they left no enduring impression on the public imagination.

Ultimately, this change in consciousness had less to do with the assassination of JFK than with the official response to his murder. The report issued by the Warren Commission in September 1964 satisfied almost no one at the time and the passage of half a century has done nothing to quell either the public's dissatisfaction with its explanation nor its search for a missing truth. Consciousness shifted when a distinguished bi-partisan body, headed by the Chief Justice of the U.S. Supreme Court and aided by the all-seeing FBI director J. Edgar Hoover, issued conclusions most people found incredible. On the night the Warren Commission's findings were announced, CBS News anchor Walter Cronkite, the avuncular voice of common sense and good judgment, echoed popular sentiment by saying, "Perhaps there will forever be questions of substance and detail." He added: "We are the jury—all of us."

The jury of public opinion has continually issued its verdicts on the Kennedy assassination, even if the court of establishment media and academia continues to set those rulings aside. The result, beginning in the 1960s and continuing through the present, is the proliferation not only of "conspiracy theories" relating to the assassination of JFK and other public figures, but a host of alternative narratives seeking to explain the deep workings of an unsettled society whose official spokespeople and gatekeepers appear dishonest. In the minds of many Americans, *They*—usually identified as a cabal of powerful political and financial interests—are concealing something nefarious.

The widespread rejection of the Warren Report was only the beginning. By the end of the twentieth century large constituencies had formed in America backing a plethora of alternative theories that run contrary to official explanations. Witness such seemingly disparate phenomena as the popularity of *The X-Files* and the unwillingness of some Americans to believe that Barack Obama is a U.S. citizen (and not a Muslim). Despite the lunacy of some of the conspiracy theories that proliferated in the wake of the massive breakdown in public trust after the Warren Report, there remain intractable problems surrounding the official explanation of the Kennedy assassination. Even JFK's successor and the man who commissioned the Warren Report, Lyndon B. Johnson, raised doubts. Asked during a 1970 interview whether the assassination resulted from an "international conspiracy," he replied that he had "not completely discounted the possibility." Eight years later the House Select Committee on Assassinations, impaneled to investigate suspicions surrounding the murder of JFK as well as Martin Luther King Jr., ruled there was a probability of a conspiracy behind the 1963 assassination in Dallas. Much of the information gathered by the Warren Commission remains sealed in the National Archives. Documents that have been released are redacted in many places. Was the Warren Commission the puppet of hidden masters—or were they worried that the truth might undermine confidence in American institutions? If the latter, then the Commission failed in its objective. Confidence in most public institutions and public leaders declined after the mid-1960s and remains low.

November 22, 1963, was the turning point.

Many theories have been advanced to explain the Kennedy assassination and the response of the Warren Commission, and many (though not all) of the ideas presented by Nick Nero have surfaced in previous speculation on the murder of JFK, RFK, and MLK. What separates Nero from many earlier commentators are the details in his proposal for an overarching narrative connecting many of the most startling events of the 1960s. He proposes a unified field theory, as physicists call their search for a "theory of everything" to explain the workings of the cosmos, that finds the common basis for the Bay of Pigs, the assassination of the Kennedys and King, and even the scandals of Chappaquiddick and Watergate. In the wake of JFK's death and the doubtful conclusions of the Warren Commission, all of these events have provoked their own conspiratorial narratives. Nero links them to the activities of a host of individuals, including Frank Sturgis, E. Howard Hunt, David Morales, and Lyndon B. Johnson, as well as the FBI and CIA, the Mafia, the Joint Chiefs of Staff, and Texas oil interests. All have been implicated in previously published accounts, but Nero does Herculean work in marshaling a comprehensive set of conspirators and their motives and opportunities. In addition, Nero has sketched in several events that have eluded previous researchers, including a rehearsal for the assassination of JFK at a Miami country club in the weeks before November 22, 1963.

The fiftieth anniversary of these events has sparked a flurry of renewed interest in the story behind the official story. In a January 2013 interview with Charlie Rose, Robert Kennedy Jr. said that his father regarded the Warren Report as a "shoddy" piece of work and hired investigators who found evidence of Mob ties to the accused gunman, Lee Harvey Oswald, and his assassin, Jack Ruby. RFK did not live long enough to reveal whatever he learned or came to suspect about this turning point in the consciousness America and much of the world.

"Our darkest fantasies were pushing at a half-open bathroom door as Marilyn Monroe lay drugged among the fading bubbles," British author J.G. Ballard wrote of the era. The circle of characters in this story is as wide as in any novel, and Hollywood's biggest star was among them. The story would be fantastic as fiction, but the surviving facts are disturbing and compelling.

David Luhrssen
January 2013

David Luhrssen is a cultural historian and author of *Hammer of the Gods: Thule Society and the Origins of Nazism, Changing Times: The Life of Barack Obama*, and other books.

INTRODUCTION

By James H. Fetzer, Ph.D.

The idea of a rehearsal for the assassination of JFK is not far-fetched—Nick Nero's account makes a very plausible case based upon the death-bed confession of his marine-hero cousin, Ben Fazzino, whose own life story weaves together his associations with the CIA, Frank Sturgis, Che Guevara, Meyer Lansky, Santos Trafficante and eventually LBJ with the Bay of Pigs, the deaths of JFK, MLK, and RFK up to the Chappaquiddick event and the Watergate break-in.

There were attempts to assassinate JFK in Miami and in Chicago before they succeeded in Dallas. In Miami, he was flown to his destination by helicopter, circumventing the intended crime scene. In Chicago, a plot was broken up based upon information from a source identified as "Lee." And in Dallas, there have even been reports of rifle shots heard in Dealey Plaza the night before the assassination, which have never been confirmed, but which would not be especially surprising—a final "dress rehearsal" with sound effects.

Waggoner Carr, Attorney General of Texas, launched his own investigation and found that Lee Oswald was an informant for the FBI, that he had informant Number 179 and that he was being paid $200 a month right up to the time of the assassination. In one of the great ironies of the case, the federal government has never released Oswald's W-2 forms, which can only be for the obvious reason they would have revealed those payments by the FBI. It cannot be because they don't know where to find them.

There are more than 15 indications of Secret Service complicity in setting JFK up for the hit, where two agents were left behind at Love Field, the vehicles in the motorcade were all in the wrong order—with JFK out front, when he should have been in the middle—and the cars were of different makes, models and colors, which made it possible for the conspirators to know who was where during the procession. Nothing was left to chance.

The crowd was allowed to spill out into the street and open windows were not covered. The motorcade route was changed not long before the event, which is something that is never done so that security officials can insure knowledge of the occupants of each building along the way. The motorcycle escort was cut down to four and they were instructed not to ride ahead of the rear wheels. One officer complained it was "the damnedest formation" he had ever seen. Even the 110-degree turn onto Elm Street was in violation of Secret Service protocol.

The driver, William Greer, pulled the limo to the left and to a halt after bullets had begun to be fired. This insured that JFK would be killed. He had already been hit by a shot passing through the windshield that hit him in the throat and by another that hit him in the back. Tiny shards of glass from the windshield punctured his face. During the stop, he was hit twice in the head: once from behind; he fell forward. As Jackie eased him back up and was looking at his face, he was hit in the right temple by a frangible or exploding bullet.

That set up shock waves blowing about half his brains out his already weakened cranium to the left/rear with such force that Dallas Motorcycle Escort Officer Bobby Hargis, riding to the left/rear, when impacted with the debris, initially thought that he himself had been shot. There are some who believe that Greer might have fired that shot, because he was sitting to the left/front of JFK, but had that been the case those brains would have been blown out to the right/rear rather than to the left.

Killing Kennedy was not the problem, but covering it up to conceal the true causes and purposes of his death and to make sure that those who were responsible would never be held to account posed the challenge. To this end, the body was forcibly stolen from Dallas and removed from the bronze casket, probably during the swearing in of LBJ, which was completely unnecessary but afforded the opportunity to move the body to a compartment in the plane from which it would be removed when Air Force One landed at Andrews Field. Nero endorses an alternative account, suggesting this happened during the exchange of luggage from Air Force Two—one of a few points on which we diverge.

We now know that the body was taken to Walter Reed Army Hospital, where the best forensic pathologists in the US military removed metal fragments that would have revealed multiple shots from different locations. It was placed in a body bag and taken to the morgue at Bethesda Naval Hospital in a black Cadillac hearse. When the entourage with the bronze casket in a gray Pontiac ambulance arrived, Jerrol Custer, the Navy technician who had taken the X-rays, was surprised because he was already headed upstairs to develop the X-rays he had taken during a pre-autopsy moments earlier, before the autopsy had begun.

The conspirators would alter the X-rays to conceal a massive blow-out to the back of his head and add a 6.5mm metallic slice to implicate an obscure Italian World War II carbine, which was known as "the humanitarian rifle" for never actually harming anyone on purpose. After patching the blow-out, there was nowhere for his brains to have gone, so they substituted another brain—which was virtually intact—for that of JFK. And they made sure the home movies were revised to support the "official account."

Oswald was framed by fabricating the "backyard photographs" and altering his image in the doorway of the Texas School Book Depository, where professional AP photographer James "Ike" Altgens had captured him on film. It would take nearly 50 years to expose this deception, but the proof is now overwhelming. See "JFK Part 1: A National Security Event—Oswald didn't do it" and "JFK Part II: A National Security Event—How it was done," for some of the most important evidence.

The execution appears to have been carried out by shooters at six different locations, one of whom was a Dallas Deputy Sheriff, another an anti-Castro Cuban, the third worked for the CIA, the fourth was a Dallas Police Officer, the 5th an Air Force expert, and the 6th was LBJ's personal hit man, all of them tied together in a kind of blood oath, as I explain in a study of the shooting sequence, "What happened to JFK—and why it matters today."

Lyndon preempted other investigations, including Senate and House inquiries as well as that by Waggoner Carr, by creating the Warren Commission, which dutifully concluded that the crime had been committed by a lone assassin, who had fired three shots from the 6th floor of the Texas School Book Depository. None of it was true: there had been 8, 9 or 10 shots—JFK was hit 4 times, Connally from 1 to 3, with 3 misses—while the "magic bullet" theory is not even anatomically possible (see "Reasoning about Assassinations"). The American public would have been dumbfounded by the very idea that elements of its own government would have murdered its president.

The documents and records gathered by the commission were locked away for 75 years on the ground of "national security". No one pointed out that, if The Warren Report was true and the assassination had been done by a lone, demented gunman, then there was no national security dimension. Only after Oliver Stone's "JFK" had generated a resurgence of interest in the case did Congress pass a JFK Records Act, which created a five-member panel to declassify documents and records, leading to the release of some 60,000 of them—but not including the X-rays.

JFK had threatened to shatter the CIA "into a thousand pieces." He had offended the Joint Chiefs by refusing to invade Cuba against their unanimous recommendation and by signing an above-ground test ban treaty with the Soviet Union, against their unanimous opposition. Now he was removing our forces from Vietnam, where the Joint Chiefs believed that a stand had to be taken against the expansion of international, godless Communism.

Kennedy had antagonized big business by standing up to the steel industry and had directed the Department of Treasury to print tens of millions in United States notes, on the ground that it was ridiculous for the country to pay a private consortium of banks for the privilege. He had Bobby cracking down on organized crime and was planning to cut the Oil Depletion Allowance. Anti-Castro Cubans despised him and LBJ obsessively wanted to become "the president of all the people."

The deaths of JFK, MLK and RFK were comparable insofar as the CIA, the FBI, the Mafia and local law enforcement all appear to have been profoundly involved in each case. Although most Americans still do not know it, in the case of MLK, a civil trial was eventually held that convicted a local Memphis man of complicity in the crime. He was not James Earl Ray, but Lloyd Jowers, one of several who were involved. Nor did Sirhan Sirhan kill Bobby: he was shot three or four times from behind, while Sirhan was in front of him. And Sirhan appears to have been under hypnosis. A CIA-related physician even boasted of having hypnotized him.

The celebrated medical examiner, Thomas Noguchi, M.D., concluded that RFK had been killed by a shot that entered behind his right ear from a distance of about an inch and a half, while Sirhan was never closer than three feet in front of his body. The LAPD even dismantled the pantry where the shooting had taken place and destroyed it on the ground that the wooden beams and other structures would not fit into 3" x 5" card files. When the coroner's report contradicted the police report, astonishingly, the coroner was fired!

The assassinations of the 1960s moved this country to the right to an extent from which it has yet to recover. The emergence of principled, intelligent and charismatic leaders is by itself unusual and unexpected. The loss of JFK, MLK and RFK in short order effectively decapitated the liberal movement in the US and led to a succession of presidents who would never have held that office but for their demise, including LBJ, Nixon, Ford, and George H.W. Bush, all of whom were involved in the death of JFK or—in the case of Ford—in its cover up. And "W" would never have been taken seriously but for his father's term in office.

Before I encountered Nick Nero, it had crossed my mind how important it would be to have a book that traced these developments at just the right level to make them accessible to the American public. I was therefore astonished to discover that he had authored such a book by weaving together a personal odyssey with an historical inquiry. It conveys in an accessible and easily readable way what happened to our country during that turbulent time and achieves just the right blend of scholarly research, practical organization, and artful writing. It is thus my profound pleasure to recommend *JFK: ASSASSINATION REHEARSAL* to the nation as a book every American deserves—and needs—to read.

James H. Fetzer, Ph.D.
February 2013

James H. Fetzer, a former Marine Corps officer, is McKnight Professor Emeritus at the University of Minnesota Duluth. He organized a research group consisting of the best qualified experts to study the death of JFK in 1992 and has published three collections of expert studies—*Assassination Science (1998)*, *Murder In Dealey Plaza* (2000), and *The Great Zapruder Film Hoax (2003)*—and chaired or co-chaired four national conferences on the assassination (Minneapolis 1999, Dallas 2000, Dallas 2001, and Duluth 2003). He has given hundreds of interviews and presentations on JFK.

PROLOGUE

An urgent call came unexpectedly, and packing quickly, I was en route to Florida from O'Hare within hours.

My cousin Patti met me and we drove to her parents' house. A typical Florida ranch, except larger, it was just as I remembered it from many delightful visits in my youth. Almost speechless with grief, we commiserated and shared old memories through looks and gestures.

Patti led me past the flowery kimono under glass on the wall opposite the parlor. It was as impressive as ever, with large black stylized chrysanthemums on a field of crimson. It had been Ben's wedding gift to Hazel, bought while serving in Peking, China. Madam Chiang Kai-shek, one of the richest and most powerful women in the world at the time, had picked it out for him. It was dazzling in its sensual, silky splendor. The specter of legendary Madam Chiang Kai-shek's role covered the kimono with a palpable aura and an almost visible patina of light.

Hazel had had a stroke a few years back and Ben had moved to a spare bedroom close to the garage, so he could come and go without disturbing her. Patti gently turned me, pointing toward Ben's bedroom down the hall as she followed close behind, gently moving in sync with my rhythm and excitement, her fingertips on my back. I did not recognize the converted bedroom or the two marines sitting in the far corner, chatting and joking with Ben. But I recognized my older cousin's broad smile.

"Hi, Uncle Ben, it's been a while," I said, hopefully upbeat.

Ben smiled that huge smile I remembered so well and flashed his gold tooth.

"Uncle" Ben always flashed it when he taught me a life lesson—or when he was just glad to see me. Memories came flooding back—the time he taught me never to gamble by betting me my last quarter that "Heads I win, tails you lose." It was the last dime or quarter I ever bet or lost; the time he showed me how to handle a pistol and remove the chamber before storing it; the time he showed me a revolver in his glove compartment. A revolver he respected like a practiced pro.

"Sorry, I can't get up," he said grinning, "But I'm glad you came. I knew you would."

I shrugged. How could I not come for the man who took me by the shoulders and walked me down the funeral home aisle to say good-bye to my father for the last time?

Patti adjusted the nasal oxygen lines which kept falling off her father's ears. I slid the tightening clip up an inch under his chin trying, to be helpful.

"Hi, I'm Nick Nero—I didn't mean to interrupt," I said to his two marine friends, one of whom was a high-level officer.

"No problem, sir," they said, introducing themselves by rank and last name, without shaking hands. I half-nodded, half-held out my hand before lamely pulling it back.

Straightening up, military style, they marched to the door. "Ben, we'll see you tomorrow. Some of the others are probably on their way here now. Semper Fi, soldier." They saluted—half toward Ben and half toward the Marine Corps flag behind the low headboard. I turned and caught a glimpse of the Marine Corps flag on the wall next to the Japanese flag. I remembered them both. They were prized possessions. The Marine Corps flag was standard. The other was a rare Japanese regimental flag, not like the usual Japanese flags with a rising sun in the center and rays emanating to the edges. This one was as special as it looked. It had once belonged to Colonel Konpo, aide to Major General Kosuke Wada.[1] Now it was Ben's. The story of his heroism behind enemy lines is detailed in the appendix.

I grew up calling him "Uncle" out of respect, although he was really my older, second cousin, my father being his first cousin. In some ways I was the son he never had. In reality, I was probably more like a little brother who looked up to him like everyone did. He was magnetic. But now, he was clearly sleepy so I went to the bathroom and headed to my room, intending to close my eyes for a few minutes. Hazel was waiting for me. In a gesture that summed up the depth of our family ties, she gave me an heirloom ring for each of the grandchildren, then excused herself for a rest before dinner.

I went to the kitchen and tried not to get in the way. Patti was making dinner and I sat and watched. Patti talked about her father's cancer coming on so quickly, and I thought about his life and mine, while pretending to listen. Ben had started out working with his father's company, building major water and sewer projects in Florida. He went on to become Superintendent of Water Distribution and Sewage Collection for the city of Miami. With his experience in the building trades, and Miami growing quickly, it was a good fit. The Mafia's presence was also growing in Miami during that time, resulting in frequent visits from northern and southern Mafia families. The

---

1 Colonel Konpo was an aide to General Kosuke Wada and was presented the flag after the infamous "rape" and capture of Nanking, China during which several hundred thousand Chinese were brutally massacred. It was inscribed.

growing heroin trafficking in Miami had opened up a limitless source of added income for the Mafia. Miami was where the action was, where the heroin was. Instead of using motels or hotels, which left a paper trail, the Mafia families were building apartment buildings for their own use and coming to Ben for permits and other related favors. He frequently bumped heads with them.

By "them," I mean significant Mafia figures. Santo Trafficante Sr. and his son Santo Trafficante Jr. were among the legendary old-style Mafia bosses; they allegedly controlled organized criminal operations in Florida and Cuba, and had links with the Bonanno family and Meyer Lansky of New York City, while being even more closely allied with Sam Giancana in Chicago. My cousin knew who was who.

Yet he was an honest man, never enriching himself as he could easily have done. I don't think his neighbors really had a clue how honest he really was until one day someone showed up on his doorstep with a large brown grocery bag filled with money.

A big apartment building in his jurisdiction had gone into arrears on real estate taxes, and my cousin put the property up for auction. A pleading Bill Bonanno, son of Joe Bonanno, head of one of the five crime families of New York, called to see if something could be done. Ben told him that while he wouldn't do anything illegal, he would see what he could do to help. So my cousin made arrangements for a meeting with the mayor, the city attorney, himself and Bill. A deal was worked out to save the property from auction and the next day the bagman arrived on the Fazzino doorstep.

My cousin politely refused, but the man would not leave until a ruckus scattered the cash around the neighborhood, where it was collected by the neighborhood children and given back to the delivery man—at least most of it. My cousin wouldn't take a dime. The next day he received a thank-you call from Bill. The neighbors still talk about it. What they didn't know was that Ben was an experienced bagman himself—a bagman for the CIA. He delivered money monthly to the Watergate burglars' families in the Miami area while the burglars were incarcerated, at the request of Frank Sturgis, a CIA operative and a key figure in the Bay of Pigs events, the JFK assassination, Chappaquiddick, and Watergate, who had recommended him to the CIA.

Over the next five days, in the late, late evening hours, when we were alone, Ben would talk to me about his past, other life, which he kept secret from most of his closest friends, never telling even his daughter. A dangerous, secret life that wove through his friendship with Frank Sturgis, Che Guevara, the Battle of Okinawa, Watergate, the Mafia, the assassination of John F. Kennedy and the rehearsal for it at the Doral Country Club in Miami, weeks before November 22, 1963.

This book is his story. It's the story of an unsung marine hero of the battle for Okinawa. I dedicate this book to him in hopes of securing for him the Medal of Honor—for which he was recommended by his commanding officer but denied by General Douglas MacArthur, Supreme Pacific Commander in

World War II, for self-serving reasons. His heroism in the battle of Okinawa is not only a story of courage behind enemy lines, it is an important historical event that has been covered up by our government and the government of Japan—the death of Major General Kosuke Wada, Japan's most famous artillery specialist and head of the 5th Artillery on the Island of Okinawa during World War II.

Ben Fazzino's story weaves through the Bay of Pigs invasion of Cuba; the assassinations of John F. Kennedy in Dallas, Martin Luther King in Memphis, and Robert F. Kennedy in Los Angeles; the framing of Ted Kennedy on Chappaquiddick Island; and the break-in of the Democratic National Headquarters in the Watergate Complex in Washington, D.C., prior to the 1974 elections.

His personal knowledge and intimate friendship with persons involved in all these historic events reveals the behind-the-scene story that has never before been told. It encompasses the reasons behind the Bay of Pigs, the JFK assassination, and the Watergate break-in as well as the men behind these watershed events such as Che Guevara, Lee Harvey Oswald, David Ferrie, E. Howard Hunt, Frank Sturgis, and Santos Trafficante Jr.

If you still believe that Lee Harvey Oswald, James Earl Ray, and Sirhan Sirhan acted alone; that the Warren Commission (WC), the House Sub Committee on Assassinations (HSCA), or the Assassination Records Review Board (ARRB) told the whole truth to the public; that the CIA, FBI, Mafia, Joint Chiefs of Staff, Secret Service, the Federal Reserve, Texas oilmen, multinational corporations, and Presidents Johnson, Nixon, and Bush were not involved in some or all of the above events; that heroin, the Vietnam War, and the wars in the Middle East are not sinisterly connected—you need to hear my cousin's story and then decide.

I am not a specialist in any area that I have written about except perhaps about things my cousin told me. I consider myself a generalist in the most common understanding of the word. My overriding consideration was to show the connection between the events cited and the conspirators involved as best I could.

I view events with a wide angle lens and not a telephoto one. I admire writer/researchers who examine historical events under a microscope and wish I could do that. They are my heroes and I stood on their broad shoulders to write this work. Many of them are mentioned in the bibliography. The most notable is Dr. James Fetzer, who has been extremely generous with his time and advice even though we disagree on several relatively small points. Dr. William Pepper has also been a great asset.

Each page in this book equates to roughly 1,000 pages of research condensed, compressed, and hopefully distilled to its essence. To keep this book reasonably short, sharp and focused, in the following pages only a small number of the witnesses who disagreed with the Warren Commission have been mentioned in Chapter 13. Only a small number of the witnesses who were harassed, threatened, and murdered have been mentioned. Only a small number the films and photos of the assassinations have been mentioned.

The result is not "200 proof" but it is, at least to me, still intoxicating. By definition it is a broad, broad outline of persons and events. Many significant details, events, and people have been omitted or minimized. They can be found by reading the bibliography. I have tried to harvest the fruit while weeding out the leaves and stems.

To borrow poorly from Shakespeare's Mercutio, this work "is not so deep as a well, nor so wide as a church door: but 'tis enough, 'twill serve."[1] I hope in some small measure it does.

---

1 *Romeo & Juliet*, Act 3, Scene 1.

PART ONE. THE BAY OF PIGS: AMERICA'S LOST WAR

Chapter 1. Ben Fazzino, Frank Sturgis, the CIA and the Mafia

The Fazzino and Nero[1] families come from a small village in the province of Campobasso[2] in the region of Molise, in south central Italy, northeast of Naples. In the early 1900s, my grandfather, Bernardino Niro, married Marsillia Fazzino. In due course, Ben, her nephew, and I became cousins. Ben's actual name was "Biaggio" but the Marine Corps preferred to enlist him as Benjamin.

Marsillia's brother Giuseppe Fazzino, had been in the service of the Italian National Police, the Carabinieri. In the course of his duty as a Carabinieri soldier, Giuseppe shot and killed a member of either the "Camorra," which basically operated out of Naples, or the "Mafia," which basically controlled Sicily. The two groups were fighting for control of southern Italy at the time.

The line between the Camorra and the Mafia was indistinct and growing more so. The Camorra is believed to have existed before the Mafia, but later survived the Mafia and assimilated what was left of the group. Both groups were similarly organized into families with leaders, called "Capofamiglia," which translates as "head of the family." Each Capofamiglia was "advised" by a trusted member of the family, called a "Consigliere," who was equal to the Capofamiglia in respect but not in authority. Each Capofamiglia designated an underboss, called a "Sotocapo." Each Sotocapo commanded any number of divisions or crews, called "Decinas," headed by a "Caporegime," or simply "Capo." Each Decina, loosely translated as "ten," was overseen by a Caporegime and consisted of about ten soldiers or "Soldati," although, in modern times, that numbers has varied considerably.

Below soldiers were associates, who are not "made" or formally inducted members of the family, not having proven their loyalty, or "made their bones," by having killed an enemy of the family. Both the Camorra and the Mafia are

---

1 Originally Niro.
2 Artist Robert de Niro, Sr. and his son actor Robert de Niro, Jr. also trace their roots to Campobasso.

sometimes referred to as "Lo Mano Nera," or "The Black Hand," which used the symbol on extortion letters. More correctly, the Black Hand refers to the extortion practice of the Camorra and the Mafia rather than the name of an organization. They are all, sometimes, collectively referred to as the Cosa Nostra,[1] (literally, "our thing"), the Syndicate, or organized crime. In Chicago, the Mafia is referred to as the "Outfit." Membership today is restricted to Sicilians and members swear an oath of "omerta," a vow of silence concerning their operations, when they are formally inducted in a ceremony dating back centuries. In addition to the vow of silence, the ceremony usually centers on a gun and a knife, a pricking of a finger, usually a trigger finger, or lip, for a drop of blood, which is then spilled on a skull or sometimes a picture of a saint, after which the picture is burned. The cardinal rules of the Mafia include respect for another member's family, especially his wife; abstinence from the use of drugs; omerta, or silence, about the family's activities; and behavior befitting a man of honor, which involves avenging the death of one of their own—a vendetta.

Giuseppe knew of and feared the inevitable vendetta which usually followed such a killing. And so, with the safety of his family in mind, he made a hasty exit from Campobasso to Shaker Heights, Ohio, on the recommendation of other townspeople whose relatives had moved there. In nearby Cleveland, Biaggio Fazzino was born on February 20, 1927.

His life took off when he joined the Marines, as discussed at the end of the book. But his time with the Marines was merely the prelude to a life full of adventures and characters bigger than life.

After marrying Hazel and having two daughters, Ben re-enlisted in the marines for a short tour of duty in Korea from October 18, 1950 to September 10, 1952. It was around this time that he met his lifelong friend and associate, Frank Angelo Fiorini.

Frank later changed his name to Frank Sturgis, and under that name he is widely known as one of the convicted Watergate burglars who spent several years in prison. The first interview Frank Sturgis gave after being released from prison was conducted in the living room of Ben and Hazel Fazzino's Florida home in 1975.[2]

During the interview, Ben and Frank joked about the photographer who came to take pictures with the reporter. She had lost the keys to her car, which she said was the kind you couldn't break into. Ben told her, "Don't worry, if you don't find them, you know Frank's here." He was referring to

1 The term "Cosa Nostra" was actually made up by the FBI after being embarrassed by the Apalachin arrests. The FBI inadvertently stumbled on a meeting of top Mafia leaders in Apalachin, NY, in the late 50s, making it impossible for Hoover to ignore the fact that there was a real organized crime syndicate operating in the United States (as he had been pretending for many decades). It was the largest gathering of Mafia heads of families, their Consigliere and underbosses ever held and led to a mapping out of all the Mafia families in the country.

2 For the newspaper article, see the illustrations at the back of this book.

Frank's involvement in the break-in at the Watergate Complex.

Also during the interview, Frank received a call from the Associated Press—right after a shot was fired at Gerald Ford in California. Frank, suspected by many of having been one of the shooters in Dealey Plaza, said to the AP reporter, "How could I have anything to do with that? I'm sitting in the Fazzino home in Florida."

In earlier and later interviews, Frank said he was not in the CIA but was hired by the Special Intelligence Unit headed by E. Howard Hunt and that he used the name Edward Hamilton.[1] He said he was instructed to photograph about 200 documents in the Democratic National Headquarters. Frank did admit he was a double agent, working both for the Cuban government (after helping Castro overthrow Batista) and for our government.

Documents declassified in 1993 show that Sturgis was clearly a paid operative of the CIA. According to a memo by FBI director L. Patrick Grey, Sturgis was heavily involved with "organized crime activities," and with Santos Trafficante and Meyer Lansky in Florida. Frank Sturgis will be discussed in the next chapter.

---

1 The alias Edward Hamilton was actually an E. Howard Hunt CIA cover name. He gave Sturgis his old ID just before Sturgis was arrested in the DNC offices at the Watergate. I believe it is the only time Sturgis used that alias.

CHAPTER 2. THE FAZZINO–STURGIS–LORENZ–OSWALD–HUNT RELATIONSHIP

The hospice doctor came for a visit, listening to Ben's lungs matter-of-factly and without commenting. At the kitchen table he wrote out a script for morphine—for when the time came. Ben was too stoical to start using it while I or his marine friends were there, but we all knew it was a matter of time. It looked to me as if he had several months left. I promised him I'd be back for the holidays. He must have known that would be too late, but he never let on. He died a few weeks after my visit.

As the days passed, we spoke with more urgency. We talked about his last trip to Italy, to Campobasso, with Mike Niro, a cousin of ours in Boca Raton. And then he told me about Frank Sturgis and Che Guevara.

Frank Sturgis and Che Guevara

Frank Sturgis, my cousin said, ran guns to Castro and Guevara in the Sierra Maestra Mountains—and some of the guns came from Joseph Kennedy. Joseph Kennedy, according to my cousin, was head of the Irish Mafia and expected payment, if and when Castro overthrew Batista—payment in the form of ownership of the lucrative Italian Mafia casinos. Castro, however, made many deals which he did not honor.

Frank and Che were frequent visitors to Ben and Hazel's home[1] before and after the Cuban revolution. Ben and Frank were marines with a mutual respect and similar backgrounds. Both had been boxers before joining the marines at a young age. Both were in the 1st Marine Division and both had fought in the Pacific as teenagers.

When my mother would visit, she would cook a feast for everyone. She cooked

---

1 In actuality it was the home of Giuseppe "Papa Joe" Fazzino. Ben moved to Florida in 1965.

the old fashioned way—from scratch. Che[1] was partial to my mother's gnocchi. She made the Southern Italian version, called "cavatelli," from flour and ricotta cheese, more delicate than the Northern, more common, gnocchi made from flour and mashed potatoes that more closely resemble a traditional dumpling.

Che was an Argentinian, trained as a dentist. He was from a wealthy family, but on a well-documented motorcycle trip through South America he saw the poverty of the people firsthand. He started to read Marxist literature and the history of South American revolutionaries such as Simon Bolivar (1782–1830) and Jose Marti (1853–1895), a Cuban national hero. Raul Castro introduced Che to Fidel in Mexico, and following the revolution, Castro made him a citizen of Cuba.

Ben also told me that after the revolution and Che's falling out with Fidel (over Che's desire to continue the revolution in South America), Che had asked Frank and him to go to Bolivia with him for his next revolution. Ben and Frank couldn't go because they both had families to support. Che was later killed in Bolivia, most likely on the order of E. Howard Hunt, most likely by Felix Rodriguez[2] (and perhaps with David Morales, although he has refused to say who accompanied him), who kept Che's Rolex as a souvenir after cutting off Che's hands as proof of the execution. In his autobiography, however, Rodriguez claims he tried to save Guevara's life and that Che was killed by the Bolivian Army. Rodriguez has never adequately explained why he, a CIA agent of the United States, was sent to a sovereign foreign country, Bolivia, to track down Che, an Argentinian at the time, and bring him back alive to Langley as he naively claims. What did he think was going to happen to Che after he tracked him down?

After the revolution, Frank helped the CIA and the Mafia on one of the many occasions they tried to assassinate Fidel Castro. The program, called OPERATION MONGOOSE, was run by the Department of Defense under General Edward Lansdale[3] and the CIA under William King. Over thirty assassination scenarios were considered but far fewer were carried out. They included exploding cigars, exploding seashells, poisoned food and infected clothing such as shoes. Castro, an avid scuba diver, was also given an infected scuba diving suit.

Prior to his contact with Castro and Che Guevara, Frank was trained as a pilot after World War II. While a member of the Naval Reserves in Norfolk, Virginia (which he joined after being discharged from the Marines), he married Nora Odell Thompson, a woman with a history of arrests for prostitution.

---

1 When Che travelled out of Cuba, especially after he became an easily recognizable personality, he disguised himself and used the alias "Ramon del Gato."

2 Che was more precisely killed by the Bolivian Army but that is not exoneration of guilt.

3 General Lansdale would eventually be sent to Vietnam in the Fifties and was a major figure in the war.

After being honorably discharged from the Navy Reserves, Frank joined the Army the very next day where he became a captain and was sent to Berlin and Heidelberg. In the Pacific he had done intelligence work as a member of the 1st Marine Raider Battalion, the 1st Marine Raider Regiment, and the 1st Marine Amphibious Corps. He was a member of the legendary Edson's Raiders. His intelligence work consisted mainly of infiltrating enemy lines to gather intelligence for the Marines. In the Army he worked in intelligence, mainly aimed at the USSR, and was given a top secret clearance. After his discharge from the Army, he joined the United States Merchant Marines in 1950 and was again stationed in Europe. In 1952, Frank Angelo Fiorini[1] petitioned for and was given a name change to Frank Anthony Sturgis. Frank Sturgis is a name that has been tied to many shadowy events in modern US history. After serving honorably in several branches of the US military, he built a career as an undercover operative, working with the CIA, Castro, and the Mafia.

After his wife Nora was killed along with another prostitute in 1954, he matched up with Juanita K. Terrell, whose family was close to the family of Carlos Prio Socarras, who had been Premier of Cuba before Fulgencio Batista ousted him. He married her in 1956 and abandoned her in 1957, shortly after meeting Castro at a gathering of the Cuban community at the Flagland Theatre in Miami, where Castro had come to speak. After talking to Frank, Castro said, "I can use people with your experience."

To finance his trip to Cuba, Frank sold his half interest in the Norfolk, Virginia, bar called the Top Hat, to his partner, Sam Bass, and began writing bad checks in a check-kiting scheme.

Frank's dealing with Castro involved frequent travel to the States as Castro's emissary. He'd go to New York and Miami where Carlos Prio Socarras was living and providing funding for Castro. (In another broken promise Castro had said he would restore Carlos Prio Socarras to the presidency after Castro overthrew Batista.)

Frank purchased guns for Castro from a company called Interarmco, which sold surplus Mannlicher-Carcano rifles. In 1958, Frank was arrested for trying to illegally ship Mannlicher-Carcano rifles to Cuba. He was released on a $500.00 bond and a few months later the charges were dropped. It was around this time Frank was recruited by the CIA.

Shortly afterwards Frank purchased a plane to deliver weapons and supplies to Castro. The plane, a Curtis C-46, was paid for with a certified check for $85,000. For his efforts Castro promoted him to Deputy Commander of the Cuban rebel air force. After the revolution he was appointed Security and Intelligence Director of the Cuban Air Force. He also oversaw the gambling casinos for Castro, who first ordered the casinos to obtain licenses and tax stamps from Frank. Frank became intimately involved with the Cuban

---

1 Oswald's address book when he was arrested contained the names Fiorinis [*sic*], John Connally, and Richard Nixon.

gambling operations (which were headed by Meyer and Jake Lansky, Santos Trafficante and Norman Rothman) and the casinos themselves, especially the Tropicana, the Casino Nacional, and the Sans Souci. He also met a lot of movie stars, as he laughingly reported to the Rockefeller Commission. Although Lansky and Trafficante were the top figures in the Havana casinos, every major crime family in the US had points or shares in the casinos—each share or point being worth $30,000 to $100,000 a month.

Frank, however, was beginning to become disenchanted with Castro and his revolution and had a falling out with Raul, according to a CIA report, "over incorporating Army officers in the training program."

Fidel Castro—Before and After the Revolution

Fidel Castro has been glorified and vilified, but never completely or honestly characterized, as far as I can tell. How could a man who inspired so many to sacrifice their lives for the revolution have been demonized by so many people after the revolution? It is understandable that those who lost family, fortune, or both because of the revolution would vehemently denounce him and try to overthrow him. But even some of those who had been most inspired by him later turned against him. Why would the very people who fought for the ideas of the revolution come to despise him?

In a serendipitous meeting in Miami, as I was trying to find a way to interview a survivor of the Bay of Pigs, I was given a book by Professor Antonio Rafael de la Cova, *The Moncada Attack: Birth of the Cuban Revolution*. I was asked to read it and comment on it by Professor Tatjana Martinez JD, who teaches in the Doctoral Program at Nova Southeastern University.

The Moncada and nearly simultaneous Bayamo attacks on the military garrisons in Oriente Province were Castro's opening gambit against Batista's government and they catapulted him into a leadership role—and into prison for a fifteen-year term, of which he served less than two.

The ill-conceived, poorly planned attack featured pitifully armed attackers numbering less than 160. Their weapons consisted mainly of .22 caliber rifles, a few shotguns and even fewer pistols, some of which had no ammunition. About twenty cars, some rented, some borrowed, carried approximately 100 of the rebels to Santiago de Cuba, a symbolic and iconic town in Oriente Province from which earlier revolutions had been launched. The journey took some fifteen hours by car. The rest of the rebels arrived by train or bus carrying ill-fitting, homemade uniforms and weapons in suitcases. As planned, they arrived during carnival time[1] around July 26th, 1953, just as Castro's hero, Jose Marti, the poet revolutionary had done in 1895.

The plan was twofold. The majority of the rebel force led by Castro was to surprise the military garrison at Moncada, take the weapons, distribute

---

1 The Cuban revolution of 1959 was called the July 26th Movement.

them to the people who naturally would rise up and go on to capture the capital, Havana, and restore democracy under the Constitution of 1940. During this period Castro rarely mentioned Marxist or Leninist leanings if he, indeed, had them at this time.[1]

A second attack against the military barracks at Bayamo was to begin twenty minutes after the Moncada attack which was scheduled for 5 AM. This smaller group, less than two dozen men, was headed by Colonel Raul Martinez Araras.

In less than thirty minutes, with less than thirty shots fired by the rebels, the Moncada attack ended. Castro never fired a shot, contrary to his claims in later writings such as *History Will Absolve Me*. In fact, according to the impressively in-depth account by Professor de la Cova, Castro acted cowardly, indecisively, uninspiringly, and left more than a dozen dead and wounded in his wake as he made his escape. Some 60 rebels were killed, half after being captured[2], 51 were taken prisoner, and the rest escaped temporarily but were later captured, tried and sentenced to ten to fifteen years in prison.

The smaller Bayamo attack began and ended just as badly, but in even less time. The night before the attack, the Bayamo rebels billeted themselves in the Gran Casino Motel, which was up for sale. They lied to the owner, telling him they were interested in purchasing the property. A seedy motel which rented by the hour, it was officially closed, but the rebels were constantly awakened by lovers who tried to rent rooms throughout the night. When Castro tried to rally the Bayamo rebels that night by telling them, "We are going into history," Raul Martinez replied. "Don't you think we are going to our graves?"[3]

Colonel Martinez Araras was able to escape to Havana and eventually to Costa Rica, while aiding a wounded fellow soldier by flagging down a horse-drawn produce wagon.

Castro quietly arranged his surrender and a pledge of safe conduct with the local archbishop after abandoning wounded soldiers at Moncada. He was released from prison after twenty-one and one half months under a general amnesty.

Returning to Cuba after the amnesty, Colonel Raul Martinez Araras approached Castro on behalf of many of the rebels and asked that he step aside in favor of a balanced leadership. Castro insisted that Cuba needed a strong leader to bring order and stability before returning to a democracy and the Constitution of 1940 (which closely resembles the U.S. Constitution).

---

1 His Marxist/ Leninist sympathies may have developed during his imprisonment where he spent ten hours a day reading.
2 The brutal murder of some of the captives immediately after capture has given rise to the "Black Legend" of grisly torture, eye-gouging, and dismemberment. Castro exploited these atrocities for propaganda purposes but they have been largely disproven.
3 Cova, *The Moncada Attack*, p 123.

After being rejected by Castro, this group of early supporters broke with him and joined the Radical Liberation Movement (MRL), thus becoming, in some eyes, traitors to the revolution. After the revolution, Castro ordered Raul Martinez to rejoin him or leave Cuba. Martinez could not support a dictator and moved to Miami with his family.

Professor Martinez says Raul Martinez considered Castro "an egotistical tyrant and psychopath who hated the U.S. with a passion and loved himself above anyone, anything, and any country. He tortured, imprisoned and murdered his own faithful followers, such as Camillo Cienfuegos, Huber Matos, and William Morgan, when they disagreed with him."

Raul Martinez's brother, Mario, was one of the few who actually entered the Moncada garrison and fought. He was captured, tortured, and killed there. He was a hero of the revolution and today is a national hero[1] in Cuba.

Many of the survivors of the Moncada attack disavowed Castro although others re-joined him in Mexico, where he regrouped and met Che Guevara. He later returned to Cuba with eighty-two[2] men on a small vessel called the *Granma*. On returning to Cuba, Fidel and Raul Castro and Che set up a guerrilla camp in the Sierra Maestra Mountains, from which he again attacked the Batista government at Santiago de Cuba.

I wrote to thank Professor Martinez for the book and to give her my impressions as I had promised. It was then that she told me that her father Raul Martinez Araras, and her uncle Mario Martinez, had been part of Castro's force that attacked Moncada and Bayamo; her father led the Bayamo attack. She wrote me:

> My father was a thinker/philosopher/historian more than a fighter. But according to my father, the 26th of July Movement was conceived as a way to make a statement outside of Havana. Historically all revolts against Spain during the War of Independence had started in Oriente Province (the easternmost province—Santiago de Cuba being the capital). Jose Marti, a national hero, called the Apostle of the Cuban Revolution, was killed in battle in Oriente by the Spaniards in 1895 (Cuba's independence did not come until 1898). I guess my father's group thought that if Marti was brave enough to die there, so were they. So it made sense to them, although they knew it would be just a "statement" and probably many would not make it. They knew this from the onset.

Professor Martinez went on to describe her mother's feelings.

> My mother, Coralia Varela 'Nenita' de Martinez and her sister

---

1 There is a baseball stadium in the family home town of Colon, Matanzas named after Mario Martinez Araras.
2 The *Granma* had room for only 81 but Camillo Cienfuegos was so thin that he talked Castro into taking him as the 82nd rebel.

'Nerida' were from a prominent family in Matanzas and studied at the St. Mary Immaculate Convent in Key West, Florida, as was customary for upper class families. My mother hated Castro from the beginning because he wanted my father to just think about the revolution and nothing else. He was rude and very disrespectful to her and to all women, even his first wife, whom my mother knew very well. She is the mother of his first child, 'Fidelito.' She was also the daughter of a very prominent politician who served as Majority Leader of the House of Representatives during the presidency of Batista, Raphael Diaz Balart. This name may seem familiar because we have had two of his sons in the US Congress (Mario, currently, and Lincoln).

In his book Professor Cova summed up the Moncada incident and its legacy:

> In spite of the promises of freedom and democracy made in the *Moncada Manifesto* and *History will Absolve me* [both by Castro], the Cuban people have been subjected to a totalitarian continuity that exists today.[1]

Marita Lorenz

Enter Marita Lorenz, a petite, curvaceous, dark-haired beauty, all of nineteen. She was the daughter of an American mother, Alice, who was a second cousin to UN Ambassador Henry Cabot Lodge. Her German father, Heinrich, was captain of a luxury liner, the *MS Berlin*. Before this he captained a German U-boat.

In February 1959, a few months after overthrowing Batista, Castro and several dozen Cuban soldiers boarded the *MS Berlin* as it entered Havana Harbor to search for contraband. Invited to dinner at the captain's table, Fidel was smitten with Marita and vice versa. At dinner Marita slipped Fidel her brother's New York address, where she could be reached, behind the back of her disapproving father. Castro sent two men to New York to escort her back to Havana. A brief love affair ensued, although according to Marita's mother she was kidnapped and raped.[2]

Marita quickly became pregnant, to the displeasure of Fidel, and according to her mother she was given an abortion in her 6th month of pregnancy.[3] The abortion was performed against her will and against the will of Dr. Ferrer, who had a gun pointed at his head while performing the abortion in Havana. One of Castro's assistants, however, claimed she had asked for the abortion. In any case the abortion was botched, leaving parts of

1 Cova, *The Moncada Attack*, p.258.
2 *Confidential Magazine*, May, 1960.
3 *Confidential Magazine*, May, 1960.

the fetal skeleton inside her. Marita barely survived.[1]

Frank Sturgis, working for the US Embassy in Havana, which also housed the CIA offices, as well as working for Castro's Air Force, offered Marita a way out of Cuba. He took her to Roosevelt Hospital in New York, where an operation was performed to remove the rest of the fetus. Frank then turned her into a CIA operative and convinced her to return to Cuba to kill Castro with two poison-filled capsules prepared by the CIA. More precisely, the pills were prepared by Dr. Sidney Gottlieb of the CIA's Technical Services Division.

Fearful of being discovered with the pills at the Havana Airport, she hid them in her vanishing cream jar; whereupon they promptly dissolved. This is when she uttered the famous lines attributed to her—"To hell with it. Let history take its course."[2]

Frank and Marita became lovers around this time and she became an intimate part of his world. She met Lee Harvey Oswald, whom she called "Ozzie," as well as E. Howard Hunt, Dr. Orland Bosch, Gerry Patrick Hemming, Alex Rorke and the Novo brothers, Guillermo and Ignacio. She traveled to Dallas with Frank as they ran high-powered, scoped rifles on several occasions. The payment for these services came directly from E. Howard Hunt.

Under a grant of immunity she testified in 1983 in a deposition,[3] in the case of *Hunt* v. *Liberty Magazine*[4], that: (A) she performed intelligence work for the NYPD, FBI, and the CIA; (B) she and Frank Sturgis traveled in two[5] cars from a CIA safe house in Miami to a Dallas motel, arriving on the night before the assassination; (C) she saw, that same night, E. Howard Hunt give Frank Sturgis a large sum of cash which he counted in front of her; (D) Jack Ruby also came to their room at the motel that evening; (E) she left Dallas later that evening; and (F) sometime later Frank called and told her:

> We[6] killed the president that day. You could have been part of it—you know, part of history. You should have stayed. It was safe. Everything was covered in advance. No arrests, no real newspaper investigation. It was all covered, very professional.[7]

---

1 There is a variant of this story in which she had a child with Fidel that was given up for adoption, but that seems less credible than the version told by her mother.
2 *The Brilliant Disaster*, Rasenberger, p. 138.
3 *Plausible Denial*, Lane, pp. 295-303.
4 Liberty Lobby was the parent company of *Spotlight Magazine* which ran the article which accused E. Howard Hunt of being complicit in the assassination of JFK.
5 According to Mark Lane, Gerry Patrick Hemming told him it was a three-car caravan but that everything else Marita said was correct. *Last Word*, Lane, p. 65.
6 Sturgis was no doubt referring to himself, Hunt, Ruby, etc.
7 *Plausible Denial*, Lane, p. 303.

Under questioning by Liberty Lobby's attorney, Mark Lane, Marita also claimed that Frank Sturgis was one of the shooters in Dealey Plaza. However, her testimony before the House Subcommittee on Assassinations was dismissed because she also claimed to have known Lee Harvey Oswald during a time when Oswald was known to have been in Russia—October, 1959, to May, 1962. However she could have known him after that time.

In a slight variation of the story, retired New York detective Jim Rothstein claims that Marita, whom he interviewed in 1978, said, "the Kennedy assassination was planned at a meeting in Miami, Florida. As the meeting broke up, there was shootout. Five people left in two vehicles for the drive to Dallas, Texas. With me were Frank Sturgis, E. Howard Hunt, Orlando Bosch, and one other. Near Natchitoches, Louisiana, after crossing a bridge on Highway 1 running parallel to Interstate 20, they had car trouble and stopped to fix the car." Rothstein says he located the gas station where the car was repaired and confirmed Marita's story of the car trouble.

Marita, however, has been inconsistent as to who traveled with her and Frank to Dallas, arriving on the night of November 21. It is doubtful E. Howard Hunt would have traveled with them, as this was not his style, and also why would he give a large sum of money to Sturgis at the motel as she claims? All the other details seem credible.

The story of the assassination of JFK begins before the US invasion of Cuba at the Bay of Pigs, perhaps around the time of the planning for the invasion or slightly before.[8] The Bay of Pigs had a great deal to do with the reasons and motives for the assassination itself and the conspirators involved—many of whom came together at that time—and stayed until Watergate. The Bay of Pigs needs and deserves a close look—a very close look.

---

8 The precise time when the plan to assassinate Kennedy was conceived, is debated by researchers. Most likely, as will be explored later, it was just before the 1960 Democratic convention, a little after the invasion of Cuba at the Bay of Pigs. But some conspirators were recruited from members and planners of the invasion.

CHAPTER 3. EISENHOWER, NIXON, BUSH, KENNEDY AND THE BAY OF PIGS

Understanding the Bay of Pigs is crucial if we are to understand the major players involved in the Kennedy assassination, because the Bay of Pigs connects the roles of Frank Sturgis, E. Howard Hunt, the CIA (namely Allen Dulles, Richard Bissell, Tracy Barnes, and General Cabell), George Herbert Walker Bush, Richard M. Nixon, the Joint Chiefs of Staff, the Mafia, and the FBI. The FBI's role was more in the cover-up phase, although J. Edgar Hoover knew about the assassination from the start. Johnson's early role will be discussed later.

Background and Planning of The Bay of Pigs Invasion

The official version of the Bay of Pigs invasion, as reported in several excellent works by noted historians, relies mainly on official documents, some of which are classified. Those documents are suspect because, at least in the case of President Eisenhower, for example, official documents were rewritten, after the fact, to minimize culpability. Eisenhower said publicly in a *Newsday* interview that if he had planned the invasion, it would have succeeded. A strange statement considering the invasion was his idea in the first place.

In the case of Kennedy, there was a concerted effort immediately afterwards to minimize his role and emphasize the role of the CIA. Nixon's role is barely mentioned and George Herbert Walker Bush's role is almost unknown.

The following are critical facts about what happened before and after at the Bahia de Cochinos (Bay of Pigs) in April 1961 and how it relates to the JFK assassination.

When Americans of a certain venerable age think of bananas, we conjure up the image of Carmen Miranda with a head full of fruit happily singing and dancing "Chiquita Banana so good for you," or words to that effect. To South Americans, the banana became a symbol of repression by huge multinational corporations dominating and controlling their economies, their political structure and their everyday lives. The term "banana republics," coined by the writer O. Henry, refers to the neo-colonial domination of many South American countries by their corporate masters—the United Fruit Company, Pepsi, Ford, and others.

The United Fruit Company, an American multinational corporation, was by the 1930s the largest employer and the largest landowner in South America. The United Fruit Company owned nearly fifty percent of Cuba's arable land, farming considerably less than half and keeping the rest in reserve. It also owned 80% of Cuba's utilities, including the phone and electric companies. It exploited workers, paid little in taxes, and regularly bribed government officials. It was so hated in South America that it was called el pulpo ("the octopus").

Allen Welsh Dulles, Director of the CIA, was a board member of the United Fruit Company and his brother, John Foster Dulles, secretary of state under Eisenhower, was a member of the law firm Sullivan and Cromwell, which represented The United Fruit Company. The brother of the assistant secretary of state for Inter-American affairs, John Moors Cabot, had once been president of the company. Ed Whitman, principal lobbyist for United Fruit, was married to Eisenhower's personal secretary, Ann C. Whitman. The United Fruit Company was well-connected.

When Castro nationalized the sugar mills in Oriente Province and apportioned some of the unused land for redistribution to the landless peasants, you can imagine the pressure on Eisenhower to remove Castro—even if it meant violating international law, the United Nations Charter, and the Charter of the Organization of American States (OAS).[1] Castro had to be stopped. In August 1969, Eisenhower implemented a plan with an $18 million budget—about $100 million today. The cost of the failure was five times that amount.

Legal and moral law notwithstanding, Eisenhower, on March 17, 1960, authorized a program of covert activity to replace the government of Castro. Eisenhower logically chose Nixon to head up the committee planning the invasion of Cuba. Nixon was the Chair of the Sub-committee on Cuba of the National Security Council (NSC) set up to remove Castro from power. He understood the situation.

Nixon was only too happy to accept the assignment, under NSC Mandate 5412, because it allowed him to repay a political favor to his political mentor-godfather, Senator (1952–1963) Prescott Bush (R-CT), head of the Bush dynasty.

In the Forties, Prescott Bush and friends took out an ad in a California paper seeking a malleable, conservative Republican candidate for the 12th Congressional district to oppose Democratic incumbent Jerry Voorhis. Nixon responded and that was, as they say, the start of a beautiful friendship

---

1 The OAS charter signed by Cuba and the US requires all signatories to come to the aid of other member nations.

which continued through the election of Eisenhower–Nixon in 1952. In fact, Senator Prescott Bush was instrumental in brokering the Eisenhower–Nixon ticket as well as serving as Nixon's campaign manager through his election to the Vice-Presidency.

The official story of Nixon's entry into politics is that California Republicans of the 12th District formed a committee of 100 to pick a candidate and Nixon, living in Baltimore at the time, was suggested by the Bank of America President in Whittier, California, Herman Perry. Perry, a family friend had served with Nixon on the Board of Trustees of Whittier College. Unofficially, Senator Prescott Bush not only recruited Nixon to run for Congress but was also his campaign manager and a major fund raiser.

Prescott Bush was a banker in addition to being a politician. In 1931, Prescott Bush became a partner in the investment banking firm of Brown Brothers Harriman & Company. He was also one of seven directors of another investment bank, the Union Banking Corporation. In 1942, Union Banking Corporation was seized by the government for violating the Trading with the Enemy Act for housing assets and clearing transactions of the Nazi government. Its assets were held until the end of the war.

In 1952, Prescott Bush ran for the Senate after the death of sitting Senator Brien McMahon, winning that election and the next in 1956. Around this time, he was also on the board of Yale University, which he had previously attended, as well as on the board of CBS.

The favor that Nixon repaid had to do with the appointment of his son, George Herbert Walker Bush of the CIA to head OPERATION 40, a group of initially 40 CIA Case Officers and Cuban dissidents to head an invasion task force. The official operational officer for OPERATION 40 was the CIA's Tracy Barnes, Deputy Director of Covert Operations (DDCO), reporting to Richard Bissell, Director of Covert Operation (DCO), who reported to CIA Director Allen Dulles.

Nixon, as the White House Action Officer, was the ultimate decision maker until Kennedy was elected. Nixon personally oversaw the function of OPERATION 40 for the invasion of Cuba. It eventually grew to over two hundred leaders recruited mainly from CIA case officers and Cuban dissidents in Miami, whose properties and lifestyles had been taken away by Castro. Bandleader and TV personality Desi Arnez (Ricky Ricardo), was one of the more vocal dissidents, although there was no shortage of dissenters.

While Barnes was taking the credit, George Herbert Walker Bush recruited Felix Rodriguez. Rodriguez's uncle had been Minister of Public Works under Batista, who was President of Cuba before Castro took over Cuba. Rodriguez's assignment was to recruit Cubans in Miami for OPERATION 40 (which also went under the name of OPERATION ZR/RIFLE and was also eventually known as Brigade 2506, so named after Carlos Rodriguez Santana, who died during training with the brigade. He was the 6th man to be recruited and since the brigade thought their numbers would sound more impressive if they started with the number 2500, Carlos was given the high honor of bearing number 2506.)

Those recruits would then be "vetted" by George Herbert Walker Bush via the CIA. In this capacity Bush travelled frequently to Miami. But if you read the official records and some of the major works on the Bay of Pigs, such as *Ultimate Sacrifice* by Lamar Waldron, *Bay of Pigs: Untold Story* by Peter Wyden and *The Brilliant Disaster* by Jim Rasenberger—Nixon is given short shrift and Bush is given almost no shrift at all which is, no doubt, how they would have wanted it. Of course, had the invasion been a success they would have made sure their roles were better known. As Kennedy expressed when it was over—"Victory has a thousand fathers, but defeat is an orphan."[1]

Some of the leaders of OPERATION 40 are significant and need to be noted here as they will take on a more ominous role later. They are E. (Everette) Howard Hunt *AKA* Eduardo, CIA Case Officer, novelist, and super spy—he has been called the model for Ian Fleming's James Bond[2]; Frank Sturgis, *AKA* Frank Fiorini/Hamilton/etc., ex-marine, ex-army officer, ex-captain in Castro's Air Force, gun runner, Mafia associate, CIA operative and professional soldier of fortune; Bernard "Macho" Barker, CIA operative and Hunt's 'shadow'; David Atlee Phillips, *AKA* Maurice Bishop, CIA Case Officer in charge of counter propaganda; Felix Rodriguez, Cuban dissident and CIA outside contractor (later CIA officer); Luis Posada Carriles; Dr. Orlando Bosch; Rafael 'Chi Chi' Quintero; Virgilio Paz Romero; Pedro Luis Diaz Lanz; Porter Goss, later CIA Director; Barry Seal and David 'El Indio' Morales, CIA operatives who eventually would work out of the Kennedy White House.

E. Howard Hunt, shortly before his death, named David Morales as a key player in the assassination of JFK along with White House advisor Cord Meyer and Lyndon Johnson. John Kennedy had taken Cord Meyer's wife, Mary, as one of his mistresses—although that may have only happened after Mary's divorce from Cord.

Mary Pinchot Meyer had known Kennedy while he was attending Choate, a prep school in Connecticut, in the late Thirties. Mary was attending Brearley School at the time. They met at a dance at Choate. After graduation from Vassar she became a correspondent for the *North American Newspaper Alliance* and *United Press*. She was also Ben Bradley's[3] sister-in-law which helped her land a position as a writer for *Mademoiselle Magazine.*

Mary, known as a bit of a wild girl, spoke of having smoked marijuana and using LSD[4] with Kennedy on more than one occasion. She is reported to have had as many as thirty intimate trysts with Kennedy in the White House, according to some accounts. She was also known to keep a diary.

1 *A Thousand Days*, Arthur Schlesinger, Jr., p 289.
2 The Russian, Dusan "Dusko" Popov, a double agent working for MI 6 (Military Intelligence, and code named Tricycle) has also been mentioned as a model for 007.
3 Editor of *The Washington Post.*
4 LSD was not illegal at the time.

She was later expertly killed while out for a jog, about a year after Kennedy was killed. She was shot twice by an unknown assailant—once in the back of the head and once in the heart.[1] Someone was arrested shortly afterwards but no gun was found and the man was acquitted. The trial judge, Howard Corcoran, appointed by Lyndon Johnson, ruled that Mary's private life could not be discussed. Defense lawyer Dovey Johnson Roundtree was able to discover almost no evidence about Mary's private life. The crime remains unsolved.

Mary's house and artist's studio were searched by Ben Bradlee and the CIA for her diary immediately after she was killed. As far as the public knows, her diary has never turned up.

Cord Meyer told friends that the same people who killed Kennedy killed Mary.

More than one Youtube video on Hunt's confession naming Cord Meyer as one of the people responsible for the assassination of Kennedy was still available for viewing as this book went to press.

Like the Battle for Okinawa, the invasion of Cuba was no surprise to anyone. The Cubans, recruited and trained in Florida, Louisiana, as well as Guatemala, spoke freely to reporters who wrote of the upcoming invasion. Cuba's Ambassador to the UN, Raul Roa, also spoke about an imminent invasion by US trained forces from Florida and Guatemala at the United Nations. Radio Moscow spoke about the invasion in an English-language broadcast four days beforehand. The only people who didn't seem to know what was going on were the American people.

CIA and Joint Chiefs of Staff's evaluations of OPERATION 40/ZR/RIFLE, now called OPERATION PLUTO,[2] put the odds of success at 30% at best, provided the Cuban population would rise up at the same time as the invasion and that Castro would be assassinated simultaneously. On top of that, a second, crucial air strike to eliminate Castro's few but lethal T-33 fighter jets was cancelled at the last moment, hours before the landing. General George Custer had better odds.

Kennedy never saw the reports that assessed a 70% chance of failure; the reports were changed to say a "fair" chance of success. Kennedy thought "fair" meant fair as in "better than average." The CIA, who changed the report of the Joint Chiefs of Staff, knew better.

E. Howard Hunt's role as White House political officer was a role he played well in Guatemala when he and David Atlee Phillips overthrew the legitimately elected democratic government of Jacobo Arbenz through propaganda and a few revolutionaries trained by the CIA.

Frank Sturgis' leadership role was due to his CIA status and his intimate knowledge of Castro and of Cuba. While Sturgis' role in the invasion is not

---

1 One account claims she was shot in the face.
2 Later OPERATION PLUTO is renamed OPERATION ZAPATA, after location of the landing is changed.

clear, some reports claim his role was a diversionary one and that he did not land at the Bay of Pigs but on another part of the island.

But retired New York Detective Jim Rothstein, who was at the Bay of Pigs invasion, claims Sturgis was one of the members of OPERATION 40 that was left behind on the beaches.

Detective Rothstein personally questioned Frank Sturgis privately after arresting him in 1977 for the attempted murder of Marita Lorenz. Lorenz had assembled 10–15 boxes of files which he says she claimed were "documents relating to OP40 [sic], the Cuban invasion, Castro, planning for the Kennedy assassination, and other covert operations that she had knowledge of. These documents were going to be delivered to the House Assassination Hearings [House Subcommittee on Assassinations (HSAC)]."

Following up on the fate of the 10–15 boxes, Rothstein met with John Tunheim who was employed by the Assassination Records Review Board (ARRB 1994–1998). The ARRB was tasked with reviewing the Kennedy assassination records before they were released to the public after pressure from the Oliver Stone movie. Tunheim told him that "there were no files from Marita or Frank." The ARRB will be discussed later.

The overall leader of the expedition was José Perez (Pepe) San Roman, (although some say it was Manuel "Manolo" Artime).[1] The government-in-exile leader, who was to be brought to Cuba after the invasion force secured a beachhead, was José Miro Cardona, a law professor and president of the Cuban Bar Association. Cardona had been appointed Premier under Castro but resigned after 39 days when he realized he was only a figurehead premier.

One of the key mistakes for which Kennedy must bear some blame was the change of landing site. Originally, the heavily populated area of Trinidad was chosen by Nixon and put forth by Bissell to Kennedy. It had two out of three factors going for it. It had a harbor for unloading supplies and ammunition, and it was close to the Escambray Mountains in Central Cuba where the invasion force could escape and survive as a guerrilla warfare unit in the event they could not establish a beachhead. It had an airport (although the runway was too short for American B26 bombers, repainted as Cuban Air Force planes, to take off from and land at). Kennedy considered this to be a critical part of the invasion plan in maintaining the fiction that the invasion was a local, domestic, internal event.

Kennedy told Bissell to "tone down the noise level,"[2] and come back in three days with a new plan. Bissell assumed correctly that Kennedy wanted a less populated area which would be more "covert."

The new plan centered on the Bay of Pigs, 130 miles south of Havana, surrounded by the Zapata Swamps, with no easy way to move inland or escape to the Escambray Mountains, 80 miles away. In addition to that, U2

---

1 Mario Kohly has also been named as a leader, but mainly and perhaps only by ex-CIA agent Robert Morrow, in both *First Hand Knowledge* and *Betrayal*.
2 *A Brilliant Disaster*, Rasenberger, p. 138.

photos of the area's beaches were misinterpreted. What the CIA thought was seaweed turned out to be coral at one of the three beaches, making a landing impossible at that beach. It did, however, have a suitable airfield for B26s to land and take off.

American opponents of this, or actually of any, invasion plan, were formidable but ineffective. Dean Acheson, former Secretary of State, Chester Bowles, Under Secretary of State, Senator William Fulbright, and Thomas Mann, Assistant Secretary of State in charge of South American Affairs, voted against it. Still Kennedy pushed forward. Some of his advisors voiced the opinion that Joseph Kennedy was urging Jack to proceed. Joseph Kennedy was upset with Castro over the Havana casinos he thought he was entitled to for providing guns for Castro's revolution.

On the eve of D-Day Minus 3, the day scheduled for the air strike by sixteen B 26s, Kennedy told Bissell to cut down on the number of planes, but did not specify further. Bissell arbitrarily decided on six—six vintage bombers to eliminate Castro's entire Air Force based on three airfields!

True, Castro only had thirty-six aircraft spread out over three airfields, yet six planes turned out to be wholly inadequate even though some of Castro's planes were not operational. Half were destroyed, but the most important jet fighters, the T-33s, were not.

Hunt and Bissell assumed that the original order gave them authority to repeat the air attack and destroy the rest of the Cuban Air Force on D-Day before the landing and after reviewing aerial reconnaissance.

Allen Dulles, away in Puerto Rico for a speech, by accident or design, left General Charles P. Cabell[1] in charge. Cabell strolled in off the golf course on D-Day Minus 1 to check on progress. Listening to the discussion about plans for the second, D-Day strike, General Cabell wanted clarification or verification of the authorization for the second pass over Cuban airspace, and so called Dean Rusk. Around 9:30 that night, McGeorge Bundy, a Kennedy advisor, called Cabell to say that no further air strikes were authorized— unless they originated from the airfield at the Bay of Pigs *after* the landing, in keeping with the charade of a civil war.

Cabell assumed the order had come from Kennedy and so cancelled the critical D-Day air strike. According to Air Force Lt. Colonel Fletcher Prouty, the order to cancel the second air strike had not come from Kennedy.

Meanwhile the various plots to assassinate Castro were going nowhere, more because the plots were amateurish than because of any brilliance shown by Castro and his bodyguard, Fabian Escalante (who wrote a book about the numerous attempts on Castro's life titled *634 Ways to Kill Fidel Castro*). They included putting powder in Castro's shoes to make all his hair fall out so he would lose his iconic beard and, thereby, his Samson-like political strength; an attempt to present Castro with a scuba diving suit sprinkled with poison; injection with a fast-acting cancer cell; exploding cigars; bribed food servers;

1 General Cabell's brother Earle was the Mayor of Dallas at the time of the assassination.

poisoned milkshakes; even a serious mob attempt by Johnny Rosselli to shoot Castro. This attempt resulted in Rosselli's capture and subsequent ransoming by Meyer Lansky, who begrudgingly paid a reported $1 million.

Rosselli, known as Handsome Johnny, should have taken the $150,000 contract, about a million dollars today, offered by Robert Maheu, an ex-FBI agent on the payroll of Howard Hughes to kill Castro. Johnny turned down the money out of patriotism, but volunteered to kill Castro—although he did ask Maheu to get Bobby Kennedy, who was trying to deport him as an illegal, off his back. But Johnny was worth the million dollars to the Mafia. He was their man in Vegas and Hollywood. Not only did he look out for their interests in Vegas, he also produced movies for the Mafia. Rosselli is also said to have made Harry Cohn, the producer of *From Here To Eternity*, an "offer he couldn't refuse," garnering Frank Sinatra the plum role of Maggio which won him an Academy Award and revitalized his career. In another version of the story, Ava Gardner, Frank Sinatra's wife at the time, used her influence with Harry Cohn's wife to get Sinatra the role.

In the end the Mafia blamed Castro's revolution and Kennedy's failure to remove Castro for all their personal and business cares and woes, especially Carlos Marcello, Jimmy Hoffa, Santos Trafficante, Sam Giancana and Johnny Rosselli.

Most of this is not in dispute. What does pose a problem for some who study these events are the names of some of the ships forming the armada to attack the Bay of Pigs—because they link George Herbert Walker Bush, at the time, to the CIA, and, perhaps, to the assassination of JFK.

Secretary of the Navy John Connally, the same Governor John Connally who was riding in the Kennedy limo and was nearly killed, provided at least six or seven destroyers and one carrier, the *USS Essex*,[1] for the invasion. Two destroyers accompanied each of the three transport ships that carried the approximately 1400 members of Brigade 2506—one fore, one aft—to three landing sites at the Bay of Pigs.[2] The *USS Essex*, equipped with jet fighters and an undetermined number of marines, stayed beyond the horizon, or roughly thirty miles offshore, on the orders of Kennedy.

Here's where things become problematic. Three of the ships used by the Brigade were named the *Houston*, the *Barbara* or the *Barbara J*, and the *Zapata* (although some say there was no ship named the *Zapata*). In addition, all the ships also had code names, making them difficult to identify. The official sources say that two of the three ships were leased from the Garcia lines, owned by an anti-Castro partisan, for $600 a day plus expenses. This is in question.

Paul Kangas, in an interview in the "*Realist*," claims that Air Force Colonel L. Fletcher Prouty, who served as CIA liaison officer to the Pentagon, said,

> ...one of the projects he (Prouty) did for the CIA was, in 1961,

1 US markings were painted over on most of the ships.
2 The beaches were code-named Blue, Red, and Green.

to deliver US Navy ships from a Navy ship yard to the CIA agents in Guatemala planning the invasion of Cuba. He said he delivered three ships to a CIA agent named George Bush who had the three ships painted to look like they were civilian ships. He named the ships: *Barbara, Houston,* and *Zapata.* [1]

At the time, George Bush was Vice-President of the Zapata Corporation, an offshore drilling operation with locations in the Caribbean. The exact location seems difficult to pin down. Zapata Corporation or Zapata Oil had known ties to the CIA.

Controversy surrounds the name of those ships. Some say the *Barbara* was the *Barbara J,* and since Barbara Bush had no middle name,[2] this could not have referred to her. Some sources do not name a ship *Zapata,* which could refer to the Zapata swamps. The *Houston* could refer to the home office of the Zapata Corporation.

The most concise description of the ships involved in the invasion comes from Wikipedia and is, surprisingly, more detailed than you'll find in the major works on the Bay of Pigs:

> ...The fleet, labeled the "Cuban Expeditionary Force" (CEF), included five 2,400-ton (empty weight) freighter ships chartered by the CIA from the Garcia Lines, and subsequently outfitted with anti-aircraft guns. Four of the freighters, *Houston* (code name *Aguja*), *Rio Escondido* (code name *Ballena*), *Caribe* (code named *Sardina*), and *Atlantico* (code named *Tiburon*), were planned to transport about 1,400 troops in seven battalions of troops and armaments near to the invasion beaches. The 5th freighter, *Lake Charles,* was loaded with follow-up supplies and some OPERATION 40 infiltration personnel. The freighters sailed under Liberian ensigns. Accompanying them were two LCIs (Landing Craft Infantry) purchased [sic] from Zapata Corporation then outfitted with heavy armaments at Key West, then exercises and training at Vieques Island. The LCIs were *Blagar* (code name *Marsopa*) and *Barbara J* (code named *Barracuda*), sailing under Nicaraguan ensigns. The CEF ships were individually escorted (outside visual range) to Point Zulu by US Navy destroyers *USS Bache, USS Beale, USS Conway, USS Cony, USS Eaton, USS Murray, USS Waller.* US Navy Task Group 81.8 had already assembled off the Cayman Islands, commanded by Rear Admiral John E. Clark onboard aircraft carrier *USS Essex,* plus helicopter assault carrier *USS Boxer,* destroyers *USS Hank, USS John W. Weeks, USS Purdy, USS Wren,* and submarines *USS Cobbler* and *USS Threadfin.* Command

---

1 *The Kennedy Assassination: The Nixon-Bush Connection,* Kangas in *Uncategorized* by ce399, on 11/06/2011, p. 1.
2 Barbara Bush did have a maiden name—Pierce Welsh.

and control ship *USS Northampton* and carriers *USS Shangri-La* were also reportedly active in the Caribbean at the time. *USS San Marcos* was a Landing Ship Dock that carried three LCUs (Landing Craft Utility) and four LCVPs (Landing Craft, Vehicles, Personnel). *San Marcos* had sailed from Vieques Island. At Point Zulu, the seven CEF ships sailed north without the USN escorts, except for *San Marcos* that continued until the seven landing craft were unloaded when just outside the 5 kilometer (3mi) Cuban territorial limit.[1]

Backing up Prouty's 1961 Bush–CIA connection is US Army Brigadier General Russell Bowen, who writes in *The Immaculate Deception: The Bush Crime Family Exposed,*

> Bush, in fact, did work directly with the anti-Castro Cuban groups in Miami before and after the Bay of Pigs invasion, using his company, Zapata Oil, as a corporate cover for his activities on behalf of the agency [CIA]. Records at the University of Miami, where the operations were based for several years, show George Bush present at this time.[2]

In 1987, General Bowen, former Army liaison to CIA Director George Bush, attempted to expose George Herbert Walker Bush's drug smuggling operation. He contacted local authorities about a Boeing 707 filled with cocaine headed for Florida. He redirected the plane to Atlanta and notified the authorities. Instead of being rewarded for his efforts he was taken into custody by CIA agents loyal to George Bush and taken to a federal prison hospital in Springfield, Missouri, where he was held without a hearing and injected with codeine which damaged his heart. After protests about his incarceration, Bowen was released six and one-half years after being taken into custody. He fled to a foreign country and wrote his book.

There are several other ex-CIA sources tying George Bush to the CIA at this time. It should be noted here that George Herbert Walker Bush denied it when questioned by Congress in 1978 before his appointment as CIA Director. When years later he was shown a memo from J. Edgar Hoover[3] which revealed a briefing on the JFK assassination in late November, 1963, to a George Bush of the CIA, George Herbert Walker Bush said it must be another George Bush. A subsequent investigation by a reporter did indeed turn up a George William Bush in the CIA . But that other George Bush was a GS5-level employee, the equivalent of a senior file clerk; he worked for the CIA for a six month period in 1963–64 and he denied being briefed by the DIA (Defense Intelligence Agency) or the FBI.[4]

1 Wikipedia, http://en.wikipedia.org/wiki/Bay of Pigs Invasion.
2 *The Immaculate Deception*, Bowen, p. 31.
3 Memo is reproduced in the back of this book.
4 *Plausible Denial*, Lane, p 331.

As expected, D-Day was Disaster Day for the invading forces. Not only were they unable to land their crafts because of the coral reefs on Blue Beach—they were not able to unload enough supplies, since to be covert required them to unload under cover of darkness. Within a span of twenty-four hours, Castro had 20,000 plus men and dozens of T-34 tanks at the Bay of Pigs. The Cuban T-33 fighter jets sank one ship, damaged others, and the rest ran out to sea leaving 1,400 or so men stranded on the beaches, blocked by the Zapata swamps from moving inland and sitting ducks for Castro, who captured roughly 1,200 men, one hundred having been killed, another hundred having escaped or having never landed in the first place.

Negotiations for their release consumed almost two years. Bobby Kennedy took charge of raising private funds for their ransom, since, of course, officially the US denied its involvement—to international amusement.

The first deal came apart over the confusion involving the 500 tractors/bulldozers which Castro had originally requested. Castro had wanted bulldozers; Bobby Kennedy wanted to give him tractors. Eventually a deal was struck for roughly $53 million worth of foodstuffs and medicines plus a few million dollars in cash. The cash never arrived, yet the prisoners were released to great fanfare in Miami three or four days before Christmas in 1962.

The critical points here are: (1) Richard Nixon and George H.W. Bush were heavily involved in the planning for the Bay of Pigs invasion, although Bush's role is not as well documented. (2) The CIA and the Cubans blamed Kennedy exclusively, and they felt betrayed and turned almost rabid in their hatred of Kennedy for not rescuing their comrades with a full US Air Force and Marine invasion force after it became obvious that OPERATION ZAPATA was failing. It has been suggested that the CIA pressed ahead with the knowingly flawed invasion plan thinking Kennedy would not let it fail and would send in the Air Force and Marines to salvage the operation at the last minute. After all, why was the carrier *USS Essex* sent with a complement of jets and marines if Kennedy or the CIA did not intend to use them as backup? (3) The Mafia, having established a working relationship and tacit understanding with the CIA that was to continue for many decades, with their mutual hatred of and numerous attempts to assassinate Castro, felt betrayed by John F. Kennedy for not succeeding in overthrowing Castro and returning their casinos to them.

The Mafia, under Charles "Lucky" Luciano, had started working together with the FBI and the CIA toward the end of World War II, before the invasion of Sicily which, at the time, was under the control of Mussolini, who had sided with Hitler. During the war, the Navy contacted Luciano through Meyer Lansky, because Luciano was in prison, serving time in Sing Sing and the Clinton Correctional Facility in New York for compulsory prostitution and pandering for prostitution. Meyer Lansky told Luciano that the Navy wanted his help in preventing dock strikes or other hostile activities on the New York docks, including infiltration of Italian spies, since the Mafia controlled the docks on the east coast. Luciano was moved to Great Meadow Correctional Facility which was closer to New York City and a much more comfortable prison. Luciano contacted Albert Anastasia, who controlled the docks for Luciano, who saw to it there were no problems for the duration of the war. When the Allies prepared to invade Sicily, they contacted Luciano again for help with his connections in Sicily to insure a successful landing. After the war, New York Governor Thomas Dewey commuted Luciano's sentence but deported him to Sicily. Luciano later claimed, and others have confirmed, that he actually did very little to help the war effort—essentially scamming the government to obtain his freedom.

The Mafia was also livid over Robert F. Kennedy's intense efforts to crack down on Mafia operations such as gambling, loan sharking, and prostitution. He also deported Mafia leaders such as Carlos Marcello and attempted to deport Johnny Rosselli (born Francesco Cacco in Palermo, Italy), both of whom who were here illegally. He also targeted Jimmy Hoffa and Sam Giancana for union pension fraud, among other issues.

CHAPTER 4. THE AFTERMATH OF THE BAY OF PIGS

Kennedy was deeply embarrassed both internationally and nationally by the failure of the Bay of Pigs. Three months later at the Vienna Summit, Khrushchev perceived Kennedy to be weak, politically unsophisticated, and capable of being intimidated. Khrushchev told Kennedy he was going to sign a peace accord with East Germany which would limit Western access to Berlin. Kennedy told Khrushchev, "Then, Mr. Chairman, there will be war."

Originally, the Vienna Summit was touted as a success for Kennedy, but according to *New York Times* reporter James Reston, Kennedy told him that Khrushchev "beat the hell out of me...He savaged me."

Khrushchev decided to go ahead with the Berlin Wall without fear of being challenged by Kennedy. On August 13, 1961, barely four months after the failure of the Bay of Pigs, the wall started to go up. It would divide East and West Germany for the next 28 years—a major violation of the post-World War II Potsdam Agreement. Khrushchev knew Kennedy had lost face internationally and was too weak politically to challenge him.

Castro, too, felt emboldened. Cuba was, as he rightly claimed, the first country to ever have defeated the United States. Castro may have asked for, or Khrushchev may have suggested, the installation of Russian missiles on Cuban soil. Cuba wanted to insure against another invasion, while Khrushchev wanted a counter to the US missiles on Turkish soil aimed at Russia. During the Cuban Missile Crisis, Kennedy actually did remove the US Apollo missiles from Turkish soil in exchange for the removal of Russian missiles in Cuba. (The Apollo missiles were in fact obsolete and were slated for removal anyway. The more important strategic bombers were left in place.) However, only some of the Russian missiles were removed from Cuba. The American public was never informed about the exchange—or the fact that some Russian missiles remained in Cuba. (Most likely, Russian missiles are still in Cuba today.)

Che Guevara sent Kennedy a note through Richard Goodwin thanking him for the invasion. Che said the failed invasion strengthened a weakening revolution. He also suggested that Cuba would be willing to compensate American corporations for nationalized property, if the embargoes were lifted. Kennedy did not respond.

At the UN, Adlai Stevenson[1] made an impassioned denial of the invasion almost as it was happening. On April 15, 1961, Ambassador Stevenson vehemently denied the Cuban Ambassador's charges that the US was planning an imminent invasion of Cuba and that American planes were bombing Cuban airfields. Ambassador Stevenson displayed a photo of one the planes in question. He claimed it had taken off from Cuban airspace and pointed out the Cuban Air Force markings. Less than a day later, it became evident to the world that the plane was a repainted American plane and not a Cuban plane. Two days after Stevenson's speech, Brigade 2506 landed at the Bay of Pigs. Stevenson had believed the CIA cover story. Both Kennedy and the CIA felt his speech would be more believable if he did not know the truth. Both Stevenson and the United States were embarrassed internationally. Stevenson offered to resign.

At home Allen Dulles, Director of the CIA, Richard Bissell, Director of Covert Actions, and General Charles Cabell, Deputy Director of the CIA, were asked to leave the agency as soon as convenient. Secretary of the Navy Connally, who had been recommended to Kennedy by Johnson, left his post at the end of the year as well.

President Kennedy was so angry with the CIA that he said he would "splinter the CIA into a thousand pieces and scatter it to the winds."[2]

It is reported that Kennedy no longer trusted his generals and began to rely almost exclusively on his brother, the Attorney General, for advice. His lack of trust is somewhat unjustified, as Kennedy himself contributed to the failure, although not as much as the CIA and the Joint Chiefs of Staff. His excuse that the CIA and the Joint Chiefs of Staff should have insisted more forcefully that the air strikes were critical rings hollow. Although, if it is true, as suggested by Colonel Prouty, that Bundy, on the instructions of Bissell, made the decision to cancel the second air strike without consulting Kennedy, this would ameliorate Kennedy's culpability in the failure.

In any event, President Kennedy and his brother almost immediately, and secretly, and with only a handful of inner circle advisors, began to plan a full scale invasion of Cuba to be launched in December of 1963. They set up a back door channel with Juan Almeida Bosque, a Cuban high up in the hierarchy of Castro's government. Alameida, in terms of responsibility, was the military commander of the central region of Cuba with headquarters in Santa Clara. Che commanded the western region with headquarters in Pinar

---

1 Stevenson claimed he was never informed about the invasion but there is evidence he was briefed by Bissell.
2 *CIA: Maker of Policy or Tool?*, NYT, April 25, 1966.

del Rio. Raul commanded the eastern region headquartered in Santiago de Cuba, and Fidel commanded the rest of Cuba. Almeida was selected by the Kennedy brothers to replace Castro after their invasion succeeded.[1]

In the Cuban community, despite the ransoming of the Brigade 2506 prisoners, there was widespread and intense hatred for John Kennedy even after Kennedy's promise to return the Brigade's flag to them, in Havana, one day.

In the Mafia, the perceived ingratitude for having handed Kennedy a margin of victory, razor thin as it was with 100,000 (or 112,000) votes in the 1960 presidential election—when Nixon was favored to win—was a major point of contention. Sam Giancana, head of the Chicago Mafia, especially felt that the 100,000 votes came mainly from Cook County, Illinois, his home turf. Giancana felt humiliated and scorned by other Mafia families for having aided the Kennedy family in the election of 1960—and having been conned by them.

The seeds of the conspiracy to eliminate Kennedy were nurtured by the failure of the Bay of Pigs. Most of the forces and major players were coming together at this point. These forces included Johnson, Nixon, Bush, Hunt, Sturgis, Ruby, Oswald,[2] the Mafia, Marcello, Trafficante, Rosselli, the CIA,[3] John Connally, and the Joint Chiefs of Staff, among others.

The only thing missing were the financiers. And they would be lining up as soon as Lyndon Johnson informed them about Kennedy's intention to eliminate the mother of all tax relief measures—the Oil Depletion Allowance so dear to the hearts and wallets of the Texas oilmen—H.L. Hunt, Syd Richardson Jr., and Clint Murchison Jr.

---

1 This account is in dispute and seems to contradict the détente Kennedy was seeking with Castro although this could have been a fallback position.
2 Ruby and Oswald ran guns to Cuba under Guy Bannister in New Orleans.
3 Allen Dulles, General Cabell, Tracy Barnes are among the top leadership involved.

PART TWO. THE KENNEDY ASSASSINATION—ROUND UP THE USUAL
SUSPECTS

Chapter 5. The Interested Parties I—Lyndon Johnson and the Texans

Lyndon Johnson was obsessed with power. My cousin mentioned that to me, but many others have said the same thing. Johnson, since childhood, had talked incessantly to anyone and everyone about wanting to be president. It was a near obsession according to his friends. Johnson biographer Robert Caro writes that Johnson, at the age of twelve, said he was going to be President of the United States. At Saturday night dances he would repeat the same mantra. Caro also wrote that Johnson's maternal grandmother, Ruth Baines, on many occasions said, "That boy is going to wind up in the penitentiary—just mark my word."

He was nicknamed "Lying Lyndon" at Southwest Texas Teacher's College, a school he felt did not provide even a mediocre education let alone an adequate one. As powerful as he became, he was intimidated by Eastern universities such as Harvard, Yale, and Princeton, and the men who attended them. It was one of the sources of his frequent bouts of depression.

At Southwest Texas Teacher's College, he was not popular or even liked and could not shake the stigma of rural poverty which forced him to do menial and humiliating labor such as shining shoes at the local barber shop or herding goats for funds to finish school. Even to get to college he had to work on a road gang, digging gravel roads from Johnson City to Austin with pick ax and shovel in weather so cold the men would have to build a fire to thaw their hands so they could grip a shovel. He cut cedar or picked cotton on other people's farms on his hands and knees in the burning sun for two dollars a day. And even with all his hard work, the Johnson family was forced to accept the charity of neighbors who brought food to their door on a regular basis. They constantly feared losing their home for non-payment of taxes. Between bouts of melancholia, Lyndon yearned for a higher purpose, a destiny he felt he was owed. He took to bragging and bravado and winning school elections at any cost. His false front among his fellow workers, friends, and fellow students earned him his well-deserved nickname.

After he was elected to Congress he went back to his college and destroyed most, but not all, of the college yearbooks that mentioned it. It just wasn't good politics—nor was having his sister, Josepha, arrested for a lesbian act in a public park in the 1950s with the wife of Johnson's associate Malcolm (Mac) Wallace,[1] who was employed by the Texas Department of Agriculture owing to Johnson's influence. Mac saw to it that no one who could harm Johnson's political career, even Johnson's sister Josepha, was ever seen alive ever again. (Josepha Johnson was only one of seventeen people Johnson is said to have had killed because they threatened his all-consuming political ambitions. Kennedy was the last obstacle that stood in the way of his ultimate goal, the presidency.)

Johnson, a master manipulator, needed like-minded friends to realize his life's ambition. He found his strongest ally and soul mate in Edward Aubrey Clark.

Ed Clark, known to his friends as "Mr. Ed," was a law graduate of the University of Texas becoming, in 1935, the Assistant Attorney General and, later, Secretary of State for Texas. His law firm was the most influential in Texas and Clark was responsible for most of the judgeships in Texas. Besides his Big Oil clients, such as Clint Murchison Jr., Clark served as Johnson's main legal counsel for almost thirty years[2]—and co-conspirator with Johnson in the assassination of John Kennedy.

When Kennedy started to challenge the major institutions and corporations that run this country—the oil industry, the Federal Reserve, the CIA, the Mafia, and the military-industrial complex, Johnson saw his opportunity and seized it like a hungry jackal. Ed Clark was only too happy to help.

Kennedy, and the rest of the country, had been warned about the dangers of the military-industrial complex. Eisenhower, in his farewell address on January 17, 1961, said: "In the councils of government, we must guard against the acquisition of unwarranted influence, whether sought or unsought, by the military-industrial complex. The potential for the disastrous rise of misplaced power exists and will persist."[3]

He was never warned about Johnson.

Still, Senator John Kennedy was well aware of Johnson's influence in handing over government contracts and backing legislation favorable to the oil industry and the military-industrial complex, including NASA. Most of those interests were located in Texas and Johnson's influence was critical to

---

1 Mac Wallace's fingerprint was identified, years after the assassination, on a tip, as being found on the 6th floor of the Texas School Book Depository on 11/22/63.
2 In 1965, Johnson appointed Clark Ambassador to Australia.
3 Eisenhower's first draft included the phrase "military-industrial-congressional complex."

the survival of those interests. Thus, they would protect Johnson's influence at any cost. But when it came to Johnson, Kennedy had no idea whom he was dealing with. And Johnson took no prisoners when it came to his enemies. He kept his hired gun, Mac Wallace, and his attorney, Ed Clark, very, very busy.

Mac Wallace's first assignment from Johnson had been issued through capo head of the Washington, D.C. area, Cliff Carter. Johnson buffered himself well from direct incrimination.

Mac's assignment was to eliminate John "Doug" Kinser, who Johnson thought had threatened him. Kinser was dating Johnson's sister, Josepha, at the time, and must have had some information about Johnson's criminal activities.

Mac made some rookie mistakes that resulted in his being quickly captured, tried, convicted, but unbelievably, released, compliments of Lyndon Johnson and friends. The story is told more completely in Barr McClelland's excellent work, *Blood, Money, and Power: How LBJ killed JFK*, but here is a brief account.

Doug Kinser ran a local golf driving range called the "Pitch and Putt." He wanted to expand and add a miniature golf course. He asked Lyndon for a loan—twice. The second time Lyndon thought the request a little too forceful—probably bolstered with information from Josepha about Johnson's criminal activities.

On October 22, 1951, Wallace walked straight into the "Pitch and Putt" pro shop and shot Kinser point blank, several times, and left without bothering to see if anyone was around.

A customer wrote down the license number of Wallace's vehicle and within hours he was arrested, with the gun still smoking, as they say. Even though Mac was charged with first-degree murder, Ed Clark, Lyndon's longtime friend, political mentor, Texas political powerhouse, and recipient of nearly $8 million for his role in the murder of John Kennedy,[1] had Wallace released on bail of $10,000, reduced from $30,000—unheard of in a capital crime in Texas. Another Johnson attorney, John Cofer, represented Wallace at trial and *admitted* the shooting but, in his one-page defense and motion, claimed that Kinser was sleeping with Wallace's wife as well as with Josepha.

He was found guilty of murder with malice, after two hours of rushed testimony. Eleven jurors voted for the death penalty, one for life. Judge Charles O. Betts, presiding, overruled the jury and sentenced Wallace to five years in prison—sentence suspended.

Wallace, arrogant and smiling, was out the courtroom door with the District Attorney Bob Long before the jury knew what had hit them—the not-so-velvet-gloved hand of Lyndon Johnson who had taken a room in town for the trial.

Johnson's friends could be counted on for a variety of favors. When

---

1 *Blood, Money, Power: How LBJ Killed JFK*, Barr McClellan.

Johnson ran for the Senate in 1948, his friends came to cheer him on and help in any way necessary. About a million votes were manually counted in four days, and Lyndon appeared to be losing to popular ex-governor "Coke" Stevenson by about 117 votes. Thankfully, his friend Ed Clark (or Clark's partner, Don Thomas) located a box of missing ballots in the small Texas town of Alice just in the nick of time. Miraculously, and to the relief of Johnson's loyal but worried supporters, the box contained 200 (or 202) ballots—2 for "Coke" Stevenson, 198 (or 200) for Johnson—giving him a plurality of approximately 87 votes to become the junior Senator from Texas.

According to McClellan, the ballots were all in alphabetical order and in the handwriting of Don Thomas, McClellan's boss at Clark, Thomas, and Winters, Austin's most influential law firm at the time. It became known as the "Box 13 Scandal." He won by such a slim margin that he earned the nickname "Landslide Lyndon."

But the scandal did not end there. "Coke" Stevenson appealed to the United States Supreme Court. Johnson's lawyers, including a certain Abe Fortas, prevailed after an FBI investigation by J. Edgar Hoover which cleared Johnson. Abe Fortas was later appointed by Johnson to the Supreme Court. Hoover was Johnson's neighbor in Washington and a member of Johnson's 8F Suite group of powerful and influential businessmen and politicians.

According to a Johnson business associate, Billie Sol Estes, Ike Rogers, and his secretary, judges overseeing the voting, were killed by Mac Wallace. Johnson's almost maniacal ambition to become president had just taken a giant step forward.

Johnson, who had wanted to run for president in the 1960 election, was so power-hungry and so important to the political and business powers in Texas that when he ran on the 1960 ticket with Kennedy, he had Texas law changed to allow himself to run for two offices simultaneously—the Senate and the Vice-Presidency, illegal in all other states. It was called "The Johnson Act." It was engineered through the Texas legislature by Ed Clark.

With Johnson in the Senate, no-bid contracts of all kind flowed into Texas and into the bulging pockets of friends who had helped him—such as ex-Nazi General Walter Dornberger, head of Hitler's V2 rocket program at Peenemünde along with ex-Nazi Major Wernher von Braun, who later became head of NASA, *which, although this is not well known, is also empowered to act as a spy agency.* Von Braun was also a member of Permindex along with H.L. Hunt, Clay Shaw, and Joe Bonanno. These associations and Permindex will be discussed in the next section.

Dornberger had recently started working at Bell Laboratories, located in Texas, under founder Lawrence Bell. The company made the Bell helicopter used extensively in Vietnam. Five thousand of these slow-moving targets were destroyed in Vietnam after Johnson became President.

Having had manufactured only four helicopters at the time, Dornberger let Johnson use one of them for blitzkrieg campaigning in rural Texas. Texans, bereft of even electric power, thought Johnson a god descending to earth like a *deus ex machina* promising them dams and rural electrification. He was a tireless campaigner with a charming, magnetic personality, according to his longtime Texas mistress Madeleine Duncan Brown, who met the young congressman at a party where, after a quick dance, he pressed his room key into her hands, smiled seductively and walked away.

Another beneficiary of Lyndon's largesse was General Dynamics (Lockheed Martin), who despite having never built a fighter jet, was awarded a $6.5 billion contract to build the TFX-111 fighter plane—even though they were underbid by 100 to 400 million (depending on the source), by Boeing. The president of General Dynamics/Lockheed Martin was former Secretary of the Army, Frank Pace. The Deputy Secretary of Defense in 1962 was Roswell Gilpatric, who had been general counsel for General Dynamics—and a member of the Suite 8F Group—a group of Texas oilmen and businessmen who met regularly in Suite 8F of the Lamar Hotel in Houston to divide up the contracts that Lyndon secured through his powerful position as majority leader of the Senate.[1]

The membership of the 8F Suite Group significantly reveals Johnson's connections in the **Senate and with the rich** and powerful. They included John Connally, ex-Secretary of the Navy; George and Herman Brown of Brown and Root, later a subsidiary of Halliburton; Hugh Roy Cullen of Quintana Petroleum; Texas Governor William Hobby; Morgan Davis of Humble Oil; Congressman Albert Thomas, Chairman of the House Appropriations Committee, Subcommittee on Defense; James Abercrombie of Cameron Iron Works and William Vinson of Great Southern Life Insurance. They worked closely with Robert Anderson, Robert Kerr, Glen McCarthy, David Harold Byrd, Sid Richardson, H.L. Hunt, Eugene B. Germany—all oil men plus Billy Sol Estes, Bobby Baker and a few senators and congressman.

It follows that when Kennedy started to put together a tax reform act that would eliminate the fabled "Oil Depletion Allowance," the Texas oilmen were apoplectic because this tax loophole was worth several billion dollars a year in today's dollars. It was the most generous tax break ever devised and had allowed H.L. Hunt, the world's richest man at the time, to pay zero income tax on his 500 plus oil wells and his 500 plus corporations. It worked something like this.

A typical oil well, costing $100,000 to bring in, would produce roughly $1,000,000 in annual revenues, resulting in a tax credit of $275,000 (the 27.5% Oil Depletion Allowance[2]) against all other income. It's no wonder the Texas oil men hated Kennedy and were more than willing to finance his removal—one way or another.

---

1 There is another version saying that Kennedy was behind the awarding of the contract to General Dynamics/Lockheed Martin and that he did so through Arthur Goldberg as a means of bolstering democratic districts in which he was weak for the upcoming elections.
2 Kennedy was trying to pass legislation to reduce the subsidy to 17.5%. Nixon reduced it to 15% and Carter eliminated it.

In a disputed account (retold in a TV interview in 1990 on *A Current Affair*, available on Youtube), Madeleine Duncan Brown, in her autobiography, *Texas in the Morning: The Love Story of Madeleine Duncan Brown and President Lyndon Baines Johnson*, tells of a late night/early morning meeting at the huge Dallas estate of oilman Clint Murchison Jr. beginning on the eve of November 22, 1963. She claims that an assembly of powerful individuals arrived for a party, ostensibly in honor of J. Edgar Hoover, on the night before the assassination. This group of wealthy and politically-connected men included: Richard Nixon; J. Edgar Hoover, Director of the FBI; Clyde Tolson, Deputy Director at the FBI as well as Hoover's roommate and homosexual lover; Texas Governor John Connally; Jack Ruby; John J. McCloy[1] (World Bank president, U.S. High Commissioner for post-war Germany and Chairman of the Rockefeller owned, at the time, Chase Manhattan Bank); H.L. Hunt, and several others from the 8F Suite Group.

Johnson, who arrived late, around 11 PM, was ushered into Murchison's office. Johnson, leaving the meeting after about an hour, grabbed Madeleine hard by the arms and, more excited than she had ever seen him, said, in effect—after tomorrow those S.O.B. Kennedys will never embarrass me again...that's no threat...that's a promise.

Madeleine also wrote that the planning for the assassination of President Kennedy began on the floor of the 1960 Democratic Convention after a deal was struck between Joseph Kennedy and H.L. Hunt in California, three years earlier. Johnson had run for the presidential nomination but ineffectively. In an embarrassing but necessary compromise, Johnson accepted the Vice-Presidential nomination. Johnson realized that a Kennedy victory would have meant a Kennedy dynasty, which would have outlived his obsession to become president.

A slightly different account of this is told by Phillip Nelson in *LBJ—The Mastermind of the JFK Assassination*. He states that Johnson made only a half-hearted attempt to get the presidential nomination at the convention. He campaigned only five days before the start of the convention and then only to have his name placed on the ticket as Vice-President, knowing he could never win the presidency itself due to his conservative Southern Democratic background and lack of liberal support. His anti-civil rights reputation was despised by the Eastern establishment.

Not being on the short or even the long list of vice-presidential nominees[2] that Kennedy was considering, Johnson, according to Madeleine Brown, blackmailed Kennedy with FBI-supplied files of Kennedy's many extra-marital affairs. In addition, Johnson threatened to expose Kennedy's affliction with Addison's Disease. Kennedy's illness was not widely known and, in fact, Kennedy's doctor's office was broken into and Kennedy's files

---

1 McCloy would eventually sit on the Warren Commission.
2 Stuart Symington, Senator from Missouri, was originally asked to run with Kennedy who then had to un-ask him.

were copied by the FBI before the convention. Addison's, at the time, was incurable and carried a prognosis of a shortened lifespan. It could have meant the loss of the election if the illness were to be made public.

But Johnson's trump card was his threat to block all of Kennedy's legislation in the Senate, and Kennedy knew that Johnson, as Senate Majority leader, was in a position to do just that.

According to Nelson, Johnson planned all along to get on the ticket as the Vice-Presidential candidate—and become president by killing Kennedy in office.

Madeleine Duncan Brown's exposé of the meeting at Clint Murchison's house on the eve of the assassination was dangerous—all of the powerful people named denied having been present. One can imagine how Madeleine Brown's credibility has been attacked. Two others who were there that evening and who offered to back up her account were killed—Texas Ranger Clint Peoples and a maid at the Murchisons' home.

Nixon and Johnson were seen publicly earlier in the evening and some speculate they could not have arrived at the Murchison house at the time Madeleine says they did. Madeleine also says that she saw Lee Harvey Oswald and Jack Ruby together at the Carousel Club, Jack Ruby's strip club—prior to the assassination. Nixon had stated that he left Dallas the following morning two hours before JFK landed at Love Field. However, Mr. Harvey Russell, general counsel for Pepsi-Cola, and his son, said Nixon was in Dallas at the time of the assassination and was driven to the airport after the assassination by a Mr. Deluca, an official of the Pepsi-Cola Company.[1] Nixon had also given several differing accounts of how and when he learned of the assassination—as had E. Howard Hunt, Frank Sturgis and George H.W. Bush.

The *Report of the President's Commission on the Assassination of President Kennedy*, commonly referred to as the Warren Commission Report (WCR), says there is "no credible evidence to support the rumors linking Oswald and Ruby directly or through others."[2]

1 *JFK, The CIA, Vietnam, And the Plot to Assassinate John F. Kennedy*, L. Fletcher Prouty, 1992, Birch Lane Press Books, p. 350.
2 WCR, appendix 12, p. 661.

CHAPTER 6. THE INTERESTED PARTIES II—THE PERMINDEX–TEXAS–CIA–MAFIA CONNECTION

Lyndon Johnson's influence was not limited to Texas or even the USA. He and his friends had powerful international connections. One of those connections was with a shadowy company called "Permindex."

Permindex, a contraction of Permanent Industrial Expositions, was incorporated and based in Basel, Switzerland, with a subsidiary, Centro Mondiale Commerciale (CMC), in Rome. Also located in Basel are the banker's bank, the Bank for International Settlements (BIS), and a bank owned by Hans Seligman—the Seligman-Schurch & Co. Bank. Both of those banks have been involved with Permindex and Hans Seligman has been mentioned as a member of the board of Permindex.

Permindex had a very impressive board of directors that, by another troublesome coincidence, included members of Johnson's Dallas-based 8F Suite Group, the CIA, the Mafia, NASA, and several important out-of-office world political figures.

Permindex was incorporated in 1958 by president and major stockholder Louis Mortimer Bloomfield, an attorney specializing in international boundaries. He worked for the most powerful law firm in Canada, Vineberg and Goldman. Vineberg and Goldman's wealthiest and most famous client was the Samuel Bronfman family, best known for Canadian Club[1] whiskey which they distilled, among others.

Co-founder George Mantello, *AKA* George Mandel, is listed as the official founder on incorporation papers. The active behind-the-scenes leader of

---

[1] Joseph Kennedy is said to have started amassing his fortune by illegally importing Canadian Club during Prohibition. Together with Meyer Lansky they imported whiskey with the help of shipping magnate Aristotle Onassis.

Permindex was reported to be Ferenc Nagy, ex-Prime Minister of Hungary, who headed the Solidarists division, one of five divisions of Permindex.

A second division, the American Council of Churches, was headed by H.L. Hunt. The American Council of Churches, Dallas Chapter, has been called the real power in Dallas. Membership included all the most influential people in Dallas.

The other divisions of Permindex—the Security Division headed by Wernher von Braun,[1] head of the US space program and NASA, based in Texas, The Free Cuba Committee—headed by ex-Prime Minister of Cuba, Carlos Prio Socarras, and the Syndicate Division headed by Clifford Jones, ex-Lieutenant Governor of Nevada. This last group included Joe Bonanno, head of one of the five major crime families of the Mafia in New York.[2] Other members of this 5th division included Lewis McWillie and Bobby Baker, Secretary to Senate Majority leader Lyndon Johnson.

Baker had been forced to resign as Johnson's assistant due to numerous scandals with which he was identified. One of the most notorious involved John Kennedy and an East German hostess at Baker's Quorum Club, Ellen Rometsch. Rometsch worked at the Quorum Club which was conveniently located next to the Senate Office Building in Washington, D.C., in the Carroll Arms Hotel. It was frequented by politicians. After Kennedy was introduced to Ellen Rometsch, Kennedy is reported to have said he spent three of the most erotic, sensual nights of his life with her. Unfortunately, she was also having an affair with a KGB agent at the same time. Robert Kennedy quashed an investigation of the relationship after it became public, by making a deal with Hoover. Rometsch was quickly sent out of the country. Hoover blackmailed those senators who were investigating the Kennedy–Rometsch affair in exchange for job security and an agreement to illegally wiretap certain individuals, such as Martin Luther King.

The Chappaquiddick Bear Trap

In an odd coincidence, Baker's secretary Nancy Carole Tyler roomed with Mary Jo Kopechne. Mary Jo Kopechne was an aide to Senator Bobby Kennedy and was supposedly killed as the result of a 1969 accident in a car driven by Senator Ted Kennedy. Mary Jo had helped pack up Senator Robert Kennedy's files after he was killed. Is it possible she revealed something to her roommate, Nancy Tyler, who then reported the information to her boss, Bobby Baker, Johnson's aide, who was also known as "Little Lyndon?"

---

1 Wernher von Braun was a former SS Nazi Major who tortured, experimented on, and killed prisoners of war. He and hundreds of other Nazis traded their files on rocketry and human experimentation for a whitewash of their war crimes under OPERATION PAPERCLIP.

2 There are nineteen other Mafia crimes families throughout the US. The most notable are the Chicago family headed by Sam Giancana, The New Orleans and Dallas families headed by Carlos Marcello, and the Florida family headed by Santos Trafficante.

According to police reports at the time, the car, allegedly driven by Ted Kennedy, was on its way to the ferry to Edgartown when it veered left at a fork in the road. Instead of heading toward the ferry, Kennedy turned onto the road which led to Dike's Bridge on a small body of water called Pouch Pond. Instead of crossing the bridge, the car hit the low side rails of the bridge and landed in the water upside down, its roof resting on the bottom. The car flipped over less than five feet from the bridge into about six or seven feet of water with the rear wheels touching the waterline and the front wheels slightly lower due to the weight of the engine. The roof was slightly crushed, the rear passenger window was completely blown out except for a halo of glass shards around the rim of the window, and the driver's side window was open although the door was locked.[1]

Mary Jo Kopechne was found dead in the back seat, with alcohol in her bloodstream, blood on her collar and sleeves, wearing some jewelry, a blouse, a pair of slacks and no underwear except for a bra. She was pulled out of the vehicle through the rear passenger window. She was "one quarter positively buoyant...still a little air in her," according to scuba diver John Farrar, who extracted her through the rear passenger window after entering the window up to his waist and grabbing her rigor mortised[2] body. Farrar also claimed that she could not have been dead or unconscious at the time of the accident as her face was pressed into the rear foot well of the car which still had air. According to Police Chief Arena, "Her mouth was open, teeth gritted in a death grimace...there were no injuries that I could see."[3]

Kennedy stated that he was unfamiliar with the roads on the island; that he exited the car but could not remember how; tried repeatedly to extricate Mary Jo until he was exhausted; went back to the cottage which was 1.2 miles away and returned with two friends, Joe Gargan and Paul Markham, and unsuccessfully attempted to rescue Mary Jo a second time; swam to Edgartown—a distance of 527 feet—and went to his hotel room; was seen at around 3 AM when he asked a hotel employee the time, and at breakfast the next morning dressed and poised as if nothing had happened; did not report the accident for nine hours, at which time he went back to Dike's Bridge to use the pay phone, even though there were several phone available to him at the hotel. His friends Joe Gargan and Paul Markham—both attorneys— did not report the accident, claiming they thought the senator would do so. Kennedy claimed he was in shock.

Questions raised at the time of the incident on July 18, 1969, thirteen months after Robert Kennedy was killed, are still unanswered today. Why was Kennedy's car traveling away from instead of toward the ferry? How was Ted Kennedy able to exit the car while twenty-eight-year old Mary

---

1 Damore, *Senatorial Privilege*, pp. 7-8.
2 Rigor mortis usually commences in 3–4 hours and reaches maximum stiffness in about 12 hours.
3 Damore, *Senatorial Privilege*, p. 9.

Jo was not able to? The open driver's side window and the blown out rear passenger window have never been explained. No autopsy was performed—the drowning was "presumed"—even though legally one should have been performed. Why did the Kennedys expend so much money and effort blocking efforts to exhume the body for an autopsy when it was decided one should be done? How did Mary Jo really die?

The coroner claimed only a cup of water was expelled from her stomach when depressed—a far lesser amount than normally found in a drowning victim. Why were there bloodstains on her collar and sleeves? Were E. Howard Hunt and Frank Sturgis on Chappaquiddick to watch the Annual Edgartown Regatta as they claimed—or some other purpose? Why did Hunt, using the alias Albert Patterson, investigate the accident, requesting an operations report of the accident from police and a drawing of the scene from scuba diver John Farrar?[1] Was there a rope around the steering wheel and the rear view mirror which was nearly torn off the windshield (as I was told by a source who did not want to be identified)? Why was the driver's side window open (and the door locked)? Why did not Kennedy's driver, Jack Crimmins who was at the rented party cottage and who usually drove him, not behind the wheel? (It was speculated that Kennedy left with Mary Jo for a sexual tryst on the beach and did not want his driver along. But Ted Kennedy also had a bad back, and could have gone to his hotel or Mary Jo's, as her roommate was still at the cottage.) Why did the tire tracks seem to indicate Kennedy's car stopped and then quickly accelerated (or possibly accelerated and stopped quickly)? How did the car summersault if it was going at 22 miles per hour, as Kennedy claimed, or even 34 miles per hour as estimated by the police?

Did Kennedy lie about the rescue attempt? He claimed the strong current kept carrying him out of the harbor when the current would actually have carried him into the harbor — if there was a current at the time. According to Harbormaster Robert Morgan, who was towing a sailboat at the time, "The tide was low and quite slack, not moving in either direction."[2]

While researching this work, I was personally told by an undercover detective (to whom I am distantly related by marriage) that Mary Jo Kopechne died as the result of a gunshot wound to the head, by a .25 mm caliber bullet. He told me it was fairly common knowledge among police departments. If this is true, and I have no reason or motive to doubt it, then it is possible Senator Ted Kennedy was "set up" to take the blame for the death of Mary Jo Kopechne in order to deep-six any chance of his running for the presidency. According to retired New York detective Jim Rothstein (who arrested Frank Sturgis after Sturgis's failed attempt on the life of Marita Lorenz), Mary Jo Kopechne was dead before she entered the water. Detective Rothstein could not confirm how she was killed but stated she was definitely dead before

---

1 Ibid., p. 407.
2 Ibid. p. 419.

hitting the water and did not drown as was reported. He also told me in a telephone interview and confirmed by email that the Kopechne family was given $1,000,000 hush money.

Detective Rothstein wrote me regarding Mary Jo:

> I received this information separately from two sources — Channel 5 reporter Mark Monsky and a police official, I believe he was a sergeant, who was one of the first to respond to the scene of the accident on Chappaquiddick. The police official, at a secret meeting in Washington DC, gave me this information in the presence of Police Officer Carl Schoffler, one of the arresting officers at the Watergate break-in, myself, and my partner Matty Rosenthal. Both sources had the same information. I did not see the payoff. It was info I received and believed to be true.

The set-up damaged Ted Kennedy's personal reputation and indeed it effectively prevented him from ever running for the presidency—the only office that would have given him the power to uncover the people behind John Kennedy's assassination and that of his brother, Robert. He was the only real obstacle to Nixon's 1972 re-election run for the presidency.

In my opinion, Ted Kennedy did not even know Mary Jo Kopechne was in the car and may not have been the driver of the vehicle. Ted Kennedy had abrasions around his head and probably never swam to Edgartown, even if he was able to do so, with his bad back. He was most likely unconscious for part of the nine missing hours and did not even hear of the accident until the next morning. His family was threatened, as were the families of Jacqueline and Robert Kennedy, and Ted Kennedy was told to go to the pay phone at Dike's Bridge to wait for a phone call. The caller told him to fabricate a reasonable fiction of what actually happened. Ted Kennedy's explanations for his actions that evening are contradictory, incredible and are believed by no one. The tragedy that evening has all the earmarks of spymaster E. Howard Hunt's imagination including a Mafia-style telegram which Kennedy understood—stay out of presidential politics!

In 1973, John Dean was taped speaking to President Richard Nixon: "If Teddy knew the bear trap he was walking into at Chappaquiddick..."

Lesser board members of Permindex included: Jean Menu de Menil, owner of Schlumberger, a clone of Halliburton; Paul Raigordsky, Chairman of Claiborne Oil of New Orleans; and, among others, Clay Shaw, *AKA* Clay Bertrand of New Orleans, the only man indicted by New Orleans District Attorney Jim Garrison, but acquitted, in the late Sixties, in connection with the assassination of JFK.[1]

---

1 While Shaw was acquitted the jury found that there was a conspiracy to kill JFK but that there was not enough evidence to connect Shaw to the conspiracy.

In recently-released papers of the estate of Louis Mortimer Bloomfield, Ferenc Nagy was shown to have been working with David Rockefeller for the purpose of constructing the World Trade Center (in Spanish, Centro Mondiale Commerciale or CMC) to bolster the value of Chase Manhattan Bank's sixty-story office skyscraper in lower Manhattan, which had been declining in value. Ferenc Nagy has been called the CIA's man in Permindex. The CIA bureau chief in Rome, William "Bill" Harvey, once fired for drunkenness by J. Edgar Hoover, was involved with CMC. He was also part of OPERATION MONGOOSE, the Mafia assisted plan to assassinate Castro. He was Johnny Rosselli's "case worker and handler" in his attempt to assassinate Castro before the Bay of Pigs.

Though ostensibly incorporated to organize international trade shows or exhibitions, Permindex never showed any visible means of support. Yet means of support there were, and they included the distribution of heroin from Southeast Asia's Golden Triangle, diamonds from South Africa, and the laundering the funds from those operations. Those funds were laundered through Hans Seligman, head of the Seligman-Schurch Bank of Basel, Switzerland. Those funds were enormous—so enormous that Switzerland expelled Permindex for money laundering and also because Charles de Gaulle pressured Switzerland to do so after he accused Permindex of an attempt on his life. The 1961 assassination attempt on De Gaulle has been blamed on Algerian generals who felt De Gaulle had betrayed France by giving up French-controlled Algeria to Algerian Nationals—but the two scenarios are not mutually exclusive. After expulsion from Switzerland, Permindex moved to South Africa but was managed out of Canada by Louis Mortimer Bloomfield who preferred being close to home.

Over thirty attempts were made on De Gaulle's life. At least one attempt is said to have been carried out by Lucien Sarti, also known as "The Jackal." Sarti, an assassin with the Marseille Mafia, is said to have been offered a contract by the Bonanno crime family to kill Kennedy. De Gaulle survived all attempted assassinations and marched in Kennedy's funeral procession.

Now the laundering of the vast sums of money from the distribution of Southeast Asian heroin is tied to Marseille and needs to be considered in connection with Nixon, the CIA, and the JFK assassination.

Heroin and the CIA

The term "French Connection" originally referred to the heroin trade. When Ho Chi Minh defeated the French at Dien Bien Phu in 1954, the lucrative heroin trade controlled by the French was threatened. (According to an Air Force Colonel and CIA liaison to the Pentagon, Colonel Fletcher Prouty, one half of the unused munitions sent to Okinawa in 1945 for the anticipated 500,000-man invasion of Japan was diverted to Ho Chi Minh in Hanoi. It was with these weapons that the French were defeated. The other half of the munitions, piled twenty feet high on the beaches of Okinawa, were sent to Korea's Syngman Rhee and most likely were used against Americans in the Korean Conflict. Prouty suspects the CIA of having redirected the munitions, although at the time, FDR favored Ho Chi Minh over Chiang Kai-shek and could have given the order to redirect the munitions; then again, it may have been Truman, after FDR died.)

Heroin from Burma was refined into Number 3 heroin (80% purity) in Pepsi-Cola bottling plants which were set up exclusively for that purpose by the Corsican crime families operating out of Marseille. There were approximately seven such plants in Laos and Thailand. (At this time, Richard Nixon was acting as a corporate counsel for Pepsi and, as such, he was in Dallas attending a conference for Pepsi the day before the assassination. He claims he left the following morning—just before the assassination, according to his account. According to other Pepsi executives, as noted earlier, Nixon was driven to the airport after the assassination. Nixon also claimed he did not remember when or how he heard about the assassination, telling several variations.)

After processing in Laos and Thailand, the Number 3 heroin was shipped out of Saigon on CIA planes marked Air America, to Marseille. There it was refined into Number 4 heroin (95% purity). And from there it was sent on to Sicily, Mena, Arkansas, California, Hawaii, New York City and Washington, D.C.

Toward the end of the Sixties, factories in Southeast Asia were able to process morphine into Number 4 heroin, effectively cutting off the French Connection for a time while effectively lowering the price, especially in South Vietnam.

So sophisticated was the heroin trade that it even used a logo and a brand name—Double UO Globe Brand. The logo was a red circle in the center of which were two lions rampant astride a shield. The best account of the Golden Triangle heroin trade is found in *The Politics of Heroin in Southeast Asia* and *The Politics of Heroin: CIA Complicity in the Global Drug Trade*, both by Professor Alfred W. McCoy.

The drug traffic in the Forties and Fifties was protected by the SDECE, a French Intelligence organization similar to the American CIA. Distribution was basically handled by the Corsican Mafia in Marseille and by the American Mafia via the Bonanno crime family of New York. Vito Corleone in the Godfather saga by Mario Puzo was modeled on Joe Bonanno. The other model is said to have been Vito Genovese.

The Mafia role in the assassination of Kennedy has some of its roots in Marseille with the Corsican Mafia. A French hit man by the name of Christian David, who spoke to a reporter from prison on the promise of a transfer to a better, less dehumanizing prison, claimed that he was originally offered the contract on President Kennedy. Agreeing at first, he declined later, after learning the hit was to be made in the States; he decided an escape out of the United States would be too difficult. But he did go on to recommend three others who were also in the employ of the heroin trafficker

August Ricord of the Corsican Mafia. One of the people David recommended was Lucien Sarti. David declined to name the other two since they were still alive—as he wished to continue to be. Other members of the Corsican Mafia at the time were Antoine Guerini and Meyer Lansky, although Lansky's connection may be dubious even if highly likely. There are problems with David's story, however, in that over fifty people have been named and/or have come forward as the shooter on the grassy knoll—but there is no problem connecting Permindex, the oilmen, the CIA and the Mafia.

Chapter 7. The Interested Parties III—Ferrie, Oswald, Ruby, DeMohrenschildt

I had heard of Lee Harvey Oswald, as most people have. But the names David Ferrie and William Greer had no meaning for me at the time my cousin mentioned them, almost casually. Then he mentioned they were at the rehearsal. I spent the next seven years searching these names and other names that intersected them. I came to find out that everything I had heard about Lee Harvey Oswald was 99% to 110% wrong due to deliberate disinformation. The truth is not all that difficult to come by, with just a little research. While there are hundreds of volumes on the subject, mainly ignored by the mainstream media, just reading a few of the top sources is eye opening, jaw dropping, and very revealing.

Lee Harvey Oswald and David Ferrie met before Oswald joined the marines. Oswald joined the marines one week after his 17th birthday. He had tried to join a year earlier using forged documents prepared by his mother, Marguerite.

David Ferrie was Oswald's superior in the Louisiana Civil Air Patrol (LCAP) although he is on record denying knowing Oswald. (The gentleman who co-founded the Civil Air Patrol was David Harold Byrd, who, in 1963, owned the Texas School Book Depository or TSBD in Dallas, Texas. He was also an oilman.)[1]

David Ferrie

Ferrie was an ex-Eastern airline pilot, fired for homosexual activities on the job. He had an unusual skin condition, known as Alopecia Areata Universalis, which leaves one completely hairless. He used pasted on eyebrows and a poor quality wig, which fooled no one and startled many. He was also a serious researcher of

---

1 Ferrie denied knowing Oswald saying he left the CAP, 1954, before Oswald joined.

cancer and worked with Dr. Ochsner and Judyth Vary Baker.[1] This research was funded by the CIA because the cancer cells they were developing were to be used as a bio-weapon to kill Castro.[2] More on this later.

When not running guns to Castro and acting as Carlos Marcello's personal pilot, Ferrie worked for FBI agent Guy Bannister. Bannister had offices at 544 Camp Street, although some say it was 531 Lafayette Street in New Orleans. This was the same block where Clay Shaw, *AKA* Clay Bertrand/Lambert, the CIA, and Office of Naval Intelligence (ONI) had offices. The discrepancy in the address is immaterial as both addresses are assigned to the same building, the Newman Building, which fronts two streets and has two entrances with different street addresses. The literature Lee Harvey Oswald was distributing when he was arrested in New Orleans titled "Fair Play For Cuba," had the 544 Camp Street address, which infuriated Guy Bannister, who was in charge of Division Five of the FBI and wanted his association with Lee Harvey Oswald to remain a secret.

When Lee Harvey Oswald was arrested after the assassination, David Ferrie's library card was in his wallet. Jim Garrison, New Orleans District Attorney, arrested and released Ferrie on bond in connection with the assassination, together with Clay Shaw. Clay Shaw was the operator of the International Trade Mart in Dallas where Kennedy was to have lunch at a fundraiser after passing through Dealey Plaza. Days later, Ferrie was found dead in his apartment—with two suicide notes—before he could be tried.

Ferrie's activities on the night of November 22, 1963, and the following day are strange, to say the least. Ferrie was in court on an immigration matter with Carlos Marcello, as an advisor, having done some research work for him, when Kennedy was killed.

Immediately afterwards, during a heavy thunderstorm, Ferrie and two companions drove[3] 350 miles during the night to Texas, supposedly to go goose hunting. On the 23rd he spent most of the day at the Winterland Skating Rink near Houston, where he made and received calls at a pay phone—one of which was to Carlos Marcello in New Orleans, according to the rink manager who remembered his appearance. The speculation of some researchers is that he was supposed to have served as the personal pilot for some of the assassins and drove to Houston to fly them out on the night of the 23rd. According to Garrison, Ferrie had deposited $7,000 in his bank account prior to the assassination and afterwards someone purchased a gas station franchise for him.

Marcello claimed he paid Ferrie $7,000 for paralegal work.[4] It was also speculated that Ferrie was a CIA contractor. Ferrie's ex-roommate,

---

1 Judyth Vary Baker was also Lee's New Orleans mistress when he went there to find work after returning from Russia.
2 Jack Ruby claimed he was injected with it before he died.
3 Some accounts claim he flew.
4 Ferrie was not a paralegal but was an extremely intelligent and a capable researcher.

Raymond Broshears, claims that Ferrie told him he went to Houston on the 22nd to await a call from one or more of the shooters of JFK to fly them in a twin engine plane to Central America and then on to South Africa, the home, at the time, of the exiled Permindex, where no extradition treaties existed with the US. He also claimed Ferrie told him some of the assassins panicked and tried to fly to Mexico with another pilot, but the plane crashed and they died off the coast of Corpus Christi. Broshears also felt Oswald did not shoot Kennedy and that there were four teams of shooters in Dealey Plaza—at the Texas School Book Depository (TSBD), the Dal-Tex Building, the grassy knoll, and in the sewer in front of the motorcade.

A fourth team of shooters was also reported by Salvatore "Bill" Bonanno, son of Joseph Bonanno. Bill Bonanno claimed that while serving time in prison, he was told by other Mafia members that Johnny Rosselli was in the sewer in front of the motorcade. It is possible that Rosselli was in the sewer calling out commands to shoot to the three teams of shooters who had radiomen listening for the command to fire—the so called "communications man."[5] According to leading researcher Dr. James Fetzer, Kennedy's throat wound came from a sewer position—the shot traveling through the windshield.

Lee Harvey Oswald

Lee Harvey Oswald was trained in the marines as a radar and electronics technician with a security clearance.[6]

In spite of the fact Lee had dropped out of high school, he was exceptionally bright and read voraciously. After basic training, he was sent to the Atsugi Air Base in Japan, a CIA base that controlled the U2 spy plane.[7]

Oswald was trained in Russian and became so fluent that he preferred, according to Marina, to speak Russian.[8] Lee's defection to Russia is bizarre but not unusual as the CIA sent many defector/spies to Russia around this time and the KGB was aware of this.

Lee had saved $1,600, almost half of his $3,452.20 total pay from the Marine Corps. However, the source of those funds is doubtful and most likely part of it was subsidized, as his bank account held about $200 at the time. He arrived in Moscow on Friday, October 10, 1959, with a five-day luxury tourist visa, and was met with a driver, a car and a lovely twenty-

---

5 A man standing at the corner of Houston and Elm photographed with a two-way radio has also been called the "communications man." His name is James Hicks. Another account claims the communications man was in a room overlooking the plaza.

6 The WCR claims he was only an operator and not a technician.

7 After the Gary Powers incident, the U2 project would be taken over by NASA and Wernher von Braun in 1960.

8 This ability to speak Russian so well has been the basis of a theory that instead of the real Lee Harvey Oswald, a Russian look-alike was sent from Russia back to the United States. It is unlikely, however, that his mother and brother would not have noticed this switch.

two-year old Intourist representative, Rima Shirokova, a graduate in English and Arabic from the Moscow Foreign Languages Institute. Rima acted as his personal twelve-hour-plus tour guide and probably his KGB handler; he stayed at the Hotel Berlin, a luxury hotel.[1] She called him Alek, because Lee sounded "too Chinese."

Within days Lee, asked Rima to help him defect. She did—but unsuccessfully, as Lee was told to leave Russia when his visa expired—which was just two hours away. Bolting himself in his room, although knowing Rima was coming to meet with him soon, Lee superficially slit his wrist and was taken to a hospital—first to the psychiatric ward and then to a regular ward. Ten days later he was released from the hospital. Rima had him driven to his hotel after stopping by an official tourist office where Lee was questioned and told to await a decision on his second request to defect.

After a few days of waiting impatiently in his room for a call, Lee decided to take matters into his own hands. He went to the American Embassy to renounce his US citizenship. He turned in his passport to the embassy on October 31, a Saturday. Some researchers speculate he picked this day because it was the day he got his passport back from the Russians, where the hotel ordinarily would hold a visitor's passport for a period. Others conceive a more complex motive. Technically, citizenship cannot be renounced unless the Ambassador is officially present—Monday through Friday. That would mean that Lee left his passport with the Embassy without actually renouncing his US citizenship. Some claim this was to keep it out of the hands of the Russians. Others claim it was to keep it handy for his return to the United States.

From November to December 30, his whereabouts are obscure. In his diary[2] he wrote that he stayed in his room and studied Russian. On January 4th, he was issued a temporary Soviet Internal Passport and given a one-year residency permit. He was sent to work at a radio and electronics company with over 5,000 employees in Minsk. Lee was given $500 in rubles and was told he would receive a $70 stipend from the Red Cross[3] monthly in addition to his salary of $70 at the Minsk Radio Factory.

He was assigned to the Experimental Shop Division which produced consumer radios, televisions, and electronic components for the Russian space program. He was also given a private apartment with a balcony, rent-free, although some say it was only partially subsidized. He received the equivalent of the factory director's salary and an apartment equivalent to that of a high-ranking member of the Communist Party, a rare privilege. The Warren Commission Report (WCR), in the section titled "Speculations and

---

1 As his money ran low, he would switch to less expensive hotels.
2 His diary may not have been written contemporaneously but over several days at a later time.
3 There is confusion over the term "Red Cross." The WCR claims it was the "Russian" Red Cross, others claiming it was the "International" Red Cross. Both interpretations are problematic and raise the obvious question.

Rumors," claims it was standard Soviet policy to subsidize foreigners who defected so their standard of living would not be too much lower than in their own country.

Lee cried when Rima told him of the Russian plans for him. Supposedly, he was disappointed at not being assigned to Moscow. However, compared to how he was living with his divorced mother before he joined the service, this seems to have represented a considerable step up in lifestyle.

He worked in Minsk for twenty-eight months, during which time he married Marina Nikolayevna Prusakova, a nineteen-year-old pharmacology student who lived with an uncle and aunt who had raised her. Her uncle was a colonel in the Russian intelligence services, the MVD—Ministry of Internal Affairs—equivalent to the FBI.

Lee had a daughter with Marina, approximately ten months after a six-week romance. According to his diary, he married Marina to hurt Ella Berlin, a Russian beauty with whom he had been smitten but who had turned down his marriage proposal.

When he decided to return home, he contacted the American Embassy in Moscow for the return of his passport, and, since he never technically renounced his citizenship, the undesirably discharged[1] marine's passport was returned and he was given a $435.71 repatriation loan, which he eventually paid back.

Six months after his arrival in Moscow in 1959, the U2 spy plane, which was controlled out of the Atsugi Air Base in Japan but flown out of Pakistan, was downed by the Russians. As mentioned, Atsugi was the air base where he had been stationed at before defecting to Russia.

This marked the very first time this type of American spy plane had been downed. U2 pilot Gary Powers was paraded around before the television cameras for all the world to see, giving the lie to Eisenhower's statements. Eisenhower had said publicly that U2 planes did not fly over Russia. The next day the Russians produced not only parts of the plane but the pilot as well. The disarmament talks between Eisenhower, Khrushchev, and MacMillan were scuttled after Khrushchev withdrew.[2]

The U2 incident accomplished its purpose or, more exactly, the purposes of those who wished the "Cold War" to continue.

Could Oswald have been trained and sent to Russia by the CIA to

---

1 Originally, Oswald was given an honorable discharge after having served three years in the marines. One year after his defection it was changed to "undesirable" discharge, a classification below "dishonorable." He tried to have it reversed several times after his return to the States.

2 According to some accounts, the U2 developed engine troubles. This was reported by Allen Dulles to Eisenhower in closed sessions, according to Col. Prouty. Prouty was the Air Force's liaison to the CIA assigned to the Pentagon. It is also reported that Eisenhower had given specific instructions to cancel U2 flights over Russia before the Paris Disarmament talks scheduled for the middle of May, 1960. The U2 with pilot Gary Powers, who survived, was captured around May 1, 1960.

provide sensitive information about the U2 that would lead to the first-time downing of a spy plane at a sensitive time to keep the "Cold War" going? Did Oswald have that type of sensitive information to give to the Russians? According to the WCR, Lt. John Donovan, in a reply to a question as to intelligence information that Oswald possessed, said:

> He [Oswald] had access to the location of all bases in the west coast area, all radio frequencies for all squadrons, all tactical call signs, and the relative strength of all squadrons, numbers and types of aircraft in a squadron, who was the commanding officer, the authentication code of entering and exiting ADIZ, which stands for Air Defense Identification Zone. He knew the range of our radar. He knew the range of our radio. And he knew the range of surrounding units' radio and radar...There are some things which he knew on which he received instructions and there is no way of changing, such as MPS 16 height-finder radar gear...He had also been schooled on a piece of machinery call [sic] a TPX-1, which is used to transfer radio-radar and radio signals over a great distance. Radar is very susceptible to homing missiles, and this piece of equipment is used to put your radar antenna several miles away, and relay the information back to your site which you hope is relatively safe. He had been schooled on this.[1]

In June of 1962, Lee returned to the Fort Worth/Dallas area where his mother, Marguerite Oswald, and his brother, Robert Oswald, lived. While in Dallas, the Oswalds were befriended by a George DeMohrenschildt whom they met while socializing with members of the "White Russian" community in Dallas. (The White Russians were fervent anti-Communists.) After a short stay and several jobs, Oswald left Marina and his young daughter and returned to New Orleans the following April—supposedly to find work—a distance of over 500 miles from his family.

George DeMohrenschildt

DeMohrenschildt was a highly educated individual with a Master's in International Finance and Maritime Transportation from the Institut Supérieur de Commerce in Belgium, a Master's in Petroleum Engineering and Geology, and a Doctorate in International Commerce from the University of Liege. DeMohrenschildt introduced the Oswalds to Ruth Paine and her recently divorced husband, Michael. A close friend of the Paines', Mary Bancroft, was the mistress of Allen Dulles at the time.

Ruth, a very charitable woman, drove Marina to New Orleans months later when Lee asked her to come and stay with him. Ruth also drove Marina back to Dallas when Oswald was ordered to go there after his mission for

---

1 WCR, Vol. 8, p. 298.

the CIA in New Orleans ended. (Oswald's assignment for the CIA in New Orleans will be discussed later.)

Marina and her daughter, June, moved in with Ruth, and Marina gave birth to her second daughter while living at the Paine home. Michael and Ruth were amicably separated or divorced and Michael visited frequently. The Paines had CIA connections and about this time received an inheritance of some $250,000. Michael Paine worked for Bell Helicopter and Ruth was a student of Russian. One day Ruth mentioned to Oswald that there was a job opening at the Texas School Book Depository.[1]

George DeMohrenschildt also secured one of Lee's Dallas jobs at the graphic-arts firm of Jaggars-Chiles-Stoval as a photo print trainee. The company did mappings of U2 photos for the CIA. Subsequently, Oswald was fired for allegedly using the equipment to make forged documents. DeMohrenschildt may have also gotten him the job at the Reiley Coffee Company in New Orleans as a machine greaser. The Reiley Coffee Company was located around the corner from Bannister's 544 Camp street offices, the Office of Naval Intelligence and the CIA.

George DeMohrenschildt,[2] a practicing geologist and occasional professor, was a friend of George Herbert Walker Bush and his nephew Edward G. Hooker, both having attended Phillips Academy in Andover, Massachusetts. DeMohrenschildt later formed an oil investment firm with Hooker. He was also close to the Bouvier family and Jacqueline Bouvier Kennedy grew up calling him "Uncle George." He was a member of the Dallas Petroleum Club, the Dallas Council on World Affairs, and the Texas Crusade for Freedom. The Texas Crusade for Freedom included the mayor of Dallas, Earle Cabell, brother of fired Deputy Director of the CIA, General Charles Cabell, and Harold Byrd, owner of the Texas School Book Depository. Reportedly, DeMohrenschildt was also a good friend of Clint Murchison Jr., Syd Richardson, and H.L. Hunt.

DeMohrenschildt had once applied to the CIA, but was turned down because he was suspected of spying for the Nazis. Oddly enough, after a trip to Yugoslavia in 1957, he was debriefed by the CIA in Dallas and again in Washington. After he received a call from the House Subcommittee on assassinations (HSCA) investigator, Gaeton Fonzi, in the late 1970s, concerning the JFK assassination, he committed suicide by putting a shotgun in his mouth and discharging it. In his address book was an entry, "Bush, George H.W. (Poppy) 1412 W. Ohio also Zapata Petroleum Midland."

---

1 Marina stayed with Ruth up until the time she was taken into custody by the Secret Service after the assassination. It is in Ruth's garage that Oswald's rifle and several incriminating photos of Oswald holding a rifle were found. Oswald claimed the photos were doctored and his head superimposed on someone else's body.

2 Jesse Ventura on his program *Conspiracy Theory* called George the CIA handler of Lee Harvey Oswald. The friendship between the two is otherwise difficult to imagine.

Jack Ruby

Jack Ruby, born Jack Leon Rubenstein in Chicago in 1911, changed his name in 1947 to Jack Leon Ruby. He served in the Air Force and was discharged in 1947. After that he moved to Dallas and managed the Singapore Club for his sister, Eva Grant—one of his seven siblings. After failing at managing several nightclubs of his own, he opened the Carousel Club in Dallas which featured an MC, a small band and four strippers. He told friends that he operated the club for Carlos Marcello, whom he visited frequently in New Orleans. He was called "Sparky" because of his volatile temper. His violent and mercurial personality caused Ruby many employee union problems and he turned to the Mafia for help, mainly through the Campisi[1] brothers who were lieutenants in the Carlos Marcello family. Ruby had connections with Lewis McWillie, an associate member of Permindex, who worked for Meyer Lansky at the Tropicana Club in pre-Castro Cuba. McWillie is reported to have treated Ruby to a short vacation in Havana in August of 1959 at the Tropicana Club. According to Madeline Duncan Brown, McWillie and Ruby were at the home of Clint Murchison on the eve of November 22, 1963.

The Warren Commission claimed no or minimal underworld connections for Jack Ruby.

Ruby's connection to the CIA was through FBI Agent Guy Bannister, who has been called the Southern United States' head of Division Five of the FBI, a supposedly secret division of the FBI in charge of covert operations. Ruby, Oswald and Ferrie both worked under Bannister. Ruby ran guns to Cuba and to the Cuban (pre-Bay of Pigs,) training camps around Louisiana's Lake Pontchartrain, Florida, Alabama, Texas and other states for the CIA.

On November 22, 1963, Ruby was spotted by several witnesses immediately after Kennedy was killed as he ran from the west end[2] of the TSBD to the grassy knoll. Among those witnesses was a young woman, Jean Hill, who was standing within feet of Kennedy as he was fatally wounded. Witness Hill also claimed to have heard six shots—some coming from the grassy knoll, as well as having seen Ruby run from the TSBD to the grassy knoll immediately after the shooting. Jean Hill was the first to use the term "grassy knoll" to describe the small hill in Dealey Plaza.

Hill maintained that she was interviewed almost a dozen times by the FBI who tried, in vain, to convince her she was mistaken. Agents insisted that Ruby was seen elsewhere and that she could not have heard six shots and certainly not any from the grassy knoll. According to her book, *JFK: The Last Dissenting Witness*, the record of her interrogation by Arlen Specter, Assistant Counsel of the Warren Commission, was altered. She said her answers were halted and the stenographer signaled to stop recording whenever she tried to talk about Ruby, the grassy knoll, or the six shots. She was not allowed

---

1 According to the WCR, Ruby visited the restaurant of the Campisi brothers on the night of November 21, 1963.
2 The "sniper's window" was located on the east end of the TSBD.

to see her transcribed testimony nor sign her name to it before having it included in the final report. She claimed the transcript of her testimony is "a pack of lies."[1] Her story is consistent with many eyewitnesses to the assassination who were pre-interviewed by the FBI before being allowed to testify before the Warren Commission.

The brake lines on her car were cut and the steering rod bolts removed from her car among other instances of foul play. Her son was almost killed because his car had been tampered with by unknown person or persons. Her married boyfriend, J.B Marshall, one of the motorcycle officers in the Dallas Police Department who was riding in the president's motorcade, informed her there was a contract on her life.[2]

Marshall also told her that he too heard shots from the front right of Kennedy, but he refused to testify.[3] In 1989, Marshall agreed to be interviewed by a national historical magazine. He died before he could be interviewed—from a fast-growing cancer.[4]

Dallas Policeman Tom G. Tilson Jr., never testified before the Warren Commission but he claimed to have seen Ruby when, being off duty and approaching Dealey Plaza from the west as JFK's limo rushed past him on the way to Parkland Hospital, he observed a man running down from the grassy knoll on the west side of the triple underpass. The man threw something into the rear of a black car which was parked on the shoulder of Elm Street. The man then jumped in and sped off. Tilson followed the car as it turned left, or south, on Industrial Boulevard. He instructed his daughter, who was riding with him, to write down the license plate number. Shortly afterwards he lost the car in traffic. He claimed the driver was Jack Ruby. He reported the license plate number, but his report was ignored and he was never called to testify. The Warren Commission in the Section on "Speculations and Rumors," Appendix 12, page 640, claims there was no corroborating evidence of Jean Hill's "recollection" that she saw Jack Ruby at Dealey Plaza at the time of JFK's assassination.

Hours before the assassination, Ruby was spotted by another witness, Julia Ann Mercer. Ruby, she declared, was in a pick-up truck blocking traffic at the base of the grassy knoll where she saw a companion of Ruby's walking up to the grassy knoll with what appeared to be a rifle case.

On the set of Oliver Stone's *JFK*, Jean Hill met Beverly Oliver, a dancer/singer at the Colony Club next door to Ruby's Carousel Club. Oliver told her that Ruby introduced her to Lee Harvey Oswald and David Ferrie in Ruby's club—she has been identified as the "Babushka Lady," because of her scarf. She was filmed in the Zapruder film as she was also filming the assassination. She claimed the film from her Super-8 Yashica movie camera was confiscated

---

1 *JFK: The Last Dissenting Witness*, p. 102.
2 Ibid. p 136.
3 Ibid. p 136.
4 *JFK: The Last Dissenting Witness*, p. 249.

by an FBI agent. Oliver testified at the trial of Clay Shaw in New Orleans at the request of DA Jim Garrison. She also claimed her testimony had been altered by the Warren Commission. There are dozens of similar stories by witnesses to the assassination.

Some witnesses placed Ruby at Parkland Hospital immediately after Kennedy's body was brought there. This testimony was considered "unreliable" by the Warren Commission.[1]

Ruby's killing of Oswald captured on television is only in dispute as to the method whereby he entered the Police station garage to shoot Oswald. It appeared to be a set-up according to many, but not considered unusual by the Warren Commission.

Ruby's second attorney, the flamboyant Melvin Belli, defended him by claiming Ruby was legally insane. Ruby did have a family history of insanity but the jury did not agree that Ruby was legally insane when he shot Oswald. Ruby was given the death sentence. Belli could have used the "unpremeditated" murder defense which carried a five-year sentence. Anyway, Ruby's death sentence was overturned on October 5, 1966, and a new trial was ordered for February 1967. On December 9, 1967, Ruby, who had been in excellent health according to doctors who regularly visited him in the hospital, suddenly developed cancer—an unusually fast-acting cancer—and died before the end of the year. Ruby himself claimed that a doctor injected him with cancer while supposedly giving him an injection to treat a cold.

Ruby had offered to tell everything he knew about the assassination to the Warren Commission, who would not have even have come to Dallas to talk to him had not Eva Rubenstein Grant's letters to the Warren Commission been published in the press. Ruby said he would open up—but not in Texas, where he feared for his life. He asked to be taken to Washington. Warren refused, claiming the Commission did not have such authority—which was not completely truthful. In fact, it was an outright lie.

Following a 1965 interview that Ruby granted to Dorothy Kilgallen of the *Journal-American*, she told several people, including her agent and producer, that she was going to break the JFK assassination story wide open. On November 8, 1965, she was found dead of a lethal combination of alcohol and three barbiturates.[2] She did have a prescription for Secanol, a barbiturate; however, the other vials were never found and all her notes were missing. Kilgallen had given some notes to her best friend and next door neighbor, Florence Smith. Florence Smith died two days later.

Kilgallen was also a regular panelist on the popular network TV show

---

1 There is speculation that Ruby was at Parkland to plant the "magic bullet", exhibit 399, on Connally's stretcher. Dr. Crenshaw of Parkland Hospital says that Kennedy's back wound in the area of the third thoracic vertebrae was a shallow wound barely entering three inches when he palpated the wound with his finger and most likely that bullet fell out when resuscitation and CPR was attempted on Kennedy. The WCR, namely due to Congressman Gerald Ford, placed the back wound at the base of the neck.
2 Marilyn Monroe died the same way.

What's My Line. On the next airing of the show, the name "Dorothy Kilgallen" was not mentioned—nor was it mentioned in any subsequent airings. As far as the press was concerned, she never existed from that point on. The panel moderator, John Daly, was also the director of *The Voice of America* radio network—as well as the son-in-law of Chief Justice Earl Warren.

Even before Dorothy Kilgallen's death, another name associated with the media, Irv Kupcinet, a well-known Chicago syndicated columnist and TV personality, was connected to the assassination. According to unsubstantiated, but troubling, stories circulating at the time of the assassination, Irv Kupcinet's twenty-two-year-old daughter Karen, a promising fledgling Hollywood actress, made a call from Oxnard, California to a an unidentified person and claimed Kennedy was going to be shot. The call came in twenty minutes before Kennedy was shot, according to an AP wire service story. The story was told by Penn Jones Jr., in a book called *Forgive My Grief II*. The author claimed that Irv Kupcinet had been told of the assassination by a man he had met in Chicago in the 1940s by the name of Jack Ruby—before the assassination happened. Penn wrote that Kupcinet's daughter was trying to warn someone about the assassination before it took place. Miss Kupcinet was found dead six days later from a crushed hyoid bone in her throat, the result of strangulation. Most likely it was a Mafia hit to send a message to her father. Irv Kupcinet has denied any prior knowledge of the Kennedy assassination.

CHAPTER 8. THE INTERESTED PARTIES IV—THE FEDERAL RESERVE AND JOHN J. MCCLOY

Although not a direct cause and effect of the JFK assassination, John Kennedy's war on the Federal Reserve was a significant contributing factor to his death and its subsequent cover-up.

Kennedy's Executive Order 11110, signed on June 4, 1963, drove a wooden stake into the heart of the Federal Reserve System's prerogative to print money, although not its prerogative to set interest rates for the country. These prerogatives were enjoyed by the Federal Reserve Bank, unchallenged for fifty years since the Federal Reserve Act of 1913 was signed into law by Woodrow Wilson.

After years of clandestine maneuvering and after spending millions of dollars in bribes and public relations campaigns to pass the Federal Reserve Act, the obscenely wealthy and influential men behind the privately owned Federal Reserve Banking conglomerate were not about to surrender trillions of dollars to an idealistic Kennedy without exhausting any and all countermeasures.

The machinations necessary to pass the act in the first place were shrouded in intrigue befitting a Dashiell Hammett or Mickey Spillane novel. It all began with a secret meeting of the most powerful bankers in America. Assembled at a deserted railway platform in Hoboken, New Jersey, the group boarded Senator Nelson Aldrich's private rail car, shades drawn tightly. Members of this influential financially- and politically-connected cabal were: A. Piatt Andrew, Assistant Secretary of the Treasury; Frank Vanderlip, president of the National City Bank of New York; Henry P. Davidson, senior partner of J.P. Morgan Company; Charles D. Norton, president of First National Bank of New York; Paul Warburg, of the banking house of Kuhn, Loeb and Co.; Benjamin Strong, considered a lieutenant of J.P. Morgan; and Senator Aldrich, a member of the Rockefeller family through the marriage of his daughter Abigail to John D. Rockefeller Jr., only son of John D.

Rockefeller. They left for J.P. Morgan's private island/club on Jekyll Island, Georgia. At the time the Jekyll Island Club's membership represented one sixth of the world's wealth, according to the *New York Times*. Membership was by inheritance.

When they arrived the group referred to themselves as the "First Name Club." To avoid being identified, the regular staff of Jekyll Island was given time off. A temporary staff, composed of employees who were unfamiliar with any of the attendees, was hired to replace them. During this time on the island the members referred to themselves only by their first names so the temporary staff could not identify them.

After nine days they drafted the plan which was to become the Federal Reserve Act. Paul Warburg, a German immigrant working for Kuhn, Loeb, wrote most of the plan which at the time was known as the "Aldrich Plan." Five million dollars was budgeted for the campaign to pass the legislation and three universities were selected as propaganda centers to convince the American public the Aldrich Plan was good for America—Princeton, Harvard, and the Rockefeller founded and financed University of Chicago.

The Aldrich Plan was opposed by several outspoken senators and congressmen such as Charles A. Lindbergh, Sr., who called it "a Wall Street Plan...It means another panic, if necessary, to intimidate the people."

Since the Aldrich Plan was perceived by most Americans as a Wall Street-backed bill, the originators decided to introduce the Federal Reserve Act as an alternative to the Aldrich Plan. They mounted a cleverly orchestrated campaign by big banks and legislators to strenuously oppose the Federal Reserve Act—even though the Aldrich Plan and the Federal Reserve Act were, in fact, identical. The public then backed the Federal Reserve Act, believing they were voting against the Aldrich Plan favored by the big banks and the wealthy elite of the country. But to further insure passage of the Federal Reserve Act in Congress, senators backed by the banking interests used parliamentary procedures and outright lies.

The Federal Reserve Act of 1913 was passed on December 23, 1913, when some thirty of the most vocal senators opposing the bill were on Christmas holiday. They had been assured that the bill would not be voted on until spring. President Wilson signed the bill one hour after passage by the Senate. Many have claimed that Wilson was elected by the powerful banking interests specifically to pass the Federal Reserve Act by fixing the election against President Taft. Taft, a popular Republican incumbent, would have won re-election had not ex-President Teddy Roosevelt decided to run as a late entry third-party candidate for a recently formed party, the Bullmoose Party, after it was apparent Taft would win re-election. Roosevelt's extremely well financed campaign split the Taft vote and ushered in Wilson.

The significance of the Federal Reserve Act was that it set up a privately owned corporation with an official sounding name which could (A) set the nation's interest rates without oversight, and, equally important, (B) print money for its own use. For example, the Federal Reserve Bank can, at any time for any reason, order the US Mint to print money for its own use at a cost of 2.3 cents per denomination, usually $100 bills, so that it costs the Federal Reserve Bank just $230.00 for every $1,000,000.00 printed or created by book entry. It then uses some of that money to purchase US Treasury obligations, i.e., bonds, notes, bills, for which the US Treasury pays interest to the Federal Reserve Bank—interest on its own money. The rest of the money is loaned out in what is termed "fractional lending." Fractional lending is the leveraging of deposits by a factor of ten. For every million dollars the Federal Reserve banks, or banks belonging to the Federal Reserve Banking System, have on their books, they are able to loan out ten million dollars. And, unbelievably, *the Federal Reserve is exempt from all federal and state taxes.* The Federal Reserve is the only for-profit corporation in the United States that is exempt from all federal and state taxes—taxes on about one trillion dollars of estimated net profit annually. In case you think this is a misprint, think again.

So how did the bankers who spent so much time and effort passing this legislation profit personally and why was Executive Order 11110 so threatening?

The Federal Reserve System, a for-profit (not a non-profit) corporation and a true central bank like many European central banks, is owned by the twelve regional Federal Reserve Banks around the country—New York, Chicago, Philadelphia, Kansas City, Boston, Cleveland, St. Louis, Atlanta, Minneapolis, Dallas, San Francisco, and St. Louis. By far the most important and most influential of the Federal Reserve branch banks is the Federal Reserve Bank of New York—since Manhattan is where most of the largest banks are headquartered. Some have compared the other eleven Federal Reserve banks to mausoleums, merely giving the impression that Eastern wealth is equally distributed around the country.

Of the 203,053 shares issued by the Federal Reserve Bank of New York, the largest block was purchased, at a price that is difficult to ascertain, by National City Bank, which was controlled by Rockefeller, Kuhn and Loeb. J. P. Morgan's First National Bank bought the second largest block, and when the banks merged in 1955, they owned a quarter of the stock in the Federal Reserve Bank of New York. Chase National, Marine National, National Bank of Commerce, among others bought substantial shares. Approximately eight banks[1] and three hundred individuals control the Federal Reserve Bank.

Kennedy's Executive Order 11110 essentially returned to the Treasury Department the right to print/create money, bypassing the Federal Reserve and competing with it by printing United States "Treasury Notes," as opposed to "Federal Reserve Notes" printed by the Federal Reserve. Everyone realized that the US Treasury Notes, which were debt-free currency backed

---

1 Rothschild Bank of London and Berlin, Lazard Brothers Bank of Paris, Israel Moses Seif Bank of Italy, Warburg Bank of Hamburg and Amsterdam, Lehman Brother Bank of New York, Chase Manhattan Bank of New York, and Goldman Sachs Bank of New York.

by silver reserves, would eventually phase out the Federal Reserve Notes, backed by nothing.

Kennedy had ordered $4,292,893,815.00 printed in $2, $5, $10, and $20 bills. The $10 and $20 dollar bills were not distributed before the assassination and most of the rest were removed from circulation after Kennedy was killed, so that less than $230 million dollars of these United States Treasury Notes still existed as of June, 2011, according to the U.S. Treasury.

Since the assassination was planned well before Executive Order 11110, it seems only a secondary issue—but that did not prevent these powerful interests from naming one of their own, John J. McCloy, president of the World Bank, chairman of Chase Manhattan Bank, trustee of the Rockefeller Foundation, and chairman of the Ford Foundation—*to the Warren Commission.*

McCloy is said to have brokered the final consensus for the Warren Commission Report, to the detriment of the minority-dissenting report favored by Representative Hale Boggs.

Boggs died some years later, under mysterious circumstances, in a private aircraft accident near Alaska. Boggs died shortly after filing a motion in Congress to re-investigate the assassination. Wreckage from the plane was never found, even after one of the most intensive searches ever conducted. Boggs' daughter, Cokie Roberts, a TV news commentator, has denied in a radio interview that her father did not want to sign the final draft of the WCR.

The Federal Reserve Bank has never been audited—at least not by outside, independent auditors. Congressman Ron Paul has been trying to introduce legislation to audit the Federal Reserve for the past thirty years. Although his bill to audit the Federal Reserve, HR 1207, has been passed in Congress, it has been blocked in the Senate. On February 26, 2009, Congressman Ron Paul introduced HR 1207 with these words:

> I rise to introduce the Federal Reserve Transparency Act. Throughout its nearly 100-year history, the Federal Reserve has presided over the near-complete destruction of the United States dollar. Since 1913 the dollar has lost over 95% of its purchasing power, aided and abetted by the Federal Reserve's loose monetary policy. How long will we as a Congress stand idly by while hard-working Americans see their savings eaten away by inflation? Only big-spending politicians and politically favored bankers benefit from inflation.

CHAPTER 9. THE MOTORCADE, DEALEY PLAZA, AND THE DORAL COUNTRY CLUB REHEARSAL

JFK's motorcade could have taken a different route in Dallas. The first question was where the luncheon should be held. Following a brief parade along Main Street, Kennedy was to address local business and civic leaders at a lunch meeting. The White House and Kennedy staffers preferred to have the luncheon scheduled at the Women's Building on the Dallas Fairground. But that would not take the motorcade to Dealey Plaza.

Deciding on lunch at the Dallas Trade Mart was the first critical step in manipulating the motorcade route. Governor Connally became "unbearable and on the verge of cancelling the trip" if the Dallas Trade Mart, the relatively new local business center, was not chosen. The Dallas Trade Mart was run by the same man who ran the New Orleans Trade Mart, Clay Shaw. And on November 15, the White House announced that Kennedy would indeed be lunching there.

The fact that Johnson and Connally were so adamant about the luncheon being held at the Dallas Trade Mart shows that Dealey Plaza had already been picked as the killing zone. The logical route from Main Street to the Dallas Trade Mart would take them through Dealey Plaza in order to reach the entrance to the Stemmons Freeway.

It is difficult to determine when the details of JFK's route were finalized. My cousin didn't mention dates. But at some point before the assassination, the original route was changed. And it was changed to detour through Dealey Plaza. The White House Staff was probably not told about the zigzag detour until the morning of the assassination, after Johnson had a heated argument with Kennedy.

According to the hotel staff, Johnson was badgering Kennedy about the seating arrangements in the motorcade, insisting that Senator Yarborough[1] be seated in the Kennedy car instead of Governor Connally. Johnson disliked Yarborough intensely, whereas Connally was a valued ally. In hindsight many commentators suggest Johnson was thinking about the possibility of stray bullets during the shooting. It is also possible that Johnson deliberately put up a fuss so he could order the detour through Dealey Plaza without too much opposition, having already given in on the seating arrangements.

The Doral Country Club was a newly built country club that had Mafia affiliations; it would have been under the control of Santos Trafficante.

My cousin said that David Ferrie, a personal pilot for Carlos Marcello, flew Lee Harvey Oswald under the radar from Miami to Dallas after the rehearsal, and that Secret Service Agent William Greer was part of the conspiracy to kill JFK. His actions, as well as the actions of all the Secret Service Agents in Dealey Plaza during the shooting, deserve mention and will be discussed later in this chapter.

Three days before the assassination, on November 19, 1963, both the *Dallas Times Herald* and the *Dallas Morning News* described the parade route through Dealey Plaza but did not show a map. Both stories were buried inside the paper. On the morning of the assassination, the *Dallas Morning News* did print a map of the route; however, it did not show the motorcade turning right onto Houston for one block, then left onto Elm and going through Dealey Plaza. But the scale of the map was small and that may account for the confusion on the part of some researchers and many parade-goers who were lined up ten deep along Main Street, while only a few hundred were on Elm Street in Dealey Plaza.

There are two other accounts which add to the confusion. Witness Jean Hill claimed her boyfriend, motorcade motorcycle officer J.B. Marshall, told her that Johnson's aides changed the route at Love Field before the motorcade began. And James Files, a claimant to the title of "grassy knoll shooter," has said he met Johnny Rosselli and Jack Ruby at a pancake house on the morning of the assassination and that Ruby handed Rosselli a 6" x 9" envelope containing Secret Service IDs and a map of the parade route.

To coordinate a triangulation shooting would obviously require more than six hours or even three days of planning; which, by the way, this was code named OPERATION BIG EVENT.[2] Even the area where limo driver, Secret Service Agent William Greer, was to stop the car was freshly marked by yellow "no parking" paint along the curb, according to some researchers

---

1 The *Dallas Morning News* on 11/22/63 carried the headline "Yarborough Snubs LBJ."
2 Some reports claim the Kennedy assassination was code named OPERATION ZIPPER, referring to Kennedy's penchant for extramarital affairs.

and also witness Beverly Oliver, who noted yellow paint on her shoes after stepping on the curb.

Even if my cousin had not told me of the rehearsal, it is clear that the strategy and every detail were planned well in advance; it was coordinated and executed with military precision. Most likely, Dealey Plaza was chosen by the beginning of November and the rehearsal took place shortly afterwards.

In any case, Ben told me that after the route through Dealey Plaza was determined, Frank Sturgis led a group of contract killers and military types to Dealey Plaza to lay out the locations and positions of the multiple sets of shooters and radiomen that were to assassinate John F. Kennedy on November 22, 1963, at approximately 12:30 PM CST.

Then, in essence, I was told about the rehearsal. Frank Sturgis, David Ferrie, and Secret Service Agent William Greer (the driver of the presidential limousine at the time Kennedy was shot) were present at the rehearsal. Lee Harvey Oswald was also present in Miami during this time, as confirmed by John Martino, an associate of Santos Trafficante, who told *Newsday* reporter John Cummings that he had met Oswald in Miami "several weeks before the assassination."[1] Further, Ben also told me that David Ferrie, a personal pilot for Carlos Marcello, flew Lee Harvey Oswald under the radar from Miami to Dallas after the rehearsal. The actions of Secret Service Agent William Greer, as well as the actions of all the Secret Service Agents in Dealey Plaza during the shooting, will be discussed later in this chapter.

Some CIA agents and other conspirators, according to my cousin, wore railroad worker overalls, some dressed as tramps, policemen, and Secret Service Agents. Bernard "Macho" Barker,[2] CIA agent, sometimes called "E. Howard Hunt's shadow," has been identified as the man on the grassy knoll who flashed Secret Service identification and kept police and others from going behind the stockade fence and confiscated film from photographers such as Mary Moorman.

The assassin on the grassy knoll arrived via a "pumper car," a hand-operated platform propelled by pumping a handle up and down, and exited the same way on a track that was deliberately closed and guarded by CIA and other government operatives dressed as railroad workers and local policemen for that purpose. I was further informed that the assassin on the grassy knoll came with an assistant and that this was his last "job" before he died a natural death.

---

1 Groden, *The Search for Lee Harvey Oswald*, p.81.
2 He was also at the Bay of Pigs and arrested for breaking into Watergate with Frank Sturgis and E. Howard Hunt.

The Shooters

Fifty people or more have been named or have come forward and claimed to have been on the grassy knoll or at one of six possible shooting sites. All have at least partial credibility. The list of possible, if not probable, suspects can be culled down to Frank Sturgis, Charles Harrelson, Charles Nicoletti, James Files, Chauncey Holt, Charles Rogers, Roscoe White, Mac Wallace, Lucien Sarti, and Jean Rene Soutre. The last two names are associated with the Corsican Mafia. The rest, except perhaps for Roscoe White, are associated with the Italian Mafia, while Wallace was an associate of the Mafia through Washington Capo and Johnson aide Cliff Carter.

Frank Sturgis was named as a shooter by his mistress Marita Lorenz. Charles Harrelson once confessed but later denied his role in shooting Kennedy. Both Harrelson and Sturgis were arrested and released in Dallas immediately after the shooting.

James Files, serving a life sentence in an Illinois prison for murder, confessed, in 1996, to having been on the grassy knoll with another Mafia hit man, Charles Nicoletti, and said that they both fired at Kennedy. He claimed to have shot Kennedy and then bit the warm shell casing, leaving a dental imprint, his trademark. He claims he put the shell casing of the "kill shot" on the top of the stockade fence; was paid $30,000[1] for the hit; and that he was specifically told not to hit Jacqueline.

Chauncey Holt was a Mafia hit man, sometimes said to be the third man[2] in the "three tramps" photo taken in Dealey Plaza immediately after the assassination. He was also involved in the Bay of Pigs invasion and worked with Meyer Lansky.

Only one fingerprint (a partial print) found that day in the TSBD[3] was unidentified; it was on the 6th floor. Years later, after an anonymous tip, it was identified as belonging to Mac Wallace, Johnson's paid killer of over a dozen people.

Lucien Sarti, mentioned earlier as a suspect in the assassination attempt on Charles de Gaulle, was imprisoned Corsican Mafia figure Christian David (pronounced *Daveed*, in French) identified as having been offered the contract to kill Kennedy after he, David, refused.

Jean Rene Soutre was reported to have been recruited by the CIA. He was in Dallas on the day of the assassination, and was arrested by US authorities and deported. However, it may not have been Soutre himself who was present but another assassin from Corsica by the name of Michel Victor Mertz, impersonating him or in any case using his name.

Roscoe White, an ex-Marine who may have worked with Oswald at the Atsugi base in Japan, was reported by Roscoe's wife to have been involved in

---

1 Some accounts mention fees of $50,000 for the shooters.
2 The tall man in the "three tramps" photo was most likely Charles Harrelson. The first tramp is Frank Sturgis, the last probably Hunt, despite his denials.
3 Some accounts claim a hit team was on the 5th floor of the TSBD.

the planning of the assassination. At the time of the shooting, White was a member of the Dallas Police Force and worked for the CIA. His wife, Geneva White, who was said to have worked a short time for Jack Ruby at his Carousel Club, claimed to have overheard her husband discussing the plans with Ruby at the club. Roscoe White's son, Ricky, claimed that his father's diary said that he shot Kennedy with a 7.65 Mauser, the first gun identified by Dallas District Attorney Henry Wade as the murder weapon. Later Roscoe White and Officer J.D. Tippit picked up Oswald and were about to drive him to Red Bird Airport when Oswald, sensing something was wrong, left the car. Shortly thereafter, Roscoe is said to have killed Officer Tippit. Roscoe was contracted by the CIA to do the shooting, according to his son. The diary, Ricky White claims, was taken by the FBI. There are many more stories like this, but it is not within the scope of this book to try to determine the names of the actual gunmen; however, according to retired New York Detective Jim Rothstein—Sturgis was one of the shooters on the grassy knoll.

Detective Rothstein arrested Frank Sturgis "on October 31, 1977, at approximately 2130 hours" together with Detective Matthew Rosenthal in the front of the apartment building where Lorenz was living. Sturgis was on his way to kill Marita who was about to testify before the HSCA. After the arrest, he and his partner questioned Sturgis for two hours in the apartment of Marita Lorenz.

Rothstein had been a sailor on the USS *Essex* which was involved in the Bay of Pigs invasion. Sturgis seemed to feel a camaraderie with Rothstein and talked freely. Sturgis talked about the Kennedy assassination, admitting he was one of the shooters on the grassy knoll.

When asked why Kennedy was killed, he told the detectives there were three reasons. Detective Rothstein wrote me what Sturgis told him:

> Number one was that Kennedy had double-crossed OP40 [sic] in the Bay of Pigs invasion by pulling back the support. Number two was that he [Kennedy] had been told to stay away from the women, especially the Russian woman Ellen Rometsch, because he would be compromised and jeopardize national security. Number three was that Kennedy was destroying the black community through his liberal social programs.

After the arrest, Frank was booked under his Italian name Fiorini because Sturgis was well known to the media at the time. Advised of his rights, Sturgis asked Detective Rothstein to call Gaeton Fonzi, one of the investigators for the HSCA which was in session. According to Rothstein, "Fonzi was dumbfounded." Shortly after the call Rothstein was told that "a Frank Nelson [CIA and organized crime in Cuba] was at the desk and was looking for Frank Sturgis, if, in fact, Fiorini was Sturgis."

Even though the arrest was based on solid evidence including a recorded phone conversation in which Sturgis is heard telling Marita, "you know what the rules are and what happens if you talk," Assistant DA Broomer decided against prosecution and the charges were dropped.

Sturgis sued the two arresting officers and the City of New York for $16 million, claiming false arrest. During the trial, Detective Rothstein received a death threat but managed to find his way to a safe house. Before Rothstein could testify, the judge in the matter, Judge Sand, was called out of court. After an hour Detective Rothstein was called out to Judge Sand's chambers and was told an agreement had been reached for a settlement of $2500, but that he and his partner would receive a commendation for "acting above and beyond the call of duty." Rothstein was offered the opportunity to make a statement in court if he chose—an opportunity he felt was best not taken.

After the trial, Sturgis and his lawyer asked Rothstein to be "part of their organization." Rothstein declined.

The story did not end there, however. According to Rothstein:

> Sometime during the summer of 1983, I was sitting at the bar in Georgia Bar and Restaurant at 722 South Wellwood Avenue, Lindenhurst, New York, taking to customers. A well-dressed man, wearing typical "spook" attire, came in and sat next to me. He introduced himself as a former New York City police officer who had moved to Florida. During an hour long conversation, he said that after Sturgis was arrested, he was sent with a "bag of money" from Florida to get Sturgis out of jail. He did not say where the money came from. He knew everything about Sturgis. I have never heard from him again and never knew why he came to me in the first place.

In 1993, after Frank Sturgis died, Det. Rothstein contacted Gaeton Fonzi and asked him if he had called Frank Nelson. He said he had not called Nelson. He thought Marita had called Nelson. Det. Rothstein informed Fonzi that Marita could not have called because they had her under guard, with no access to a phone. Fonzi's response was, "Do you know what that means?" Det. Rothstein said "Yes, I do. It was a sanctioned hit!"

The Frank Sturgis 22-Page Confession

Also around this time Rothstein received a call from an Arthur Nazeth, whom he identified as a "reliable source in the underground of organized crime. Nazeth, Rothstein said, was not his real name but an alias or "street name." Nazeth claimed he had an envelope with Frank Sturgis's name on it—and the seal of New York Cardinal Cooke. Nazeth claimed he was given the envelope upon the death of a relative who had been a professor at a major New York university. The envelope contained a 22-page confession given by Frank Sturgis to Cardinal Cooke in 1971.

The confession was read over the phone to Detective Rothstein. Rothstein wrote in an email to me, "In the confession, Sturgis admitted to the assassination of John F. Kennedy in Dallas, Texas, and gave a full confession of what happened that day in Dallas. He claimed that police officer Tippit had been killed by G. Gordon Liddy and that James McCord (a police informant for local Police Officer Carl Shoffler, one of the arresting officers at the Watergate break-in) deliberately left the tape on the lock of the garage door at the Watergate Complex which led to guard Frank Wills calling the police."

Rothstein made arrangements to meet Nazeth at the Saston Lumber Yard on Sunrise Highway in Lindenhurst, New York. Nazeth was intercepted before he could make the delivery, although he was wise enough not to have the confession on his person.

A second meeting was scheduled for the next night at the Lindenhurst Diner. "On what was supposed to be a quiet night, it was standing-room only with Feds when I got there. When Nazeth saw the crowded diner, he aborted the drop."

Rothstein did not hear from Nazeth again until 2007 when he called to say, "the confession [was] safe and by the water, and someday they would meet to finish the drop." There has been no further contact from Nazeth. More on the contents of the confession will be revealed later.

The "Three Tramps"

Some hours after the assassination three men (and perhaps more) dressed as tramps were arrested and photographed multiple times by multiple photographers as they were led, unshackled, to the Sheriff's office. These photos are problematical for the conspiracy deniers because they place Frank Sturgis, Charles Harrelson, and several other known assassins at the scene of the crime—most of whom had CIA and Mafia connections.

The photographs would have not become an issue had not Sturgis and Hunt been captured at Watergate in mid-1972. But in January of 1973 a reporter for CBS in Atlanta, Bruce Hall, contacted the Dallas Police Department and inquired about the names of the two police officers[1] in a photo taken around 2 PM in Dallas on November 22, 1963. The officers carrying lowered shotguns were lazily escorting three tramps to the Sheriff's Office. He also mentioned he thought the first tramp was Frank A. Sturgis. By the summer of 1973 Washington was buzzing with the Sturgis–Hunt–Kennedy connection[2].

Shortly afterwards the CIA and the FBI issued reports showing that Sturgis and Hunt were not in Dealey Plaza nor were they among the tramps arrested in a boxcar (or gondola car) behind the TSBD shortly after the assassination. The reports identified three other men as being the tramps—even though there were no arrest records, mugs shots, or fingerprints taken at the time.

---

1 The officers were identified as Marvin Wise and Billy Bass.
2 Sturgis had been questioned by the FBI in 1964.

My cousin told me Frank was one of the "tramps" arrested. Saint John Hunt, son of E. Howard Hunt, believed one of the other men was his father, and the third man has been identified by many as Charles Harrelson, a known hit man, father of actor "Woody" Harrelson, later (1980) arrested for the murder of Federal Judge John Wood Jr. and executed in Texas.

The CIA, the FBI and the Warren Commission went to great lengths to find three similar-looking men to propose as alternatives, one being Chauncey Holt, who has been interviewed and claimed he went to Dallas with Charles Nicoletti, a reported Mafia hit man, James Canty, and Leo Moceri. He said he gave forged documents and guns with silencers to known assassins Charles Harrelson and Charles Rogers (*AKA* Richard Montoya). He also identified Jim Braden as the man in the Dal-Tex building. He claimed that he, Harrelson, and Rogers, were the ones in the infamous tramp photo taken in Dealey Plaza.

According to Houston Police Department artist Lois Gibson, the three tramps are Charles Rogers (*AKA* Richard Montoya), Charles Harrelson and Chauncey Holt. Holt admitted he was one of the tramps and actually went to see Gibson to confirm her identification of him as one of the three tramps! Gibson believes Charles Rogers to be one of the tramps "but not beyond a shadow of a doubt."[1]

In 1992, however, the Dallas Police Department and researcher Mary LaFontaine alleged that the three tramps were Gus Abrams, John F. Gedney and Harold Doyle. Since there are no arrest records, no fingerprints or any other official evidence, it is difficult to see what the Dallas Police Department and researcher Mary LaFontaine were using as a basis for their conclusion.

Part of the difficulty is that more than one set of tramps was arrested that day. The WC and the HSCA both claimed six to eight tramps were arrested. However, based on my cousin's account, Col Fletcher Prouty's analysis of the photos, and A.J. Weberman's research, I believe emphatically that two of the three tramps were Frank Sturgis and E. Howard Hunt—the third probably being Charles Harrelson.

Both Sturgis and Hunt were in Dallas at the time although both denied being there on several occasions. Hunt also denied it to his son. Hunt's alibis have not stood up. He claimed he was home with his wife, children and a maid and did not leave his home for forty-eight hours, sending out for food. He later admitted his complicity in the assassination but described his role as that of a "back bencher."[2]

Both Hunt and Sturgis were probably wearing disguises; this was Hunt's modus operandi. Hunt has been characterized by convicted Watergate burglar G. Gordon Liddy and H.R. Haldeman one of Nixon's Chiefs-of-Staff, as a "master of disguise." When arrested for the Watergate break-in, his safe

---

1 Craig and Rogers, *The Man On The Grassy Knoll*, p. 196.
2 Before making the movie *JFK*, Kevin Costner offered Hunt $5 million to publicly confess his role in the assassination. He refused at the time, but later decided to accept the offer—which by that time was no longer on the table.

contained face altering prosthetics and other methods of disguise.

But the most persuasive of the technical analyses in terms of probability was printed in 1975 in the German magazine *Der Stern*, which hired Professor Rainer Knussmann of the Anthropological Institute of Hamburg University to compare stock photos of Hunt and Sturgis against the Dallas photos. His translated report states:

> The given question about the identity of STURGIS and HUNT with the two designated persons on the Death Site can only be answered clearly to the extent that a firm identity denial is not possible from the photographic documentation placed at my disposal...The probable identity from the resemblance analysis is given a special weight because the margin of error is significantly reduced when both HUNT and STURGIS are analyzed in combination. This is on the common sense ground that while an accidental resemblance between HUNT or STURGIS on the one side, and one of the persons shown in the Death Site pictures would be understandable, there is a very narrow probability that STURGIS accidentally resembles one, and HUNT accidentally the other of both person shown in the Death Site photographs. Possibly what is finally expected of me is a precise probability quotient for the possible identity of STURGIS and HUNT with the questioned persons on the Death Site pictures. Such a numerical probability estimate can certainly be produced by mathematics, but would show false exactness. However, to give a preliminary examination, I estimate that the positive resemblance between STURGIS and the questioned person #1 in the Death Site photographs has a probability of 0.1 (10% error, that is 90% for identity). The similar value for HUNT being person #2 [the back or 3rd tramp], I estimate at 0.3 (that is a 30% chance of error and 70% probability of identity). From this a theoretical error probability for the combined results figures at only 0.003 (that is 3%, therefore 97% probability). In closing I should like to assure you that in preparation of this evaluation I have taken pains to work according to the best conscience and knowledge without any political presumptions.
>
> —Prof. Knussmann, Officially Registered Court Hereditary Biology Expert, Examining Laboratory, Duesseldorf, Markenstr. 5, West Germany.[1]

These photos are a significant part of the assassination story so the obfuscation[2] by those involved is understandable. It is no coincidence that

---

1 Re-quoted from A.J. Weberman's website, *The Photographic Evidence: The Tramp Shots*. Article not paginated.
2 There is reason to believe that the photos may have been doctored.

the photo of the three tramps in Dealey Plaza was one of the main reasons E. Howard Hunt, Frank Sturgis and others (also connected to the Kennedy assassination) broke into the Watergate offices of the Republican National Committee.

Sturgis is quoted in a 1977 interview in the *San Francisco Chronicle*, "The reason we burglarized the Watergate was because Nixon was interested in stopping news relating to the photos of our role in the assassination of President John Kennedy."

Since there were no other photos of Frank Sturgis taken in Dallas that day, Sturgis had to be referring to himself as one of the three tramps. And since Sturgis and Hunt worked closely together on the assassination including meeting the night before, according to Sturgis' mistress at the time, Marita Lorenz, it is not unreasonable to assume Sturgis was referring to Hunt when he said "our role."

Dr. Fetzer, however, who knew Chauncey Holt and held a symposium on the identity of the three tramps in Dallas, disagrees that either Sturgis or Hunt were photographed. While Dr. Fetzer agrees with me that Sturgis was one of the shooters, he also agrees with Lois Gibson that the three tramps are Charles Rogers, Charles Harrelson, and Chauncey Marvin Holt.

The Non-Actions of the Secret Service

The prior activities and immediate actions of the Secret Service Agents, dedicated to protecting the life of the president, are highly unusual and suspect. The night before November 22, 1963, many of the agents were inebriated, according to an article by Drew Pearson written shortly after the assassination, enjoying a night of drinking first at the Fort Worth Press Club and later at an all-night club called The Cellar, until at least 3 AM.

Moments before the limo entered the "kill zone," the two Secret Service Agents running alongside the presidential limo were called back to the Secret Service car immediately behind the limo by Assistant to the Special Agent in Charge, Emory Roberts. The Special Agent in Charge was Roy Kellerman, who sat in front of Kennedy. A video on Youtube, called "Secret Service Standdown," clearly shows this strange behavior on the part of Secret Service Agent Emory Roberts in the follow-up car filled with Secret Service Agents whose job was to protect the president at all cost—even at the cost their own lives.

Secret Service Agent Greer drove Kennedy's limo directly to the center of the deadly triangle, stopped, and twice turned to look as Kennedy was shot. He was filmed by Abraham Zapruder as turning and watching after the first shot. Next to Greer, in the passenger seat, was Secret Service Agent Roy Kellerman, whose actions or lack of actions seems premeditated. Kellerman's sole responsibility was to protect the life of the president with his own. It was his only responsibility. Yet he sat still in his seat looking straight ahead[1] until after the last shot was fired.

In contrast, Agent Rufus Youngblood, assigned to protect Lyndon Johnson, has been claimed to have jumped over the front seat immediately after the first shot and covered Johnson's body with his own. Johnson, of course, was already crouched down behind the front seat as his car turned onto Elm Street, before any shots were fired. The story of Agent Youngblood jumping on top of Johnson appears to be fiction—no one else reported it, there wasn't enough room, and Senator Yarborough, who was there, has debunked the story—but it is far closer to the kind of behavior we would expect of a Secret Service Agent.[2]

Agent Greer, trained to distinguish the sound of gunfire, claimed he thought he heard a firecracker. Before the Warren Commission he claimed he accelerated immediately after the first shot. The extant Zapruder film does not show that. As most viewers can easily see, the Zapruder film does not show the car accelerating—it shows the car slowing down.

Stopping the limo was such a blatant indication of Secret Service complicity in the crime that it absolutely had to be removed from the Zapruder film, which absolutely required the film to be altered. To accomplish this two versions of the Zapruder film were taken to the National Photographic Interpretation Center—the original, an 8mm, already-split film developed in Dallas, was taken to the NPI on early Saturday and the revised, un-split 16mm film developed in a secret CIA lab at Kodak Laboratories in Rochester, New York, on Sunday, November 25th. Once the frames showing the limo stop had been removed there was no time left in the sequence for Secret Service Agent Clint Hill to have rushed forward, pushed down Jackie, laid across their bodies and given the "thumbs down" to his associates, so they removed that sequence, too—and other activities taking place—from the revised version. (A fuller detailing of the Zapruder film will be found in Chapter Seventeen, *The Zapruder Film.*)

I was told by my cousin that Greer stopped the limo for *two full seconds*, although Dr. Fetzer and others believe it may have been four or more seconds—further proof that the Zapruder film was altered, if indeed further

---

1 Some observers claim Kellerman appeared to turn to look at Kennedy but as seen on the Zapruder film, Kellerman is looking straight ahead as Kennedy is killed.

2 The Youngblood story is told by Johnson (and backed-up by Mrs. Johnson and Johnson aide Cliff Carter) in his written testimony to the Warren Commission which did not require him to testify under oath or in person. Since all three were party to the conspiracy the story is most likely a contrived fabrication to cover up Johnson's ducking down behind the front seat before the first shot.

proof is required after *The Great Zapruder Film Hoax: Deceit and Deception in the Death of JFK*, by James H. Fetzer, Ph.D.

A standing target is a much easier target for a kill shot, especially with nothing standing in the line of fire.

CHAPTER 10. THE "WHYS" AND WHY IT MATTERS

The necessity of showing that no conspiracy existed cannot be overstated. Almost every president, high government official and "official" historian has echoed the "lone nut, three shot assassination" scenario. It is both a mantra and a secret password to those involved in the assassination and the cover-up. They have echoed this talking point from the beginning even though the majority of Americans and the rest of the world believe, by a 5 to 1 ratio, that there was a conspiracy to kill JFK. A 2005 poll by AOL of over 200,000 subscribers showed that 80% believed that Lee Harvey Oswald did not act alone; 11% believed he did; and 9% weren't sure. These numbers have remained constant since the end of November 1963.

The reason, actually multiple reasons, for the continued charade of a non-conspiracy raises the enormously more important issue, namely, if there was a conspiracy, *why* was there a conspiracy? And the answer to that is frightening in its implications.

If a lone nut shot Kennedy, no reason is necessary or implied, and the question never surfaces. So why was Kennedy killed and, by association, who killed him?

There are nine reasons why Kennedy was killed. Not all are equally important, but all definitely contributed to the overall, absolute imperative that Kennedy (and the inevitable dynasty of Robert and Teddy which would have followed) had to be eliminated and Johnson had to replace him.

One of the lesser reasons centers on J. Edgar Hoover. His imminent retirement, by Kennedy, upon Hoover's 65th birthday, looming approximately in two years, was probably the least significant reason yet it deserves a brief explanation.

Hoover could not afford to retire, politically, although he was well-off financially.[1] He lived across the street from Lyndon Johnson in Washington

---

1 Hoover's estate at the time of his death was around $550,000.

and was one of Johnson's best friends as well as a member of the 8F Suite Club mentioned earlier. He was a compulsive gambler who was photographed at the two dollar window at the racing track while betting thousands with Mafia bookies. Those bookies subsidized his vacations with his live-in lover and heir to Hoover's estate, Clyde Tolson, who was also his Deputy Director at the FBI.

The Mafia also had compromising photos of Hoover which documented his homosexuality and his cross-dressing. The fact that Hoover claimed throughout his entire public life that there was no organized crime or Mafia in this country should have raised a red flag. Hoover simply could not retire. He had photos and files compromising to Kennedy (and many politicians), but the Mafia photos trumped Hoover's Kennedy files. Hoover was also so arrogant that he referred to himself as the "SOG"—the "Seat of Government." He intended to die in office of a natural death.

A second lesser reason was the sealed indictment of Vice-President Lyndon B. Johnson by Attorney General Robert F. Kennedy for the murder of Henry Marshall that was to be unsealed on December 1, 1963. Johnson was going to be *arrested for murder* by Attorney General Robert Kennedy with federal marshals—had Kennedy lived. The murder of Henry Marshall will be discussed in a later chapter. At the time, Johnson was also being investigated by Congress for criminal acts in connection with Bobby Baker, his senate aide.

Johnson knew he was not going to be on the 1964 ticket with Kennedy. Nixon was even quoted in *The Dallas Morning News* on November 22, 1963, predicting that JFK would not run for re-election with Johnson. Not only was there bad blood between Johnson and Robert Kennedy, but Johnson had lost his Texas base after stepping down as Senate Majority Leader after a six-year run, so could no longer help Kennedy's re-election chances. His numerous scandals involving Billy Sol Estes and Bobby Baker were becoming known and investigated by the Congress. Johnson was now a liability to Kennedy's own reputation. Kennedy's last conversation with his secretary, Evelyn Woods, was to that effect—that Johnson would not be on the 1964 ticket with him.

No doubt that was in the back of Johnson's mind, but, like Executive Order 11110, plans for the assassination were already well along by that time and nearing completion. The imminent murder indictment and the inevitable removal from office may have affected the timetable of the assassination but not the underlying reasons.

The third minor reason was Attorney General Robert Kennedy's war on organized crime, which he was waging vigorously against Carlos Marcello, Johnny Rosselli, Santos Trafficante, Jimmy Hoffa, and Sam Giancana. The Mafia's reason for killing Kennedy was minor in the broad scope of historically significant reasons. Their participation in the nuts and bolts—the physical aspects of the assassination—was quite major and their participation has been told and re-told by many authors.

Carlos Marcello was livid when, on Robert Kennedy's direct orders, he was unceremoniously arrested and immediately deported to Guatemala. His passport was taken away and he was given no opportunity to notify anyone before his instant deportation: no warning and no hearing. He returned to the States in a few weeks, his hatred of both Kennedys escalating exponentially. He is reported to have told friends that if he had Robert Kennedy killed, John would just appoint another Attorney General. But if he had John killed, Bobby would not be a problem. He likened Bobby to a dog's tail and John to its head. Cutting off the head, he reckoned, was the better solution.

Johnny Rosselli faced the same deportation problem as Marcello and felt a sense of betrayal from the Kennedys. After all, he had tried to help by trying to kill Castro for the CIA.

Sam Giancana (*AKA* Mr. Gold[1]), had his reasons as well, both personal and professional. He was sharing[2] Judith Exner with John (and Frank Sinatra and, perhaps, Bobby), wasn't he? And those 100,000 votes from Cook County, Illinois, his home turf, had put Kennedy in the White House, hadn't they? Ingratitude is a fatal sin in Mafia eyes.

Jimmy Hoffa and Bobby Kennedy were mortal enemies and that was no secret to anyone who watched the Senate racket hearings and the heated exchanges between the two.

Santos Trafficante, head of the Tampa and Miami Mafia, was heavily involved in the Havana casinos and their loss was a major deduction to his family's bottom line. The Mafia had more than enough reasons in their mind to kill Kennedy. But they needed friends in high places to cover it up—just as Johnson needed friends in low places to carry it out.

A fourth reason was Kennedy's intention to reduce the Oil Depletion Allowance from 27.5% to 17.5% (mentioned earlier).

A fifth reason was Executive Order 11110, which would have destroyed the Federal Reserve Bank (also mentioned earlier).

A sixth but rarely mentioned reason (or reasons) was the thawing of the Cold War with Russia, which Eisenhower had tried to do in Paris, with Khrushchev and MacMillan in June 1960, before the CIA-engineered downing of the U2 spy plane which scuttled those talks. Kennedy, more artful than Eisenhower, held secret back-door negotiations with Khrushchev during, and even after, the Cuban Missile Crisis.[3] He did so through the person of Lisa Howard. Lisa Howard was a former model and actress who turned journalist and became the first TV anchorwoman for ABC. In April of 1963, she traveled to Cuba to do a special on the island nation and learned

---

1 He was also known as Momo, Mooney, Sammy, Sam the Cigar, Mr. Flood, among others.
2 There is also reason to believe he shared the charms of Phyllis Maguire with Kennedy also.
3 The CIA suspected that Kennedy was showing Top Secret reports on the Bay of Pigs and the Missile Crisis to Khrushchev and the KGB to verify the CIA accounts of those events. The CIA considered this treasonous.

that Castro was interested in improving relations with Kennedy. After debriefing by the CIA, she set up meetings in her New York apartment with Cuban diplomats and US officials during which calls were made to Khrushchev, Castro and Kennedy. She was in the process of arranging a meeting with Kennedy and Castro at the United Nations before Kennedy was killed. Not only were the two major world powers talking disarmament, but co-operation as well. Kennedy thought it a duplication and waste of resources for each nation separately to try to explore space and put a man on the moon—and Khrushchev agreed. Kennedy and Khrushchev had agreed to co-operate on a joint space venture to the moon.

But maintaining the Cold War enemy was vital to the military-industrial complex whose economic health depended on the continuation of the rivalry, which generated billions of dollars in contracts for more and more weapons, including nuclear weapons. Peace did not equal prosperity—not for the military-industrial complex. It may not have signaled extinction, but it did mean a major reduction in the military budget—one of Kennedy's stated goals.

A seventh reason was the Civil Rights Movement in the early 1960s. Although Johnson took credit for passage of the Civil Rights Act of 1964 and the Voting Rights Act of 1965, it was Kennedy who wrote the initial legislation with the advice and counsel of Martin Luther King Jr. Opposition to this legislation from Hoover, H.L. Hunt, and the Southern democrats like Russell and Byrd, was fierce. Ironically Johnson, needing a more positive legacy than Vietnam and wishing to show that he could lead the whole country, went on to pass the Civil Rights Act in 1964. Indeed, had Kennedy lived, he probably could not have gotten the Civil Rights Act through the House or the Senate, especially with Johnson and the Southern democrats opposing it or at least removing any meaningful enforcement from the legislation.

An eighth reason was Kennedy's express intention to fracture the CIA and eliminate its unconstitutional covert actions, which included the killing of democratically-elected foreign heads of state such as Jacobo Arbenz in Guatemala, Salvador Allende in Chile, and Ngo Dinh Diem in Vietnam, as well as trafficking in drugs and engaging in undeclared and covert wars around the globe.

But the ultimate reason Kennedy was killed was the conflict in Vietnam—a war Kennedy had tried to prevent. The CIA enjoyed lucrative, unaccountable revenues from the sale of heroin to the Mafia that it was using to finance its growing worldwide empire, without the need for Congressional funding or oversight, and it did not want to give that up.

CHAPTER 11. VIETNAM—THE THIRD OPIUM WAR

"Just get me elected and I'll give you your damn war."

President Lyndon Baines Johnson[1]

"No event in American history is more misunderstood than the Vietnam War. It was misrepresented then, and it is misremembered now."

Ex-President Richard Nixon[2]

The war in Vietnam has been called "the Second Indochina War,"[3] but a more accurate description would be the "Third Opium War," based on purpose rather than location. The main purpose for going to war was the protection and continuation of the heroin trafficking network commonly known as "The French Connection."

Kennedy may or may not have known about the drug trafficking in Southeast Asia, but his opposition to expanding the war and his order to withdraw all American military personnel by the end of 1965 was the most important reason Kennedy was assassinated, next to Johnson's obsession with power.

The opium wars continue today in and around Afghanistan, in the Fourth

---

1 Spoken on December 24, 1963, at a Christmas party for the Joint Chiefs of Staff, according to historian Stanley Karnow in *Vietnam: A History*.
2 Nixon was reminiscing about the Vietnam War in 1985.
3 The First Indochina War, 1946-1954, resulted in the defeat of the French by Ho Chi Minh at Dien Bien Phu.

Opium War, and it is being fought for many of the same reasons.[1] If the U.S. government is so concerned about the use of illegal drugs, why weren't the opium fields of Afghanistan destroyed, as they easily could have been?

The official reason given by our government was that the destruction of the opium fields would have caused economic hardship to the farmers. The value of the annual harvest to the local economy from the opium fields in Afghanistan is approximately $750 million—a fraction of the cost of enforcing existing drug laws, not to mention the cost in human life and suffering.

Although opium cultivation is as old as history, it was the fabled British East India Company, one of the first multinational corporations, that raised the cultivation and distribution of opium to the level of a modern commodity like rice or tea. The East India Company had its roots and its fingers in the poppy-growing regions of India as early as 1750 when British ships moved opium from Calcutta to trade with China. But the East India Company imported more from China than it made by selling goods to China, resulting in a large trade imbalance, mainly in the form of silver. To even things up The East India Company addicted 25% of the male population of China to opium, very much the way the CIA addicted American soldiers to drugs in Vietnam—by lowering the price and increasing the availability. In Vietnam heroin was so easily available, it was sold at roadside stands by Vietnamese children; at cigarette stands in downtown Saigon; and right on army bases in plain view of the military commanders. Estimates of GI addiction in South Vietnam ranged from 22 to 34% by 1969.

One of the reasons for the increased availability of heroin in the late Sixties was the fact that the CIA had started to process morphine into No. 4 heroin in Laos instead of having it processed in Marseille. For a while this cut down the Corsican Mafia's profits, but it necessitated addicting more customers locally, namely American GIs.

The Chinese Emperor Kia King had outlawed opium and destroyed major quantities of East India stockpiles of opium, resulting in the British invasion of China on behalf of the East India Company's interests, culminating in the First Opium War in 1841. The victorious British forced the Chinese, who were no match for England's modern weapons of war, to pay reparations by opening major Chinese ports for trade with England and handing over Hong Kong to British rule. The Emperor, however, refused to legalize opium in China.

Ten years later the British arrived in Burma[2]. They transplanted a large portion of India's poppy there. The French were interested in the distribution of heroin and so joined with the British. Together they attacked

---

1 The war in Afghanistan is also being fought over the installation of the Turkmenistan–Afghanistan–Pakistan–India (TAPI) gas and oil pipeline which is expected to be completed in 2014, at which time the US is scheduled to leave Afghanistan, having achieved its real purpose.
2 Modern day Myanmar.

China again to increase their sales of opium, resulting in the Second Opium War. The outcome was predictably the same and this time China was forced to legalize opium as well as pay reparations and open additional new ports to trade with the West.

The United States banned opium in 1905, twenty-five years after England passed the Opium Act which criminalized opium. Both actions increased the cost to the consumer. The French quietly colonized Southeast Asia and took over the production and distribution of opium and its byproducts, morphine and heroin.

The poppy plants were grown in Burma, the product was refined in Laos, and it was exported through Saigon to Marseille. By the 1940s, Southeast Asia's "Golden Triangle" was a major producer of opium and worldwide addiction rose to alarming rates.

In World War II, France was defeated by the Axis powers of Germany, Japan and Italy. The Japanese took control of French colonial Southeast Asia, namely Burma, Thailand[1], Laos, Cambodia, and Vietnam. After the war, the US joined forces with the French and some of the warlords of Southeast Asia to limit the spread of Communism, which it deemed more important than controlling and profiting from the spread of opium, morphine, and heroin combined.

In Marseille, the Corsican Mafia took over the heroin processing and used the Italian Mafia as their distributor in Italy, the United States, and much of the world. The arrangement was not without problems: the Corsican Mafia and the Italian Mafia fought several wars over control of the processing and distribution as well as the supply of raw morphine. At one point the Corsican Mafia started its own airline, Air Opium, to compete against the Italian Mafia which used the CIA's airline, Air America.

At the Potsdam Conference and in the Geneva Accords after World War II, Vietnam was split into North and South at the 17th Parallel with democratic elections to be held in two years. The British and Americans opposed the elections because eighty percent of the population was Buddhist while only ten percent was Catholic. The population of all of Vietnam favored Ho Chi Minh and the American-backed Catholic candidate would have lost by an embarrassing margin.

By 1954, Ho Chi Minh was strong enough to defeat the French at Dien Bien Phu and the French asked Eisenhower, or more correctly, asked John Foster Dulles, for help in preventing the Communists from taking over, and perhaps dismantling, the heroin trade. Eisenhower sent in American "advisors" under the command of General Edward Lansdale, who later would head OPERATION MONGOOSE[2] for the CIA. Sixteen thousand advisors were sent over the next few years to protect the "French Connection," although officially it was to keep the godless communists from taking over

---

1 Formerly Siam.
2 The CIA program to kill Castro.

Southeast Asia and the planet.

The French withdrew from Indochina and the CIA took over where the French left off, except that the CIA increased production.

After the Korean War, to facilitate the operation, the CIA bought a small airline, Civil Air Transport, from General Claire Chennault of Flying Tiger fame, for $950,000 to facilitate the movement of heroin from Burma to Laos to Saigon and even to Marseille. It added planes and renamed the airline Air America. At one time Air America was the largest airline in the world. Its motto was "Anything, Anytime, Anywhere." The drug trade grew rapidly under the CIA and its private airline.

Ho Chi Minh was also growing stronger. Eisenhower had warned Kennedy that after the election, Kennedy might have to send in combat troops. Kennedy had originally followed Eisenhower's advice and increased the number of advisors from 900 to 16,000.

After it became clear that victory in Vietnam was not possible, Kennedy had a change of heart. He was determined not to have another failure, like the Bay of Pigs or the Berlin Wall, on his record before the upcoming election.

On October 11, 1963, Kennedy signed National Security Action Memorandum 263 (NSAM 263), which called for the withdrawal of 1,000 advisors from Vietnam by the end of the year and the withdrawal of all advisors by the end of 1965. The Joint Chiefs of Staff told him it was an impossible timetable. Kennedy weighed this decision carefully: he could be called soft on Communism, or accused of needlessly expending American lives.

Three days after Kennedy's assassination, President Lyndon Johnson quietly ordered NSAM 263 to be reversed by a new action memorandum. NSAM 273 was prepared and signed by McGeorge Bundy—the same Bundy who had conveyed Kennedy's message to General Cabell that a second air strike over Cuba, at the time of the Bay of Pigs invasion, was not authorized.

In the summer of 2012, I had a face-to-face interview with one of my cousin's Marine friends who served in Vietnam in the late Sixties. He was also in Laos and Cambodia, fighting a war that was never sanctioned by Congress and never officially existed. He was told by his commanders that he was never there; but he told me what he saw in Laos and Cambodia.

This retired Miami detective who worked undercover in the narcotics division told me he saw CIA-piloted C147 cargo planes loaded with moist, burlap wrapped, live poppy plants being flown out of Laos. The plants were being flown to Afghanistan for replanting just as the East India Company had moved poppy plants from India to Burma years earlier.

Today Afghanistan is the world's leading grower of poppy plants, second only to Myanmar/Burma.

This gentleman's efforts in Miami during the cocaine wars resulted in a one million dollar contract on his life from Pablo Escobar, famed leader of a Columbian drug cartel. His family was put in protective custody for months until the assassins from Columbia were captured by the Miami police.

Years earlier, a friend, who asked not to be named, told me he had worked as a Navy doctor doing research on respiratory diseases for the Navy in the Seventies. He told me he was tasked with preparing for the next war—which, he was told, would be fought in the desert.

The Vietnam War was a needless, CIA-fabricated war fought to maintain the untraceable revenues derived from the production and sale of heroin around the world to finance covert smaller wars and illegal "black op" operations. The Vietnam War resulted in the death of 58,000 American soldiers, the serious wounding of 350,000 more, and the death of 3,800,000 Vietnamese soldiers and civilians—nearly fourteen percent of the population of Vietnam.

The Gulf of Tonkin Resolution, which Johnson used to justify the war to Americans, and Congress in particular, has been shown to have been a contrived and fabricated event.

This is what actually happened: Since 1961 the CIA had been trying to provoke North Vietnam to attack American forces, in a classified covert operation known as OPERATION PLAN 34-ALPHA. Hanoi had even complained to the International Control Commission (ICC), set up after the Geneva Convention in 1954, about US ships which deliberately crossed into Vietnamese territorial waters on many occasions, seeking to provoke an attack. The United States denied the attacks on North Vietnamese shores.

On August 2, 1964, the USS *Maddox* attacked three North Vietnamese torpedo boats while on patrol in the Gulf of Tonkin. Four Vietnamese sailors were killed and several others were wounded. The Vietnamese torpedo boats sustained heavy damage. No damage or casualties were incurred by the Americans.

On August 4, a radar operator on the USS *Maddox* claimed the ship was under fire. Later, it was reported that these were "radar ghosts" or false radar images. There were no North Vietnamese ships firing at the USS *Maddox* on August 4, 1964.

The Gulf of Tonkin Resolution eventually resulted in over 6,000,000[1] Americans being sent to Vietnam. Over 58,000 of them were killed, many more wounded, and many were addicted to heroin and other drugs.

---

1 There were over 8 million Vietnam era veterans but some served in the US.

Chapter 12. The WC, HSCA, and the ARRB

Three official government bodies have looked into the assassination of John F. Kennedy.[1] The first and most widely known is the Warren Commission, although it is officially titled "The President's Commission on the Assassination of President Kennedy."

I was hoping I could find something in the testimony to corroborate my cousin's description of the rehearsal for the assassination, or at least some hints about it. I went to my local library and found it in the reference section. Many libraries have all twenty-six volumes of the WCR. Fifteen volumes are devoted mainly to testimony and conclusions; the rest are devoted to documentation in no particular order. I read and read until it became painfully obvious the report was fatally flawed and, in the words of many, a total fabrication, as evidenced by a mass of internal contradictions between the evidence it collected and catalogued and the conclusions it rendered.

One week after the assassination, Johnson asked a reluctant Earl Warren, Chief Justice of the Supreme Court, to head a six-man panel of distinguished citizens to work with fourteen attorneys and a twelve-man staff to look into the assassination. Johnson had quickly called for the Commission, to ward off Congressional and Senatorial committees which were being formed to investigate the assassination as well. His appointment of a "Presidential Commission" trumped their efforts. At the same time he ordered all evidence to be taken from the local authorities in Texas and delivered into the hands of the FBI. Murder was a state crime at the time and should have been investigated by Texas authorities in Texas. Johnson was the most astute politician of his day.

To silence dissent in the Senate, he appointed two senators—Richard Russell

---

1 The HSCA also looked into the assassination of Martin Luther King but not the assassination of Robert Kennedy.

Jr., a democrat from Georgia, and John Sherman,[1] a republican from Kentucky. To silence dissent in the House, he appointed Hale Boggs, a democrat from Louisiana and Gerald Ford, a republican from Michigan. To silence dissent from the rest of the world he appointed Allen Welsh Dulles,[2] ex-CIA Director (fired by Kennedy over the Bay of Pigs) and brother of John Foster Dulles, who had been Secretary of State under Eisenhower and was a full-fledged member in good standing with the Eastern Establishment. He also appointed John J. McCloy, another well-connected and prominent member of the Eastern establishment. McCloy's resume included the presidency of the World Bank, the Chase Manhattan Bank (formerly a Rockefeller family bank[3]), and a close friendship with Adolf Hitler, having shared a box seat with him at the 1936 Olympic Games in Berlin. McCloy had later acted as Regent of post-war Germany, as MacArthur had done for Japan.[4]

Most of the members of the WC had full-time jobs and, according to recently declassified information, Allen Dulles essentially ran the commission. Some members attended only a few sessions. Most interviews were conducted in private with only one witness, a stenographer, and one attorney.

The most notable of the attorneys were Arlen Spector, later Senator Arlen Spector, Albert Jenner Jr., and David W. Belin. They interviewed the most significant witnesses. These witnesses were treated as hostile witnesses whose testimony was to be changed, modified, or completely discarded if it did not fit in with the predetermined guilt of Lee Harvey Oswald.

Many witnesses offered to testify and were interviewed by the FBI but, of these, only a few were called to actually testify and go on the record in the Warren Commission Report. The rest were not called because their testimony did not support the "lone nut, three shot" scenario the commission wanted to hear. Since their stories could not be easily modified or discredited, they were not called to testify.

Among those significant witnesses was Lee Bowers, who witnessed suspicious out-of-state cars and people behind the stockade fence from his perch in the railroad tower, fourteen feet above and slightly west of the grassy knoll. He died in a one-car accident due to monoxide poisoning.

Roger Craig, ex-army soldier and deputy sheriff in the Dallas Police Department, told reporters that on November 22, the entire sheriff's force was told they had no duties to perform for the motorcade except to direct

---

1 Sherman and Cooper were reluctant to sign the final draft of the Warren Commission although Boggs was the most vocal critic according to Jim Marrs, journalist, best-selling author, and assassination researcher.
2 Recently declassified records show that Dulles was the prime mover of the Warren Commission and Warren more of a figurehead.
3 The Rockefeller family is still the majority stockholder although it holds only 1% of Chase's stock.
4 McCloy advised the US not to bomb railroad tracks to Jewish death camps after they were discovered, which could have saved the lives of millions of Jews. The Allies took his advice.

traffic, and then only if asked. When Craig heard the shots in Dealey Plaza, he ran to the grassy knoll where witnesses had pointed. There he came across a man in a dark suit behind the fence. The man flashed Secret Service credentials and told him not to jump over the fence. He went back to the TSBD and said he saw Lee Harvey Oswald get into a light beige Rambler[1]— and later identified Oswald in a police line-up. This was minutes after the last shot was fired. He then went inside with other officers where they discovered, on the west end on the 6th floor of the TSBD (Oswald's sniper's nest was on the east side of the 6th floor), a rifle hidden in an empty carton. The carton was behind a chest-high row of cartons.[2] The rifle's stock was stamped—Mauser 7.65. A while later, a Mannlicher-Carcano rifle was found on the 5th floor of the TSBD.

Since the Commission had already decided that Oswald's gun was a 6.5 mm Italian made Mannlicher-Carcano, the 7.65 German-made Mauser could not have been fired at Kennedy, according to the WC. A deposition of his statements was taken by David Belin. He was never called to testify before the Warren Commission or any of its members. Roger Craig's experience with the WC would be repeated over and over again, with any witness whose interview or deposition did not agree with "lone nut, three shot" scenario.

Other witnesses told Craig of having seen two men on the 6th floor of the TSBD; of seeing Jack Ruby driving away from the grassy knoll with a man who threw what appeared to be a rifle into the back of the vehicle; of seeing two men, neither of whom looked like Oswald, firing at Officer Tippit; of spent cartridges being thrown in the air; and of seeing the two men run off in opposite directions.

The majority of eyewitnesses in Dealey Plaza believed shots were fired from the grassy knoll. Almost none of those witnesses were called. Witnesses who claimed a shot came from the grassy knoll, like Jean Hill, were called and treated as hostile witnesses by Arlen Spector, intimidated by the FBI, and threatened and harassed with death threats.

Roger Craig was fired by the Dallas Police Department after refusing to change his story. Two attempts were made on his life before he was shot to death. His death was ruled a suicide.

Off-duty Dallas patrolman Tom G. Tilson Jr.[3] claimed he was driving east on Elm Street as the presidential motorcade was speeding west on its way to Parkland Hospital. He saw a man run down from the grassy knoll on the west side of the triple overpass and throw something into the rear of a black car which then sped off past him. Tilson turned left on Houston then back onto Elm and chased the black car, which turned left on Industrial Boulevard. Tilson's daughter, who was in the passenger seat, took down the

---

1 Similar to one owned by Ruth Paine at whose house Marina was living.
2 The 6th floor had boxes of textbooks stacked chest high around the perimeter because the flooring was being replaced.
3 Tilson was a close friend of J.D. Tippit and served as a pallbearer at his funeral.

license number. Tilson phoned in the license number to headquarters. The license number belonged to Jack Ruby. Tilson's report was ignored. He was never called to testify before the WC.

Motorcycle patrolman J.B. Marshall claimed he saw Vice-President Johnson duck down in his seat, thirty to forty seconds before the first shot was fired—before his car even turned onto Elm Street—the kill zone. He also claimed that while protocol required a "four wheels" ride with a motorcycle escort alongside each of the four wheels of the presidential limo, the four motorcycles escorts were used only on the back wheels. Marshall never testified before the Warren Commission. In 1989, Marshall died a few weeks after agreeing to be interviewed by a national historic magazine. He died of a fast-acting cancer.

Beverly Oliver was seen in the Zapruder film as she filmed the motorcade. She is commonly known as the "Babushka Lady" after the scarf she was wearing while filming Kennedy. She says that Jack Ruby was a friend and that he introduced her to Lee Harvey Oswald in Ruby's Carousel Club. She said Ruby introduced him as Lee Oswald of the CIA. Her film of the assassination was confiscated and lost. She was never called to testify. The WC relied entirely on the resources and agents of the FBI for investigations and witness interviews.

Representative Hale Boggs was later reported to have said, "Hoover lied his eyes out to the Commission—on Oswald, on Ruby, on their friends, the bullets, the gun, you name it."[1] He originally refused to sign the Warren Commission's final report. He died in a small plane crash shortly after asking Congress to reopen the investigation into the Kennedy assassination. A thirty-nine day hunt for the wreckage turned up nothing.

Why would so many leaders, who were obviously not involved in the conspiracy, try to cover it up? For the same reason any possible involvement of Cuba and Russia in the conspiracy was covered up by the Warren Commission. The Warren Commission was told that any hint of a conspiracy to kill Kennedy would lead to Cuba and Russia and might start World War III, in which nuclear weapons would be used, resulting in the death of thirty-nine million people.

Of course, I couldn't find the faintest hint of a reference to the rehearsal.

The HSCA

I was a little more hopeful as I delved into the records and accounts of the second investigation into the Kennedy assassination. This three-year investigation resulted in the "House Subcommittee on Assassinations

---

1 Cited by Bernard Fensterwald in *Coincidence or Conspiracy*. Boggs was speaking to an aide. Fensterwald also quotes Lindy Boggs and Hale's wife and successor in Congress as having said Hale wished he had never signed the Warren Commission final report.

(HSCA) Report." The HSCA had concluded there was a conspiracy to kill Kennedy after all. My hope was premature.

In the fall of 1976, Congress passed a resolution authorizing a twelve-member committee to "conduct a complete investigation of the circumstances surrounding the deaths of President John F. Kennedy and Dr. Martin Luther King Jr." Separate committees were set up to investigate Kennedy and King.

For reasons[1] not given, the assassination of Robert Kennedy was ignored and not investigated by the HSCA.

The resolution to investigate these assassinations came about because of public pressure at the time. The pressure was a result of the first public viewing of the Zapruder film. *Life Magazine*, which had purchased the film, had kept it away from the public, in a vault, for twelve years.

On March 6, 1975, Geraldo Rivera, on his program *Good Night America*, showed it publicly for the first time. Even though he had warned his audience of the gruesome and graphic nature of the film, the audience was stunned.

At the same time the Senate was also investigating assassinations and assassination attempts, particularly on the life of Fidel Castro by the CIA. The Senate committee, called the "Hart-Schweiker Committee," issued a "Final Report of the Select Committee to Study Governmental Operations," which concluded: that the CIA was indeed responsible for numerous attempts on Castro and other heads of state; that the CIA had withheld information from the Warren Commission and had engaged in a program of censoring and withholding information from the public called "OPERATION MOCKINGBIRD"; and that the CIA had conducted counter-intelligence activities under a program called "COINTELPRO." A 1976 poll conducted shortly afterwards by the *Detroit News* showed 87% of Americans believed there had been a conspiracy to kill Kennedy.

Before the House Select Committee on Assassinations (HSCA) could begin hearings, several important witnesses were murdered or committed suicide.

Sam Giancana and Johnny Rosselli were murdered in typical gangland style. They had been told that they would be called to testify. Giancana was murdered in his Oak Park, Illinois home. Since the outside of the house was being guarded by FBI and local police, and Giancana was in his basement kitchen preparing food for more than one person, it was suspected he knew his killer and let him in. According to Giancana's younger brother Chuck Giancana, Sam was killed with a bullet to the back of the head, another in the mouth and five more bullets under the chin—the typical Mafia signature-killing for someone who talked too much. Annette Giancana was convinced her father was murdered by the FBI.

Rosselli was found floating in the Gulf of Mexico, in pieces, in a fifty-five gallon drum. Most likely both men were killed on the orders of Santos

---

1 Some sources have reported that the Black Congressional Caucus would only agree to reopen the JFK investigation if MLK's assassination was also investigated.

Trafficante Jr. Trafficante was the Mafia leader with the most to lose if either of the men talked. Trafficante, however, would have had to have the blessing of the New York Mafia to order the hits.

George DeMohrenschildt, Oswald's handler mentioned earlier, apparently took his own life when contacted by the same committee.

Almost immediately, the committee's investigation ran into problems. Funding issues, rotating chairmanships, rotating lead counsels, and parliamentary delaying tactics plagued the committee which was first headed by Senator Frank Church, then Richard Schweiker, and finally by Louis Stokes. The hearings, as usual, were held in secret. The evidence was sealed until 2017, but a public report was issued in March 1979, entitled, "Report of the Subcommittee on Assassinations of the United States House of Representatives."

One major piece of evidence did leak out—the existence of a Dictabelt tape found in the Dallas Police Department in a storage box. It had inadvertently never been turned over to the Warren Commission along with all the other evidence. It was a recording from an open microphone on the motorcycle of one of the police officers in the Kennedy motorcade. Acoustic evidence showed four shots were fired at Kennedy over a total period of 7.91 seconds. The first, second and fourth shots came from behind; the third shot came from the grassy knoll. The committee had no choice but to conclude Kennedy was killed as the result of a conspiracy.[1]

These conclusions issued in 1979 were startling, strange, and original. They concluded that the shot from the grassy knoll missed, that Lee Harvey Oswald had indeed fired three shots, the last two hitting and killing Kennedy. Yes, there was a conspiracy but no, it didn't really change anything since the identity of the man on the grassy knoll could not be discovered. But, "on the basis of the evidence available to it," the committee believed that the Soviet Government was not involved; that the Cuban Government was not involved; anti-Castro Cuban groups were not involved; the "national syndicate of organized crime (i.e., the Mafia), as a group," was not involved. Neither was the Secret Service, the Federal Bureau of Investigations or the Central Intelligence Agency involved—although it's possible, the committee concluded, that individual members of these groups might have been involved.

The ARRB

In 1992, after Oliver Stone's movie *JFK* was released, Congress passed the "President John F. Kennedy Assassinations Records Collection Act (JFK Act),"

---

1 The tape was discovered as the hearings were concluding. Although two sets of acoustic experts found four shots fired, the FBI conducted additional tests and determined, based on computer recreations, that the motorcycle in question was "mis-located" by the first acoustic experts and therefore not accurate.

which led to the formation of "The Assassination Records Review Board (ARRB)." The ARRB was not tasked with re-investigating the assassination, but it was empowered to examine all the classified records from the WC and the HSCA with the purpose of declassifying them after review. Those records were to be placed into the JFK Collection at the National Archives. The ARRB did, however, interview witnesses, some under oath, concerning the completeness and the authenticity of some documents, especially the autopsy photos and X-rays, which are not yet available to the public. (The X-ray technicians and photographers at Bethesda Naval Hospital, as will be shown later, failed to authenticate the photos and X-rays shown them by the ARRB—because the photos and X-rays they were shown were not the same ones they remembered having taken.) More on this later.

CHAPTER 13. THE OFFICIAL WC AUTOPSY REPORT AND THE MISSING BRAIN

I received a copy of the "Warren Commission Appendix 9: Autopsy report and Supplemental Report," by mail. Some of the WCR is available for download on the internet. The autopsy report required filling out a specific request form which required a name and mailing address. A touch of paranoia elbowed its way into my frontal lobe, vacationing there for a few weeks.

I requested the report because if someone were to attack my cousin's credibility, the medical evidence, mainly the autopsy, would provide evidence of the truth. If the medical evidence showed that three shots, and only three shots, came from behind, then that would pretty much make my cousin a liar. I was a little apprehensive. This was hard, scientific evidence, not easily dismissed. I read with rapt attention.

The autopsy was performed by Commander James J. Humes, MD, USN. He was assisted by Commander J. Thornton Boswell, MD, USN, and observed by Dr. Pierre Finck who arrived thirty minutes after the autopsy had started, around 8:30 PM.

Drs. Humes and Boswell were essentially Bethesda Naval Hospital administrators and had not performed an autopsy in years, had never performed forensic autopsies, and were unfamiliar with basic bullet wounds. Dr. Finck, an Army doctor from nearby (walking distance) Walter Reed Army Hospital, while a qualified forensic pathologist, was not an expert in bullet wounds. Requests by Dr. Humes for civilian forensic bullet wound specialists were denied.

The report was not as technical or as complete as I expected it to be, considering the significance of the event. This report, it turns out, is the second one typed by Dr. Humes. He burned the first autopsy report, along with his notes, in his fireplace at home. He burned them, he told the WC, because he didn't want them to become macabre curiosities like the blood-stained doilies from Lincoln's rocking chair in the Ford Theatre. Dr. Boswell's notes disappeared while he was cleaning up after the autopsy was completed.

I can understand that Dr. Humes' notes, which were probably written while the autopsy was in progress, might have blood on them. I can't understand why the first *typed* autopsy report would have blood on it...or why he burned it as well.

The report begins with a clinical summary of the events preceding the autopsy based on "available evidence," and a telephone conversation with Dr. Malcolm Perry, trauma surgeon at Parkland Memorial Hospital where Kennedy was first taken.

> Dr. Perry noted the massive wound of the head and a second much smaller wound of the low anterior neck in approximately the midline. A tracheostomy was performed by extending the latter wound. At this point bloody air was noted bubbling from the wound and an injury to the right lateral wall of the trachea was observed. Incisions were made in the upper anterior chest wall bilaterally to combat possible subcutaneous emphysema. Intravenous infusions of blood and saline were begun and oxygen was administered. Despite these measures cardiac arrest occurred and closed chest massage failed to re-establish cardiac action. The President was pronounced dead approximately thirty to forty minutes after receiving his wounds.

It then addresses the back, neck, and head wounds.[1]

> Three shots were heard and the President fell forward bleeding from the head. (Governor Connolly [sic] was seriously wounded by the same gunfire.) According to newspaper reports (*Washington Post* November 23, 1963) Bob Jackson, a Dallas *Times Herald* photographer, said he looked around as he heard the shots and saw a rifle barrel disappearing into a window on an upper floor of the nearby Texas School Book Depository Building.

According to the WCR section titled "Summary and Conclusions," and the "Autopsy Report," the first shot missed completely,[2] struck the curb, bounced up and hit James Tague in the face, causing a minor scratch. The bullet was never found although the FBI had that section of the curb cut out and flown to Washington to verify a bullet had struck the curb. What the WC failed to mention was that James Tague (sometimes seen as Teague) was not on Elm Street but on Main Street near the triple underpass—several hundred feet in front of the presidential limo. The significance of Tague's position when he was struck is that it is an indication that a trajectory from the 6th floor of the TSBD missed JFK by thirty-three feet above his head and twenty-one feet to the right of his head. The trajectory is more logical if fired from the Dal-Tex building at a lower level.

---

1 Page two, Pathological Examination Report—A63-272.
2 Tague claimed it was not the first shot that hit him but the second.

The second shot struck Kennedy in the back (and exited the neck below the Adam's apple) and the third struck him in the head—all the shots coming from behind and above.

The last two shots are, of course, controversial but the back wound is the most controversial, provoking curiosity and disbelief. A bullet that is claimed to have caused that wound was recovered from an empty stretcher/gurney[1] at Parkland Memorial Hospital and flown to Washington by two FBI agents, Siebert and O'Neil. It is known the world over as Warren Commission Exhibit 399 (WCE 399), the so-called "stretcher" or "magic" bullet.

While the autopsy report locates the neck wound ("third and fourth tracheal rings") technically and medically, it does not locate the back wound in the same way. It says:

> ...situated on the upper right posterior thorax just above the upper border of the scapula there is a 7 x 4 millimeter[2] oval wound.

But here's the problem.

Admiral George Gregory Burkley, Kennedy's personal physician, placed the back wound at the 3rd thoracic vertebra on an autopsy descriptive sheet.[3] Dr. Humes palpated the back wound with his finger in another example of his inexperience as a forensic pathologist. (The proper method would have been to insert a probe so as not to destroy any trace evidence). He reported he was able *to touch the end of the wound with his fingertip.* It was reported, as well, by several assistants at the autopsy that the bullet which entered Kennedy's back at the 3rd thoracic vertebra[4] to the right of the spine did not penetrate *more than 3–4 inches*—and the autopsy report[5] seems to agree...and disagree:

> The second wound presumably of entry is that described above in the upper right posterior thorax. Beneath the skin there is ecchymosis of subcutaneous tissue and musculature. *The missile path through the fascia and musculature cannot be easily probed* [emphasis mine.]

But when it summarized its findings[6] it says:

> The other missile [referring to the back wound] entered the right superior posterior thorax above the scapula and traversed

---

1 Some witnesses claim Ruby planted this bullet on the gurney of John Connally; others say it was found on an empty gurney not used by Kennedy or Connally.
2 7 by 4 millimeters is 9/32" by 5/32" the size of a bullet.
3 Reproduced in the back of this book. Admiral Berkley was never called to testify before the WC.
4 The 3rd thoracic vertebra is approximately four inches below the base of the neck.
5 Kennedy autopsy report, page 3.
6 Kennedy autopsy report, Page 6.

the soft tissues of the supra-scapular and the supra-clavicular portions of the base of the right side of the neck. This missile produced contusions of the right apical parietal pleura and of the apical portion of the *right upper lobe of the lung* [emphasis mine]. The missile contused the strap muscles of the right side of the neck, damaged the trachea and made its exit through the anterior surface of the neck. *As far as can be ascertained this missile struck no bony structures in its path through the body* [emphasis mine].

If it struck the "right upper lobe of the lung," wouldn't that indicate the bullet ("missile") entered the back at the 3rd thoracic vertebra rather than the base of the neck? Was Dr. Humes trying to reconcile the fact with the fiction?

Dr. Crenshaw, who attended Kennedy in Dallas, surmised in his book *Trauma Room One*[1] that when doing cardiac compressions to keep Kennedy alive, the bullet, most likely a World War II vintage cartridge[2], was a dud and fell out of the wound and onto the gurney. Other researchers have speculated that the pristine bullet was fired into a barrel of water, retrieved and planted on the stretcher by Jack Ruby.

Dr. J. Thornton Boswell said that a general he did not know, and who claimed to be in charge, was not interested in a full autopsy but only in trying to find the bullet that entered the back. FBI Agent O'Neil called the FBI lab when the bullet could not be found during the autopsy and was told a bullet had been found in Dallas. O'Neil further claimed that at the end of the autopsy everyone involved believed the bullet found at Parkland was the one from Kennedy's back.

Most likely this was the magic bullet—an almost pristine bullet that the WC claims entered Kennedy's back, exited his neck, entered Connally's back (he was sitting in the front seat), struck a rib, exited below his right nipple, passed through his right wrist and lodged in his left thigh virtually undamaged and then fell out onto Connally's gurney. One bullet, two victims, seven wounds.

But entry at the 3rd thoracic vertebra is problematic. How could a downward trajectory from the 6th floor of the TSBD enter Kennedy's back at a point *lower* than the exit point, turn 90 degrees upward, change course again, and exit his neck at the level of the 3rd and 4th tracheal rings, all without having "struck no bony structures on its path through the body?" Simple physics says it's impossible.

Nevertheless, Congressman Gerald Ford,[3] a member of the Warren Commission, thought it *was* possible—especially if the back wound were somehow moved up four plus inches from the 3rd thoracic vertebra to a non-

---

1 A rewrite of *Conspiracy of Silence* which morphed into *Trauma Room One*.
2 The manufacturer claims this bullet was not manufactured since WW II.
3 Later, President Gerald Ford. As Vice-President he replaced Nixon upon the latter's resignation. He is the only unelected US President.

descriptive, non-exact location at the base of the neck.[1]

Ford ignored the evidence from Parkland doctors, the shirt and jacket[2] Kennedy was wearing (which lined up with the 3rd thoracic vertebra), and Admiral Berkley's autopsy diagram (showing the lower location in the WC exhibits) and *changed the location of the back wound moving it up 4 plus inches.* Years later in a telephone interview with a reporter he claimed, "My changes had nothing to do with a conspiracy theory. My changes were only an attempt to be more precise." Arlen Spector[3] took it from there and evolved the "magic bullet" scenario outlined above.

The final shot (the third shot, according to the WC) that killed Kennedy also presented problems for the WC and the Navy doctors at Bethesda Naval Hospital. The official Bethesda autopsy report states:

> There is a large irregular defect of chiefly the parietal bone but extending somewhat into the temporal and occipital regions. In this region there is an actual absence of scalp and bone producing a defect which measures approximately 13 cm. in greatest diameter.

Dr. Robert McClelland of Parkland Memorial Hospital in Dallas supervised an artist's rendering[4] of the head wound. It showed a large gaping hole in the rear of the skull—the occipital-parietal area. McClelland was also photographed during a press conference, immediately after the assassination, as he showed the location of the head wound at the back of the head with his right hand.[5] The WC says the head wound was on the top and side of the skull (the temporal region)—a discrepancy of 10 centimeters. Once again, the location of the wound had moved nearly 4 inches.

In the days following the assassination, several other doctors from Parkland described the head wound as Dr. McClelland had—"in the rear of the skull where the cerebellum is located." They were quoted in the press and interviewed on TV saying the head wound was in the back of the head behind the right ear.

Months later they were "pre-interviewed" by the FBI or Arlen Spector *before* testifying before the WC. By this time the doctors at Parkland had seemingly contradicted their earlier statements to the press, and now agreed that the head wound was four inches away from where they first thought they saw the wound.

Thirty-three years later Drs. Baxter, Jones, McClelland, Perry, and Peters

---

1 Ford changed the initial WC draft to read "A bullet had entered the back of his neck slightly to the right of his spine."
2 Ford claimed that when Kennedy lifted his arms to his throat he pulled up the shirt and jacket thereby proving the back wound was at the base of neck. The autopsy doctors were denied an examination of Kennedy's clothing at the time even though the clothes were nearby.
3 Later Senator Arlen Spector.
4 The drawing appears in Josiah Thompson's book, *Six Seconds in Dallas*.
5 Photograph is reproduced in the back of this book.

of Parkland Hospital were deposed for the ARRB. However, instead of being deposed individually, they were deposed as a group casually sitting around and "reviewing" their original testimony immediately after the assassination. They also discussed the interviews some of them had given to various researchers which basically consisted of their memory of the neck wound and the head wound and whether they were intimidated into changing their testimony before the WC. They were supposed to be there to review and authenticate the "original autopsy materials."

But before starting the review of the photographs, there was a problem:

> We, the Assassination Records Review Board, as part of its work mandated by Congress, was [sic] able to digitize the original autopsy materials by very high-quality digitization process. We hoped that we had been able to bring some of these photographs with us today to show you and get your observations on those. Unfortunately, at the last minute we were not able to make the necessary security arrangements.[1]

Mr. T. Jeremy Gunn, the attorney who questioned the doctors "not in a typical deposition format" said that photographer John Stringer and his assistant Floyd Riebe "confirmed that the photographs were authentic photographs."[2] The non-typical format consisted of a discussion rather than a question-and-answer deposition.

In summarizing the discrepancy between the doctors at Parkland and the doctors at Bethesda, Dr. Crenshaw said:

> 1. At Parkland the wound to the right rear of the President's head is a large gaping hole extending from behind the ear all the way around to the back of the head. At Bethesda Naval Hospital the back of the President's head is intact with only a small puncture just to the right of the midline near the base of the skull. The large gaping hole is only on the upper right side with no damage to the rear of the head.

> 2. At Parkland Hospital, a small wound of entry is seen in the President's throat just below the Adam's apple and slightly enlarged to accommodate the tracheal tube. Upon examination at Bethesda this wound has become a three inch wide gaping gash. At Bethesda, pathologists discover a wound in the President's upper back near the spine.[3]

---

1 ARRB, 8/27/98, Answers and Depositions of Charles Baxter, M.D., Ronald Coy Jones, M.D., Robert M. McClelland, M.D., Malcolm Perry, M.D., Paul Peters, M.D. Uncorrected Copy, p. 6, lines 8-17.
2 Mr. Gunn did acknowledge that Mr. Stringer had said the supplemental brain photographs were not as he recalled.
3 *Trauma Room One*, p. 97.

The Supplemental Autopsy report on the brain was conducted several days later, as is customary to allow formalin fixation, a procedure to preserve and solidify tissue. Dr. Humes examined the President's brain with Drs. Pierre Finck and J. Thornton Boswell[1] and concluded:

> ...the wound of the skull produced *such extensive damage* [emphasis mine] to the brain as to preclude the possibility of the deceased surviving this injury.

Reinforcing this description the WC said that concerning resuscitation effort at Parkland:

> There was a great laceration on the right side of the head (temporal and occipital), causing a great defect in the skull plate so that there was herniation and laceration of great areas of the brain, *even to the extent that the cerebellum*[2] *had protruded from the wound. There were also fragmented sections of brain on the drapes of the emergency room cart* [emphasis mine].

Kennedy's brain weighed in at 1500 grams—the upper weight of a normal, un-traumatized brain. FBI Agent Francis X. O'Neil told the ARRB in 1997 that Kennedy had only half a brain when he observed its removal. So did assistant autopsy photographer Floyd Riebe, Dr. Boswell and Dr. Humes. Jacqueline Kennedy carried a handful of brain matter into Parkland Hospital. Kennedy's brain should have weighed considerably less than 1500 grams at the time of the brain autopsy, given the extensive loss of brain matter described in the autopsy report.

Photographs of the brain were taken at the Supplemental Autopsy.[3] Navy photographer John Stringer said he took pictures of the brain two to three days after the autopsy. In 1996, while examining photographs and negatives of the brain for the Assassination Records Review Board (ARRB), Stringer said he remembered having used Ektachrome E3 color positive transparency film and B & W Portrait Pan negative film in 4 x 5 format using duplex film holders—*not Ansco film in a film pack (or magazine) format.*

Customary microscopic sections of the brain were not done or are not available and the brain has since gone missing. One account says the brain was given to Robert Kennedy and that it was buried with the body.

However, on May 26, 1992, a legal investigator, Joe West, interviewed, by

---

1 Testifying on two different occasions, Dr. Humes claims two different scenarios. To the WC he claims to have examined the brain with Boswell and Finck. To the Assassination Records Review Board (ARRB) in 1996 he claims Finck was not present. Dr. Finck has testified he examined the brain with Humes several weeks (not days) after 11/22/63. It has been suggested that two separate brain examinations occurred.
2 Evidence of cerebellum (brain matter in the lower rear of the brain) reinforces the parietal-occipital location versus the occipital-temporal location.
3 And only at the autopsy, according to Boswell.

telephone, Mr. Thomas Evan Robinson, one of the morticians who embalmed Kennedy before burial. Following his death in 1993, Mr. West's handwritten notes were published. Copies of his handwritten notes which are difficult to read are shown in the appendix along with a typed version for clarity.

The notes taken during the telephone interview mention a large gaping hole in the back of the head; a smaller wound in the right temple; adrenlin [*sic*] gland and brain removed; other organs removed and put back; wound in back 5–6 inches below shoulder to the right of backbone.

Besides supporting the original reports of Parkland Hospital doctors regarding the head wound and back wound, Mr. Robinson told Mr. West he was in favor of exhuming the body "to settle once and...for all."

The brain would have shown the trajectory of the head shot(s). Mr. Robinson was never subpoenaed to appear before the AARB.

Dr. Crenshaw was never called to testify before the Warren Commission, although he was cited multiple times in the Warren Commission Report. In his best seller, *Trauma Room One*, Dr. Crenshaw writes:

> Had I been asked to testify, I would have told them that there is absolutely no doubt in my mind that the bullet that killed Kennedy was shot from the front.[12]

I never really doubted my cousin for a minute.

---

1 *Trauma Room One*, p. 14.

2 Dr. Crenshaw also writes about a personal phone call from LBJ while he was operating on Lee Harvey Oswald in Trauma Room Two (instead of Trauma Room One, out of respect for Kennedy) two days later, telling him that a large man—Crenshaw referred to him as Oliver Hardy—would be taking a death bed confession from LHO.

Chapter 14. Dr. Mary and the Galloping Cancer

Little has been written about Lee Harvey Oswald's true activities in New Orleans in the months preceding the assassination, approximately mid-April to mid-October, 1963. Why was he there at all, when his wife and baby daughter were in Dallas most of that summer?

The official story is that Lee left Dallas around mid-April, after having lost yet another job, to find work in New Orleans, more than 500 miles away, leaving his wife (and baby) who spoke no English, had little money, and was staying with a relative stranger. I suppose it's possible.

The unofficial version is strange, horrific, frightening, but true—and fits my cousin's account of Lee Oswald, David Ferrie, and the rehearsal for the assassination of Kennedy in Miami.

The unofficial story of Lee's time in New Orleans in the summer of 1963 concerns the worldwide epidemic of cancer—cancer that was *knowingly* allowed to be inflicted on millions of people, mainly young children—in the form of a polio vaccine—incredible as that may seem.

The Polio Vaccine–Cancer Connection

In the 1930s, lung cancer was so rare it was not even listed as a disease. By the 1980s there was an epidemic of lung cancer as well as many other cancers such as breast, colon, and skin. These cancers started in the early 1960s as a result of the subcutaneous and muscular injection (Salk vaccine) and oral ingestion (Sabine vaccine) of a polio vaccine which, unknowingly at the beginning, contained Simian virus #40 (SV40). These cancers started to appear just after tens of millions of children around the world were inoculated with the polio vaccine.

The developer of the first polio vaccine, Dr. Jonas Salk, head of the Virus Research Laboratory at the University of Pittsburgh, knew that several monkey viruses were present in his polio vaccine, but thought that he had "killed" all the monkey viruses with formaldehyde.

Shortly afterwards, Dr. Albert Sabine, developed a cheaper and easier-to-manufacture and administer oral (as opposed to injectable) vaccine which contained several live monkey viruses. One of those viruses was the yet unidentified SV40 virus. The vaccines were considered safe because the viruses were in an attenuated or weakened state—just enough to stimulate the immune system to create antibodies to kill all similar viruses in the body. It was not thought possible, at that time, that viruses could cross species. The ability of simian viruses to cross species, i.e., infect humans, was discovered only after tens of millions of doses were cultured, packaged, and distributed around the world.

In 1959, Dr. Bernice Eddy, PhD (University of Cincinnati), working with Dr. Sarah Stewart, M.D. (Georgetown University), PhD (Microbiology, University of Chicago), at the National Institute of Health (NIH) discovered the presence of SV40 in monkeys[1] *and* that it was capable of causing cancer in humans. The NIH refused to let her publish her findings, took away her lab, and demoted her.

In 1961, a federal law was passed requiring polio vaccines to be free of SV40. It did not, however, require the recall of the millions of doses of unused stocks of vaccines which the government and the NIH knew contained SV40. It was used to inoculate an unsuspecting populace until 1963 when all the previously distributed doses had been used up.

After a few rushed studies by the NIH showing that SV40 was not present in the vaccine, the matter lay dormant until the mid-1990s, when a researcher for the National Cancer Institute (NCI), Dr. Michele Carbone, reviewed Dr. Eddy's research and re-tested the vaccines and published the results. In a February 2000 edition of *The Atlantic Monthly*, Carbone is quoted as saying, "There is no doubt that SV40 is a human carcinogen."

Dr. Carbone, considered the leading expert on mesothelioma, has written over twenty papers linking SV40 to cancer in humans and worked at one time at The Cardinal Bernadin Cancer Center at Loyola University in Maywood, Illinois, before moving to Hawaii to practice.

Rather than recall the infected vaccine in 1961 and cause a panic as well as create distrust of the medical and scientific communities, the National Institute of Health (NIH) went ahead with the vaccination program.[2] The twisted rationale was—alleviate the public's fear of polio[3] *now* and find a

---

1 So named because it was the 40th monkey virus discovered. Drs. Maurice Hilliman and Benjamin Sweet, scientists working for Merck, one of the makers of the polio vaccine, in the 1960s, confirmed the presence of SV40 in the polio vaccine. The other company making the polio vaccine was Parke-Davis.
2 Estimates range as high as 200 million children inoculated with polio vaccine containing live SV40 from 1955-1963.
3 The polio epidemic, roughly 30,000 cases at its height, was already disappearing and continued to do so at the same rate in countries which did not inoculate their populations as those who did inoculate their populations.

cure for the cancer, which it was certain to cause in a large number of the world's population, *later. The NIH kept secret the contamination of the polio vaccine infected with SV40 for forty years.*

The government funded over 150 secret laboratories[1] around the country to find a cure for the cancer it had knowingly introduced around the world in over 100 countries via the polio vaccine.

A few of those secret labs, however, were funded for different purposes and by a different government organization—the CIA. Those labs were looking for a way to *speed up* the growth of cancer cells as an untraceable biological weapon to kill enemies of the United States—such as Castro. This weaponized cancer would eventually be used to kill Americans as well.

One of those labs was in New Orleans and Lee Oswald was, in his own words, loaned by the CIA[2] to the New Orleans laboratory of Dr. Alton Ochsner, New Orleans' most famous cancer researcher and head of the American Cancer Society. More specifically Lee was ordered to New Orleans by the CIA to learn how to safely handle this cancer virus and how to keep it viable outside the lab. Later, he would be instructed to take it to Cuba via Mexico and deliver it into the hands of anti-Castro doctors to kill Castro.[3] This explains a lot about Lee's activities in New Orleans and his real reasons for being there in the summer of 1963. Oswald was sent by the CIA to work with Dr. Ochsner to report on the progress of the experiment and to familiarize himself with handling of live deadly cancer viruses.

Dr. Ochsner was, by all accounts, a brilliant surgeon. He worked and taught at Tulane Medical School on the campus of Tulane University. He owned several huge clinics that catered to wealthy South American clients such as Juan Peron. He had influential friends like Richard Nixon and Louisiana Congressman and House Whip Hale Boggs, among others. But he was too well known and had too much at stake to risk being identified with a potential career-destroying project. Instead, he put the trusted and respected orthopedic surgeon Dr. Mary Sherman (affectionately known as Dr. Mary), a partner in one of his clinics, in charge of supervising the testing which was to take place off campus and outside the hospital. Dr. Mary lived alone and could work in relative secrecy—secrecy and plausible deniability being critical to the project.

Most of the basic testing was done on sterile mice. Later, larger animals such as monkeys were used. Testing was carried out in various unlikely and non-suspicious locations in New Orleans. Reports were regularly sent to Dr. Ochsner, sometimes by Lee, after which they were routinely destroyed.

---

1 CIA Director, Admiral Stansfield Turner, in congressional testimony has stated that approximately this number of secret government labs existed, mainly to further the aims of OPERATION MK-ULTRA. Some of these were used for other purposes as seen at Tulane Medical.
2 He was being paid approximately $400 per month by the CIA during this time.
3 Later his assignment would be changed to deliver the virus to a contact in Mexico City rather than take it to Cuba himself.

Aside from various Cuban helpers who moved cages and burned the animals after dissection, three people ran the routine animal testing—David Ferrie, Judyth Vary Baker, and Lee Harvey Oswald who was, basically, an expeditor, observer, errand boy, and CIA watchdog.

David Ferrie, an ex-seminarian who completed all six years of Catholic studies for the priesthood but was denied ordination, housed the test mice at his two apartments in New Orleans. He sometimes dressed as a priest and kept several sets of priestly garb in his apartment, along with several dresses. He also studied medicine from unaccredited schools and mail order houses and listed himself as Dr. David Ferrie in the New Orleans phone book. His studies also ran to law and he consulted for Carlos Marcello, head of the Dallas and New Orleans crime family, who was having immigration problems compliments of Robert Kennedy. He also acted as Marcello's personal pilot when not flying guns to anti-Castro rebels in Cuba. In his spare time, he ran a laboratory for Dr. Mary Sherman out of his apartment, where he kept caged test mice, sometimes as many as 400 at a time. There were so many cages, in fact, that he had to rent a second apartment in a nearby building for some of them.

To help Dr. Mary conduct the tests, a brilliant nineteen-year-old student was recruited by Dr. Ochsner—Judyth Vary Baker.

Judyth had distinguished herself even in grammar school. She found her calling in cancer research after watching her grandmother die slowly of the disease. She vowed to find a cure for cancer. In high school she consistently won science awards on a state and national level. Her science fair exhibits demonstrating ways of extracting magnesium from sea water and her innovative exhibits in cancer studies were widely publicized in the press, especially in Florida and Louisiana. She caught the attention of Dr. Ochsner and several other prominent cancer researchers when she discovered a ground-breaking way of rapidly growing cancer cells to expedite her search for a cure. She was barely seventeen at the time.

Her discovery was simple but original and her research was exactly what Dr. Ochsner was looking for when the CIA came calling.

Baker had discovered that by radiating the subjects, in this case mice, before injecting them with cancer cells, the cancer cells would grow to maturity in seven days—instead of the usual several plus weeks. This was just what the doctor ordered—a brilliant and, more importantly, an untraceable, un-suspectable, research assistant.

Although offered scholarships to many universities, Judyth Vary chose the University of Florida. After a few semesters there, she met and married Robert Baker, III, hastily. She married Baker after a dramatic falling out with her domineering father, who kidnapped her to prevent her from attending college. Shortly after her marriage, Dr. Ochsner offered her an internship at Tulane Hospital with a small stipend but a large inducement—early entry[1] to Tulane Medical School without having to finish her undergraduate work—*after* she helped with his project.

Married two days, her new husband Robert Baker left to work on an oil rig, leaving her with no money (even though he was from a well-to-do family), no way of reaching him (even though a phone was available), and no estimated time of return. He wrote infrequently and was away for up to three weeks at a time.

In New Orleans, one month before beginning her internship, she met Lee (by design, as it turns out) and a strong friendship quickly turned into a passionate love affair. Lee found her a place to stay and provided basic necessities.

The first place he found her to stay was called the "Mansion." Lee had called his old friend, Jack Ruby, in Dallas, to find a place. Ruby recommended the Mansion as a joke, thinking Lee knew it was a bordello. The bordello was promptly raided, Judyth left, and the madam refused to return her rent. When Ruby came to New Orleans to see Carlos Marcello about hiring a New Orleans star stripper known as "Jada," he repaid Judyth for the lost rent plus a little extra, apologizing for the joke. Lee introduced Jack Ruby to her as "Sparky Rubenstein," and she only knew him by that name until after she saw Ruby kill Oswald on TV.

Dr. Mary Sherman was to direct and supervise Judyth's work, which consisted of injecting the test animals with live cancer cells, dissecting the animals after euthanizing them, extracting the cancer cells, preparing slides, and writing reports. Judyth's first informal and accidental meeting with her was emotionally hurtful. Invited to a party at David Ferrie's apartment, Lee pointed out Dr. Mary. When Judyth approached her, Dr. Mary refused to speak to her, ignoring several attempts at an introduction. The following week Dr. Mary explained to Judyth that the party consisted mainly of homosexuals and, if she had talked to Judyth, she might get the reputation of being a lesbian in ultra-conservative New Orleans society. Judyth later attended several such parties at Ferrie's apartment as well as at the elegant home of Clay Shaw, a former military officer with CIA ties and a homosexual tendency.

Judyth later met Carlos Marcello through Lee's uncle, Michael Victor "Dutz" Murret, who worked for Marcello. The Murrets had raised Lee because he was too young to go into the orphanage after Lee's mother, Marguerite, gave him and his brothers up for adoption. Dutz was a bookmaker for Carlos Marcello and occasionally ran errands as well. Such errands usually involved carrying large sums of cash. Marcello, who took a liking to Judyth, let her and Lee eat at his restaurant every week on the house.

To obscure her role in the research project, Judyth was given a day job working mornings at the Reily Coffee Company around the corner from the FBI offices of Guy Bannister at 544 Camp Street, the offices of Naval

---

1 Early entry to medical school without an undergraduate degree was rare and only a man with Dr. Ochsner's stature could make this happen.

Intelligence, and close to David Ferrie's apartment. She and Lee were hired on the same day, Lee being assigned to maintenance work in the multi-story building, giving him ample places to escape from without too much notice from the other employees. Most days Judyth clocked him out at 5 PM, with the knowledge of her boss, Mr. Monaghan, an ex FBI agent. On other days Mr. Monaghan clocked them both out.

During their free time Lee complained to Judyth, whom he affectionately called "Juduffski" (because she had a passing knowledge of Russian and Russian literature) about his troubles with Marina. He told Judy that he had only married Marina so he could stay in Russia and that she had had numerous affairs right from the start. He told her Marina only married him to come to America and always carped about money. He admitted he had hit Marina when provoked by her emasculating comments, and this prevented a physical relationship with the frightened Judyth—for a while.

Judyth complained to Lee about Robert, who was insensitive, oversexed, domineering, and miserly, asking for her paychecks and giving her less than she needed to even pay her rent while indulging himself. He barely wrote, never asked how she was managing, and never told her when he would be off the rig and home. She decided to divorce him.

Lee decided to divorce Marina as well and they made plans to run off to the Yucatan and study Mayan culture when the cancer project was over. She would become a doctor in South America and Lee would become a sociologist and continue his hobby of writing short stories. They would live on the money Lee was saving—money being held for him by his friend, George DeMohrenschildt, in Dallas.

Although a high school dropout because of his slight dyslexia[1], Lee was a voracious reader with a near photographic memory which he displayed on several occasions. Once he named every city in Cuba for Judyth, recited from a Russian opera, *The Queen of Spades* by Tchaikovsky, which the CIA made him memorize as an exercise, and memorized a chess game in progress. His hero was Herbert Philbrick, the real-life triple agent, whose life was portrayed in the TV series *I led Three Lives*. He also imagined himself the Scarlet Pimpernel, a hero playing the role of a bumbling idiot. They fell deeply in love.

Judyth's experiments on larger animals[2] were as successful as her experiments on mice. By August of 1963, the research was coming to a head and would soon be completed. Lee prepared his cover story for entry into Cuba by building a pro-Castro image with the help of his friends. He passed out pro-Castro leaflets titled "Fair Play For Cuba."[3] The pamphlets bore the 544 Camp Street Address of Guy Bannister's office, which infuriated Bannister. Next, Lee arranged for a public brawl and arrest to be filmed by

1 Lee was punished in school for being dyslexic and hated school.
2 After mice, marmoset monkeys, then rhesus monkeys, and finally African green monkeys were experimented on.
3 At a Dallas press conference Ruby corrected the Dallas DA asserting the correct name of the pamphlets- Fair Play For Cuba.

the local TV station and later did a radio debate on the subject of Marxism. He also traveled to Mexico to apply for an entry visa to Cuba.[1] All this was to build a pro-Castro image he could use to enter Cuba.

The tests on thousands of animals were extremely successful and Judyth was told that a "terminally ill volunteer" from the Angola Penitentiary was going to be injected with the vaccine after being radiated (to lower his immune system and speed the growth of the cancer cells).

The Jackson Mental Hospital in Clinton, Louisiana was chosen.[2] This was the final phase of her internship after which she expected to enter Tulane Medical School in the fall.

Judyth was brought to Clinton to insure that the "volunteer" was properly radiated and injected with viable cancer cells. She was given collected blood samples to see that the cancer had taken. So many samples, in fact, that she suspected more than one volunteer had been infected. She was horrified, later, to see the man, in pain, tied to his bed at the hospital. He died within twenty-eight days. He was of the same age and body mass as Fidel Castro.

Although warned from the start of her internship that no paper trail was to exist on this project, she wrote a letter directly to Dr. Ochsner. She delivered it to Dr. Ochsner's secretary, without marking it "personal," complaining about the human experimentation. Dr. Ochsner's secretary opened the letter. Dr. Ochsner was furious, canceled her internship and refused to honor his commitment to enroll her into Tulane Medical School. Judyth and Lee were fired from the Reily Coffee Company on the same day, August 16, 1963.

The project, having been successfully completed, was dismantled and the cleanup begun. While Dr. Mary was out of the country at a conference, her apartment was burglarized. Instead of expensive jewelry and furs, only her computer was stolen. She was not upset and filed a police report to collect on the insurance. David Ferrie's two apartments were cleaned out and all evidence of any experiments was destroyed.

Within a year Dr. Mary would be found dead in her bed, naked, with her right arm and right side of her rib cage missing. The right arm and rib cage appeared to have been burned completely off. Her mattress was on fire but it was a minor fire with a little smoke which aroused the neighbors who called the fire department. The case has never been solved and the autopsy is unavailable. Researchers have speculated that her wounds were inconsistent with a small mattress fire but were consistent with destruction from a particle accelerator—such as used in the testing she was doing on cancer cells.

Within four years David Ferrie would be found dead in his apartment

---

1 He let the visa expire after plans were changed for him to go only so far as Mexico City to deliver the virus.

2 As a cover, Clay Shaw drove Lee and David to Clinton in a big black Cadillac (which was sure to stand out in the small town) so Lee could register to obtain a voter card and attract attention while doing so. This was justify his visiting the Clinton penitentiary without suspicion.

---

after being notified by District Attorney Jim Garrison that he was to be arrested in connection with the JFK assassination. Two suicide notes were found in the apartment.

Lee was told by the CIA to wait for the signal to go to Mexico City to deliver the fast-acting cancer, known as the "galloping" cancer, to a contact. The call came on Monday, September 23, 1963.

His assignment was to travel to Mexico City[1] by bus and to meet a Cuban medical technician at a souvenir shop who would continue to keep the cells alive and deliver them to anti-Castro doctors in Cuba—doctors who had studied under Dr. Ochsner. He carried them in two thermos bottles given him by Clay Shaw.

But something went wrong. His contact failed to show up. Lee attempted to get a visa to Cuba to try to salvage a seemingly botched operation. He was told the visa would take a month—too long for the cancer cells to survive. Lee called the local CIA office in Mexico City for instructions. He was told the operation had been cancelled because a tropical storm had destroyed their safe houses in Cuba. He was shown pictures of the destruction. Later he learned that the storm had not happened at the time when the CIA told him it happened. He became suspicious.

He was told by the CIA to stay in Mexico City as a CIA "asset." Soon he was told to report to Dallas for "debriefing." Lee worried that if the mission to assassinate Castro has been compromised, he knew too much to be left alive.

In Dallas he was directed to check into the YMCA and not to talk to Marina until he was debriefed. He was directed to report to the Texas School Book Depository for a cover job—an inventory clerk. His boss, Mr. Truly, was told he was working undercover for the FBI. The building was owned by Mr. Byrd, a close friend of LBJ, Clint Murchison, and H.L. Hunt.

By mid-October, shortly after he turned 24, he told Judyth he probably wouldn't see another birthday because he'd been "invited" to be a participant in the assassination of JFK at one of three locations in Dallas, one location in Chicago, and one location in Tampa. The three locations in Dallas were Love Field Airport, Dealey Plaza, and the International Trade Mart.[2]

---

1 Lee's time in Mexico City from mid-morning, Friday, September 27, 1963 until Thursday October 3, 1963 as Judyth Vary Baker relates in *Me & Lee*, is controversial but critical. Mark Lane, the most famous and trusted researcher, claims emphatically, in dozens of pages in his latest work, *Last Word*, that Lee was never in Mexico City during this time, and that the CIA fabricated Lee's trip to Mexico City for several reasons including the pretense that Lee contacted the Cuban and Russian Embassies to facilitate his escape from the US after he killed Kennedy thereby providing the charge of premeditation. Much as I respect Mr. Lane, his writings and his tenacious quest for the truth, I believe Judyth Vary Baker's version of Lee's trip to Mexico City during the above-mentioned period and his reasons for going there. I have written to Mark Lane twice but he has not replied.

2 Kennedy was scheduled to speak at a fund raiser at the International Trade Mart in Dallas at 1 PM. The Mart was managed by Clay Shaw of New Orleans.

According to Detective James Rothstein, "Big Al" Carone, a New York City police officer, CIA asset, US Army Colonel, Brooklyn Mafia bagman, and a "made Mafia man" was part of the back-up team at Love Field. "Carone was a close associate and friend of Bill Casey. Casey attended Carone's daughter's wedding at the Narragansett Inn on Montauk Highway in Lindenhurst, New York on Long Island."

Kennedy was scheduled to attend the Army–Air Force Game in Chicago, Illinois on November 2. The route was planned through a neighborhood of tall buildings. The trip to the Army–Air Force game was called off because of a tip from a source identified by local Chicago authorities only as "Lee."[1]

The attempt in Tampa, Florida was to be made during a long motorcade ride. Kennedy was scheduled to speak at the Al Lopez Stadium to the Cuban community on November 18. The motorcade was unexpectedly cancelled and Kennedy was helicoptered to the site.

---

1 There is also an account that says the FBI or Chicago Police were notified by the owner of a motel who saw rifles with scopes and a map of Chicago on a bed in a room he had rented to two Cubans. Professional hit men would not be so careless.

CHAPTER 15. THE ZAPRUDER FILM

If my cousin were correct regarding a planned and rehearsed triangulation shooting in Dealey Plaza, the Zapruder film would confirm or deny it. It did, and then again, it didn't.

Abraham Zapruder was a Jew born in Kovel, in the Ukraine, who immigrated to Manhattan. He worked in the garment district of Manhattan as a pattern maker. His expertise caught the attention of a high-end clothing design firm, Nardis of Dallas, which moved him and his family to Dallas in 1959. There he worked with a designer, Jeanne LeGon, for whom he cut patterns and material. He joined the "Dallas Council on World Affairs" and "The Crusade for a Free Europe." Both organizations were considered CIA proprietary organizations and included George DeMohrenschildt, Clint Murchison, George H.W. Bush, and H.L. Hunt. He was also a 32nd degree Mason as were Gerald Ford and J. Edgar Hoover.[1] In 1959, Jeanne LeGon married George DeMohrenschildt.

Eventually, Zapruder started his own company with partner Erwin Schwartz, in Dallas, called, "Jennifer Juniors," which occupied the 4th and 5th floors of the Dal-Tex Building across from the TSBD. Zapruder decided, he claimed, to film the motorcade almost as an afterthought.

An avid photographer, he had left his camera home and had to go back to retrieve it at the last minute. He decided on a closer view than his office window could provide and so walked down to Dealey Plaza and stood on a four-foot pedestal with help from his receptionist, Marilyn Sitzman. Due to his vertigo, he asked her to stand behind him on the pedestal to steady him as he shot.

The camera was one of the best home movie cameras available—a 414 PD Bell & Howell Zoomatic Director's Series. It had a Viramax 9-27 mm, F 1.8 lens. The film played on an 8mm film projector, although it used 16mm film in the camera.

---

1 Ford and Hoover may have been 33rd degree Masons.

The camera exposed one side of a 16mm 25' filmstrip at a time. After exposing one side of the 25' film, the film had to be reloaded, under dim lighting, and then the other side was exposed.

When developed, the film was split down the middle, glued or cemented together, and returned to the customer in a 50' strip.

Zapruder had inserted a new roll of film and had shot only a few test frames before filming Kennedy. The film of Kennedy took less than 30 seconds and used 6' of film. The rest remained unexposed. The camera had two settings—normal (16 frames per second) or slow motion (48 frames per second.) Zapruder used Kodachrome II 8mm color film. According to the WC he shot 486 frames running at 18.3 frames per second. Three hundred and forty-three frames (18.7 seconds) show the presidential limousine, known as SS-100-X.

Immediately after filming Kennedy, Zapruder returned to his offices. He locked the camera in his safe and told his secretary to call the police or the Secret Service. When the Secret Service arrived, he promised them a copy of the film, and then went out and tried to have copies made. After several futile attempts to find a lab capable of developing the film, he arrived at the Dallas Kodak Lab, which developed the film for him but did not slit it or make copies. They did give him the three rolls of unexposed film he would need to make copies. He wanted six but the lab only had three strips of film in stock.

Finally finding Jamieson's lab, he asked them to make three copies (actually three new exposures) from the original with the film he had brought with him. He insisted on being in the dark room while the copies were made and then asked everyone to sign an affidavit stating that no bootleg copies were made. Jamieson's equipment was not able to reproduce the images around the sprockets as on the original.

Zapruder then went back to Kodak to have the copies developed. The original and perhaps one copy were slit and cemented together in a continuous 8mm strip capable of being shown on a small projector. The next day he showed the film to his employees on a projector in his office.

Altogether, Zapruder had five affidavits signed on the advice of his lawyer, whom he had called several times during his search for a developer. He knew he had something valuable and that its value lay in its exclusivity. He said he intended to sell the film for as much as he could get.

He gave two of the copies to the Secret Service with the stipulation that they could only be used for official use and that he was not conferring or transferring any other rights. He kept the original in his safe, intending to sell it to the highest bidder. He gave another copy to his business partner, Erwin Schwartz. Three days later, Zapruder sold a copy to *Life Magazine*, a subsidiary of *Time, Inc.*, for $50,000, but maintained the movie rights. Shortly afterwards he sold all the rights to *Life Magazine* for $150,000 to be paid in six annual installments on the third of January for the next six years. The first $25,000 he donated to the Fireman's and Policeman's Benevolence Society to ward off criticism of a Jew's profiting from the death of a Catholic president.

There was a stipulation that *Life* protect the copyright. That stipulation proved so cumbersome in later years that *Life Magazine* sold the rights back to the Zapruder Family for $1. Eventually the Zapruder family sold the film to the government for $16,000,000.00, after arbitration. The family had been seeking $30,000,000.

Four days after purchasing the film, *Life Magazine* published thirty frames of the film in black and white due to deadline restraints that prevented preparing the color separations. One week later *Life* published some of the frames in color.

The next time the film was shown publicly was at the trial of Clay Shaw in New Orleans by District Attorney Jim "Jimbo"[1] Garrison. *Life* had fought the subpoena but lost. In 1975, Geraldo Rivera showed it for the first time on national television. In 1991, Oliver Stone incorporated the Zapruder film into his film of the assassination, called *JFK*. Stone paid $85,000 for the rights to show the film in his movie. The outrage sparked by this showing led to the creation of the Assassination Records Review Board (ARRB) in 1992.

What seems like a straightforward film of the critical 18.7 seconds of the assassination, however, has turned into another proverbial can of worms raising questions about Zapruder himself; the sale price of the film; the speed at which the film was shot; the inconsistencies and "jumpiness" in the film; the evidence of alterations; and the reality of what it appears to show.

Originally Zapruder claimed to have set the camera at the slow motion speed of 48 frames per second. The FBI and the Warren Commission said the film ran at 18.3 seconds, a slight deviation from the 16 frames per second advertised by the manufacturer of the camera, Bell & Howell. The rate of 18 frames per second formatting *was* adopted by Bell and Howell for the P414 camera—but not until 1966.

When viewing the film, concentrating on everything but the limo, several problems appear to "pop up." The frames seem to "jump." This could be explained by Zapruder's natural unsteadiness due to vertigo; his reaction to the shots fired; alteration of the film for sinister purposes; or a combination of the three.

The driver of the limo, William Greer, turned to face Kennedy so rapidly that his movement has never been duplicated in terms of speed. The car does not appear to slow down in the film, although dozens of witnesses testified that the vehicle came to a full stop. Other claimed it came to a near stop and others said they saw the brake lights on the limo light up.

My cousin told me that during the rehearsal the driver was told to stop in the "kill zone."[2]

The first seven seconds (132 frames) are of the lead motorcycle escort. Then, to conserve film, Zapruder stopped filming until the presidential limo

---

1 "Jimbo" was a comic combination of Jim and jumbo due to Garrison 6", 6" frame.
2 Some witness accounts mention that the curbs in the kill zone were painted yellow; that would have helped the driver to know exactly where to stop.

appeared.

The Zapruder film is silent and does not record any gunshots. Originally Zapruder claimed the shots came from his right side (the grassy knoll). Later he claimed he heard the shots with his left ear and that they originated from the direction of the TSBD.

When *Life Magazine* ran frames from the film, it captioned them by saying that the head shot had come from the front. Some subscribers received that issue, but then the caption was rewritten to say the head shot came from the rear. Hoover admitted he gave the WC still photos from the film which showed Kennedy falling forward after being hit in the head. Later Hoover told the WC that a technician had made an error.

The WC relied on the Zapruder film to establish that 2.3 seconds elapsed between the second and third shots—a feat neither FBI nor Army marksmen were able to duplicate even under enhanced conditions such as using oiled gun mechanisms, multiple practices, a re-sighted and re-aligned scope[1], a re-machined trigger action, and a closer distance—thirty feet in the air instead of sixty feet. In addition, they shot at a stationary target[2]. The FBI tests were in the range of 4.8 to 9.0 seconds between shots while the Army managed 4.45 to 8.25 seconds between shots.

The Zapruder film was not the only film of the assassination. Dozens of spectators were filming with movie and still cameras. Some of these were confiscated and destroyed but some survived and they contradict the Warren Commission's conclusions outright.

Two films are notable for what they did not show—the Robert Hughes and the Charles Bronson films. Both show that, at the time of the shooting, no one was in the 6th floor window on the east side of the TSBD. The supposed sniper's nest of Lee Harvey Oswald, captured on 8 mm motion picture film and 35mm portrait film, show that at the time Kennedy's car was beneath the window—no one was in the 6th floor window.

The WC dismissed these films by saying they did not show the building from which the shots were fired and they were not of sufficient clarity to have identified anything, when the opposite was painfully true.

Other professionally shot photographs show Oswald watching the motorcade from the doorway of the TSBD. As AP photographer James Altgens took pictures of the presidential limo, he captured the doorway of the TSBD. His black and white photo went out over AP lines the next day. The WC claimed the man in the doorway was a fellow worker, Billy Nolan Lovelady—except the shirts on the two men were different and could easily have been used to identify one from the other. Although there are two photographs of Billy Lovelady wearing two different shirts, researchers such

---

1 The scope was, in fact, so badly misaligned that three shims had to be placed under one end of the scope to sight it.
2 There is a major difference in shooting at a positioned target as opposed to a target moved into position at the last minute.

as Dr. James Fetzer[1] have confirmed that the shirt Lovelady was wearing at the time of the assassination was a vertically striped red and white short sleeved shirt, the one which he had shown to the FBI on February 29, 1964, and they photographed him wearing it at the time. Billy Lovelady did not testify before the Warren Commission. Lovelady's supervisor at the TSBD did testify before the Warren Commission that he observed Lovelady sitting on the steps of the TSBD—not standing in the doorway.

If Lovelady was sitting on the steps at the time of the shooting, then he could not be the man in the TSBD doorway. And if he was wearing a red and white striped short-sleeved shirt, he could not have been the man in the doorway who appears to be Oswald. Conversely, if Oswald was standing in the doorway, he could not have been on the 6th floor, shooting at Kennedy. He could not have been one of the shooters.

---

1 Dr. Fetzer has also written that the man wearing a fedora hat in the same Altgens photograph may have been Jack Ruby.

CHAPTER 16. THE COVER-UP—IMMEDIATE AND CONTINUING

Not only was the assassination executed with military precision; equally well rehearsed and executed was the framing of Oswald and the subsequent cover-up.

First, fifteen minutes before Kennedy was even pronounced dead, shortly after one o'clock, a bucket of water was brought to the limo and the limo was cleaned. Then the limo was covered with a quarter-inch plastic two-piece bubbletop[1] which was stored in the trunk in the event of rain. The top was then covered with a fitted black cloth covering which was also stored in the trunk in the event of excessive heat. These efforts took about twenty minutes. Later the limo was whisked away to the C-130 cargo plane which accompanied Air Force One. Why?

The limo was washed, covered and removed after medical students and reporters began noticing the bullet hole or hole-like crazing in the windshield, the creased chrome, and the bullet fragments on the front floorboards. Some researchers, such as Dr. Fetzer, credibly claim that photographic evidence of the windshield clearly shows a hole the size of a pencil cratered on the inside indicating entry from the front. This would have had to have come from an above-ground sewer position in front of the limo.

The Secret Service has argued that the photographic evidence shows only a grazed windshield but there is also evidence that the original windshield was removed at the Ford Motor Company and replaced with a new windshield. The Secret Service, in turn, produced a grazed windshield and maintained that the grazed windshield had been the original windshield.

Next, immediately after Kennedy was pronounced dead, six Secret Service men removed Kennedy's body—against Texas law. Murder, not a federal crime at the time, was required to be investigated in Texas. The autopsy was also required

_____

[1]There were several tops for the limo including a stainless forward top and a formal rear top.

to be performed in Texas to preserve the chain of evidence. But when the Texas chief medical examiner, Dr. Earl Rose, informed the Secret Service that the body had to remain in Dallas, he was knocked to the ground, weapons were drawn and the body was removed from the legal jurisdiction of Dallas.

Within fifteen minutes of the assassination a description of the assassin was broadcast over police radios. He was "identified" by Howard Brennan who was sitting atop a low concrete wall at the corner of Elm and Houston. "He was a white man in his early 30s, slender, nice looking, and would weigh about 165 to 175 pounds," testified Mr. Brennan. Brennan also testified he saw Oswald, standing up and resting against the left window sill and actually shoot Kennedy from the window on the 6th floor, even though the photographic evidence shows no one in the window at the time of the shooting, as mentioned earlier. Brennan was approximately 120 feet away when he said he saw Oswald. The *Washington Post*, on the day after the assassination, reported that a Dallas newspaper photographer saw a rifle barrel being pulled back into the east 6th floor window of the TSBD.

Several detectives and police officers ran up to the 6th floor of the TSBD and found three[1] shell casings, perfectly lined up on the east side of the building behind a stack of cartons which they dubbed the "sniper's nest." On the west side of the 6th floor buried beneath a stack of boxes and surrounded by a chest-high stack of other cartons they discovered a rifle. The rifle, however, was, as noted earlier, stamped "Mauser," a popular German made rifle well known to the police and detectives who found it. It was photographed and displayed to the press the next day.

Unfortunately for the conspirators, it was the wrong rifle and a retraction had to be issued the next day. The rifle DA Wade should have displayed at the press conference was an Italian Mannlicher-Carcano rifle—a rifle so poorly made that it was cited by the Italian Army as the reason they lost the war. It was called a "humanitarian rifle" as it rarely killed anyone it was aimed at. Production of the Mannlicher-Carcano rifle was halted after the Italian Army surrendered.

In Washington, DC, telephone lines went dead around noon on November 22nd and service was not restored for over an hour. When service was restored, Johnson telephoned Robert Kennedy from Air Force One for a legal opinion as to whether the swearing in should take place in Dallas or Washington. Johnson reported that Robert had said to go ahead with the swearing-in in Dallas. Kennedy later denied saying this.

In another odd coincidence, most members of the Kennedy Cabinet were in flight to Honolulu to attend a convention at the time.

At the moment Oswald was taken into custody, the *Star*, a New Zealand newspaper published in the town of Christchurch, hit the newsstands with a front page story on JFK's assassin, replete with photos of Oswald dressed

---

1 Originally only two shell casings were found and photographed. The third shell casing turned up later. A photograph of the two shells is shown in Groden's *The Search for Lee Harvey Oswald*, p.166.

in a suit. Oswald's life story was detailed, including his time the marines, his time in Russia, and his association with the Fair Play For Cuba Committee. Before Oswald was charged with any murder, New Zealanders were told, in print, that Oswald was Kennedy's killer.

The ensuing press coverage was a masterfully conceived and very effectively executed program, carried out with typical military efficiency and money. It was called "OPERATION MOCKINGBIRD," a mopping-up-and-eliminating-of-messy-details operation to cover up "OPERATION BIG EVENT."

PART THREE. WHY WATERGATE?

CHAPTER 17. MARTIN LUTHER KING AND THE VIETNAM WAR

Martin Luther King was killed because he spoke out against the war in Vietnam, thereby threatening those forces having a vested interest in the war. Kennedy had done the same, except behind the scenes, and not as eloquently as Dr. King, through his National Security Action Memo 263 (NSAM 263). NSAM 263 was the order for the withdrawal of American "advisors" from Vietnam. The outcome for both men was the same—martyrdom in the prime of life.

Dr. King had made many enemies including J. Edgar Hoover and the Southern Democrats when he formed the Southern Christian Liberation Movement (SCLC). His Civil Rights Movement, his peaceful marches, and sit-ins across the South had made serious enemies in federal, state, and local governments. But when he spoke out publicly, emotionally, and elegantly against the Vietnam War, he brought forth the hounds of hell—the military-industrial complex.

Dr. King's decision to come out against the war was not universally supported by his followers in the SCLC or similar organizations. Dr. King was criticized for taking away time, resources, and money from the Civil Rights Movement. Vietnam was not their fight, many argued. Still, Dr. King felt morally compelled to speak out against the war, even though, by this time, the U.S. was three years into the war.

Dr. King spoke out against the Vietnam War in a major address at the Riverside Church in New York City on April 4, 1967. A year later, to the day, he was killed by elements linked to the Mafia, the FBI, the CIA, H.L. Hunt, Carlos Marcello, the military—and, in the opinion of author and barrister, Dr. William Pepper, who was James Earl Ray's last attorney, members of Martin Luther King's closest inner staff were also complicit in the conspiracy to kill Dr. King.

King's memorable and moving address, *Beyond Vietnam: A Time to Break Silence*, was the most forceful and significant expression of opposition to the war at the time. In it he spoke of the "madness of Vietnam," the killing of civilian Vietnamese.

"So far we may have killed a million of them—mostly children," he said. He called for the U.S. to "End all bombing...Declare a unilateral cease-fire...," and "Set a date that we will remove all foreign troops from Vietnam in accordance with the 1954 Geneva Agreement."

In his address, Dr. King also spoke of France's defeat at Dien Bien Phu and America's intervention to prop up the government of South Vietnam President, Ngo Dinh Diem, against the wishes of the majority of the people of Vietnam. Dr. King spoke out against U.S. support of French efforts to re-colonize Vietnam. He spoke of crimes against humanity—"We watch as we poison their water, as we kill a million acres of their crops... Somehow this madness must cease. We must stop now."

The Reverend Martin Luther King was killed exactly one year after he spoke those words, on April 4, 1968, and less than twenty-four hours after his memorable "mountaintop" speech, in which he predicted his imminent death or, at least, a short life for himself.

Dr. King's Last Two Days in Memphis

Dr. King had come to Memphis on April 3rd, arriving around 10:30 AM. He had come to lead a peaceful march in support of the Memphis Sanitation Workers Union who had been on strike since February. Dr. King had come to Memphis twice before in the past several weeks. The first time, on March 22nd, a rare sixteen-inch snowfall cancelled all activities in Memphis. The second time, on March 28th, the march was aborted due to window breaking and vandalism by some younger marchers. When the police tried to forcefully break up the march, Dr. King was ushered away to safety and back to the Riverside Motel where he was staying. He left town the next day.

He had come again to march with the sanitation workers, whose difficult work, unsafe equipment,[1] sub-standard pay, and inhuman treatment had caused them to go on strike after the newly-elected mayor of Memphis stood adamant against any compromise and began recruiting strikebreakers. The thousand-plus striking sanitation workers carried signs that read, "We are men."

Dr. King was scheduled to speak that evening at the Mason Temple, which was the headquarters of the Church of God in Christ. He had decided at the last minute not to speak because the weather had turned stormy, and he was certain that no one would show up. When an overflow crowd of approximately 10,000 people showed up, he was quickly called to the church. In this emotionally-charged speech, which turned out to be his last, he spoke of being thankful that God had allowed him to live a few years in the second half of the twentieth century. He said that longevity had its place, but he didn't care about that, because he had been to the mountaintop and had seen the "promised land." He nearly collapsed from exhaustion after speaking and

---

1 Two sanitation workers were crushed to death by a defective trash crusher.

had to be helped from the podium.

The next day was filled with meetings about the upcoming march on Washington that the SCLC was planning for May. Previously, on August 28, 1963, 250,000 people had marched on Washington. The march planned for the next month was to be a more dramatic event, with demonstrators pitching tents and staying in Washington until Congress acted. The upcoming "March on the Capitol" added to Washington's paranoia and no doubt was a factor in Dr. King's assassination, along with the anti-war sentiments Dr. King was espousing.

The details surrounding King's assassinations are all too despicable and all too familiar. Once again, we have a "lone nut" patsy, in the form of a felon or person of anti-social leanings (or perceived anti-American leanings, in the case of Oswald), this one by the name of James Earl Ray. We have no apparent or discernible motive for the killing. "No motive" again equates to "no conspiracy," at least in the minds of the conspirators. (After all, the concept had worked well before, with the assassination of John F. Kennedy.) Large sums of money were involved. Federal and local government agencies worked hand in hand with the Mafia. Handlers carefully maneuvered the patsy into position. Federal and local government agents were planted at the scene of the crime ready for damage control and obfuscation of the evidence—before the crime was committed. We have instantaneous identification of the patsy moments after the crime occurs. We have instant discovery of evidence which implicates the patsy. We have a murder weapon which proves not to be the murder weapon, a fact which seems not to matter to official forensic experts. We have no real trial of the patsy and the patsy is quickly neutralized and effectively silenced, as are any unfortunate, honest witnesses to the crime. We have a systematic pattern of suppressing any exculpatory or contradictory evidence, or publicity about such evidence, by sealing it for decades, for no compelling reason. We have numerous, lengthy behind-closed-door, official investigations that are forced to admit a conspiracy, due to evidence which cannot be hidden or denied—but which still deny the existence of conspirators. And, we have researchers who try to expose the inconsistencies and failures of multiple official investigatory bodies and bring forth the true testimony of suppressed witnesses (those who have not been permanently and criminally silenced). These researchers are forever branded with the scarlet words "conspiracy theorists" or, worse yet, "communist," which justify, at best, intellectual stoning. If this does not sound all too familiar, it should. We've heard it before—and will again.

Some months after the shooting of Dr. King, James Earl Ray was captured in England. He was extradited, tried in a matter of hours, and convicted on the basis of his own confession, which was given, he claimed, to avoid the death penalty. Case officially closed—except for a few stubborn details.

James Earl Ray's Story

This is James Earl Ray's story—the unofficial story.

Ray was a high school dropout. He joined the army and served in the closing years of World War II. In 1949, at the age of 21, Ray was arrested for his first burglary in California, a half continent away from his Alton, Illinois roots. A series of petty crimes, arrests, and convictions led to a twenty-year sentence for armed robbery, for stealing $120 from a Kroger grocery store in St. Louis, Missouri, in 1959. He escaped eight years later from the Missouri state prison.

According to Ray's brother, John Larry Ray, who wrote *Truth at Last*, Ray was aided in his escape from a maximum-security prison in late 1967 for only one purpose—to be used as the patsy in the murder of Dr. King. One day a fellow inmate, Ronnie Westberg, convinced Ray to escape. According to his brother, Ray escaped by hiding in an empty bread box that was wheeled out to a bakery truck that regularly delivered bread to the penitentiary. John Larry Ray suspected Richard Helms of the CIA of arranging the escape with Ronnie Westberg's help. Westberg, no doubt in a fit of remorse at having helped Ray escape, hanged himself in prison—but not before managing to break both his arms and legs.

John Larry Ray also claimed that Warden Donald Wyrick told an inmate and a trustee, Gene Barnes, that he, Donald Wyrick, had helped James Earl Ray escape, so that the Feds could use him as the fall guy in the King murder. Barnes gave James Earl Ray a signed affidavit, which he turned over to the HSCA in the late 1970s. The warden also told Barnes that an escaped prisoner was the best sort of fall guy, because he couldn't go to the police, or any official source, for assistance.

According to his brother, James Earl Ray was given shock treatments as well as LSD, in prison, for "therapy." He claims that Dr. Donald B. Peterson, co-author of a scientific paper entitled, "Applied Hypnosis and Positive Suggestion,"[1] worked out of State Hospital No. 1, a mental hospital in Fulton, Missouri—the same hospital that James Earl Ray was sent to, on several occasions, while incarcerated at the Missouri State Penitentiary in Jefferson City.

While a fugitive, Ray travelled to Chicago, Toronto, and Montreal. He had learned in prison that it was easier to get a new identity in Canada. In Montreal, James met a man called Jules "Ricco" Kimble, an admitted CIA agent and member of the Canadian Mafia run by the Cotroni Family. Kimble promised Ray a new identity and passport.

According to the FBI, the Canadian Mafia family, headed at the time by Vic "The Egg" Cotroni and Luigi Greco, answered to New York crime boss Joe Bonanno. The "Egg" was headquartered in Montreal.

Both Ricco and Ray were taken to a Holiday Inn in Montreal where they were both hypnotized by someone from McGill University in Montreal.

1 Published in 1965 and co-authored by George A. Ulett.

McGill University, according to John Larry Ray, was the home of a CIA program called "SUBPROJECT 68," part of the program MK-ULTRA.

MK-ULTRA was a CIA-sponsored human behavioral modification program, begun in the early 1950s and officially halted in the early 1970s. CIA Director Richard Helms ordered all records of its existence destroyed, but 20,000 documents which had been misfiled earlier were uncovered, subpoenaed, and investigated by the Church Committee and by the Rockefeller Commission in the late 1970s.

The MK-ULTRA program was originally started by CIA Director Allen Dulles and headed by Sidney Gottlieb, the same Sidney Gottlieb who prepared poison capsules for Marita Lorentz with which to assassinate Fidel Castro. MK-ULTRA was a continuation or offshoot of World War II OPERATION PAPERCLIP which whitewashed the background of Nazi scientists, notably SS General Walter Dornberger and SS Major Wernher von Braun, and gave them U.S. citizenship in exchange for their "research" files on brainwashing and torture techniques that had been acquired in Nazi concentration camps.

MK-ULTRA is also known under several other names, such as MK-SEARCH. There is speculation that the program, although officially cancelled, never really ended, but was renamed OPERATION MK-NAOMI and continues today but probably under a different name.

Research for MK-ULTRA was conducted at over eighty colleges and universities in the U.S. and Canada, as well as in a similar number of prisons and hospitals.[1] The research centered on behavior modification through the use of drugs, such as LSD, barbiturates, amphetamines, and sodium pentothal, plus torture, electroconvulsive shock treatments, and hypnosis. The hypnosis experiments in Canada were conducted by Dr. Donald Ewen Cameron at the Allan Memorial Institute of McGill University in Montreal.

In Montreal, Kimble introduced James Earl Ray to a man who would provide him a new identity. Unbeknownst to Ray, the man would also become his "handler" in the same way that George DeMohrenschildt became Lee Harvey Oswald's handler.

The identity Ray was given was that of "Eric Stavro Galt," an actual, living native of Toronto, who looked surprisingly like Ray, had a highly classified security clearance, and worked on top-secret U.S. Defense Department projects. The handler was a man known to Ray only as "Raoul."

According to an article in the *Chicago Reader*[2], Kimble, in an interview from El Reno, Oklahoma, in June, 1989, confirmed that:

> In July 1967, on orders from a Louisiana FBI agent, he flew Ray from Atlanta to Montreal, where Ray was given an identities

---

1 According to Congressional testimony by CIA director Admiral Stansfield Turner.
2 *Chicago Reader, The conspiracy to kill Martin Luther King: New Testimony Implicates the CIA*, John Sergeant and John Edgington, March, 1990.

package by a CIA specialist. An ex-CIA agent with knowledge of Canada in the 1960s recently confirmed in an off-the-record interview that there was an agency "asset" specializing in false identities in Montreal in 1967. He was known as Raoul.[1]

According to English seaman Sid Carthew, Raoul hung out at a dockside bar called The Neptune, in Montreal. He identified him as 5'8", 145 pounds, dark hair and a Mediterranean complexion. James Earl Ray claimed he met Raoul in a bar in Montreal—and that Raoul was the man who shot King. The HSCA investigation concluded no such person ever existed.

Raoul, Ray claimed, had recruited him and provided false identities for him to help run guns to Mexico. Raoul also gave Ray money to buy a specific whitish Ford Mustang[2] before traveling to Memphis. Ray purchased the Mustang in Birmingham in August, 1967, under the name Eric S. Galt and gave a Birmingham address.

In Memphis, Raoul had told Ray to take a room at Bessie Brewer's Boarding House across the street from the Lorraine Motel, a few days before the assassination. The seedy rooming house was located above Jim's Café, owned by Lloyd Jowers. Ray registered as "John Willard,"[3] although he had been using the alias Eric Stavro Galt since late 1967.

Ray also claimed that Raoul had also asked him to buy a deer hunting rifle at a gun shop, Aero Marine Supply Company, in Birmingham, Alabama, on March 30. He purchased the rifle under the name Harvey Lowmyer. It was the second rifle he bought for Raoul, who had made him return the first one for the more powerful 30.06 with a scope. The gun shop owner remembered Ray because Ray had asked for a rifle with which to hunt deer in Wisconsin with his brother, but seemed to know nothing about rifles or deer hunting.

On the day of the shooting, Raoul told Ray to meet him in front of the boarding house at around 5:30 PM.[4] Around that time Ray went to get the spare tire of the Ford Mustang fixed. Ray had changed a flat tire that morning and didn't want to be left without a spare. Ray suspected he was to be the getaway driver for a crime Raoul was about to commit. Ray went to a local gas station and, while waiting to have the spare fixed, heard police sirens. An escaped convict, he could not take the chance of being captured and so he left the scene. Within thirty minutes, an APB[5] went out for a "John Willard." Shortly afterwards the APB was changed to an "Eric Stavro Galt."

Some witnesses reported seeing two identical white Ford Mustangs parked outside Jim's café within a few hundred feet of each other, hours earlier. It may have been part of the plan to somehow implicate Ray in the conspiracy, according to some researchers.

1 Sometimes spelled "Raul."
2 The "white" Mustang was actually "Springtime Yellow" but looked white.
3 Some sources say Ray checked in as John Williams.
4 Some accounts say Raoul gave him $200 and told him to go to a movie.
5 An APB for LHO went out with similar haste in Dallas.

Ray eluded capture by driving the back roads, which were not blocked. He soon learned that he was wanted in connection with the killing of Dr. King and drove to Atlanta, where he abandoned the Mustang on April 5th; the car was not found until the 11th. From there he flew to Montreal and then to London, where he tried to fly to Rhodesia, which did not have an extradition treaty. He was captured in a London airport on June 8th, using a passport in the name of a Canadian by the name of George Raymon Sneyd who lived in the same area of Toronto as the real Eric Stavro Galt. Sneyd's passport picture had a strong physical resemblance to Ray—as did Galt's.

The existence of Raoul was denied by all government agencies that investigated the assassination of Dr. King:

> The task force [Department of Justice] views the exculpatory of these varying and patently self-serving tales [regarding Raoul] to be unbelievable.[1]

Although the HSCA admitted a conspiracy,[2] no conspirators were named, except to say they were not members of the FBI, the CIA, the military or the Mafia. In 1979, the HSCA committee investigating the assassination of Martin Luther King issued its findings. It concluded that James Earl Ray fired one shot at Dr. Martin Luther King; that the shot was fired from a bathroom window at the rear of Bessie Brewer's Rooming House where Ray had rented a room for the week; that James Earl Ray fled the scene; that his alibi, his story of "Raoul," and other exculpatory evidence, was not worthy of belief. It also stated in its findings:

> B. The committee believes, on the basis of the evidence available to it, that there is a likelihood that James Earl Ray assassinated Dr. Martin Luther King as a result of a conspiracy.

Four sentences later, it put to rest any involvement by the government:

> D. No Federal, State or local government agency was involved in the assassination of Dr. King.

The King Assassination Set-Up

Dr. King had been invited to dinner at the house of Reverend Billy Kyles on the evening of April 4, at 6 PM.

Dr. King was staying in Room 306, an outside room, of the Lorraine Motel, facing Mulberry Street. Originally, he was booked into an inside room, Room 202, next door to his brother, A.D. King, who did not arrive until early the next morning.

Walter Bailey, manager of the Lorraine, said he received a call the night

---

1 Report of the Department of Justice Task Force to Review the FBI, Martin Luther King, Jr., Security and Assassination investigations, p. 89.
2 The above report did not admit a conspiracy.

before Dr. King's arrival from the Atlanta office of the Southern Conference Leadership Council (SCLC), which Dr. King headed. The caller, whom Bailey refused to identify, insisted that Dr. King's room be changed to an outside room. Bailey explained to the caller that the inside room was closer to the motel offices and would be the safer choice. Unable to dissuade the caller, Bailey moved King to Room 306 before Dr. King checked in. A.D. King's room was not changed and he checked into Room 201.

Dr. King, according to a surveillance team report, was in his brother's room, Room 201, at 1:30 PM and returned to his room at 5:45. This timeline, however, conflicts with Reverend Abernathy's FBI interview in which he said that he and Dr. King spent most of the day in Room 306, only leaving for one hour between 4:30 and 5:30 PM to dress for dinner. Reverend Abernathy said Dr. King was trying on different ties and asked him to call Reverend Kyle's house to see what they would be serving for dinner. The Reverend Kyle had just purchased a new home and Dr. King joked that he hoped the Kyles had furniture. He was pleased to hear that dinner was to be "prime rib and soul food," and not, he joked, "Kool-Aid and ham sandwiches."

Reverend Jesse Jackson, staying in Room 305, had gone down to the pool area below and was observed by several people nervously looking at his watch.

The Reverend Samuel "Billy" Kyles, in a recent documentary called "Witness," claims he originally told Dr. King that dinner was at 5 PM, so that the notoriously late Dr. King would be relatively on time. He says, in the documentary, that he came to Dr. King's room at 5 PM and spent about fifty minutes talking with Dr. King and Rev. Abernathy about "preacher talk." He said he helped Dr. King pick out his tie. Reverend Abernathy has consistently denied Reverend Kyles was in the room with them at any time during that day.[1]

At 5:45 PM, a maid knocked on the doors of rooms 315 and 316 where Dr. King's self-appointed, informal but armed local bodyguards, a group calling themselves "The Invaders," was staying. The maid told them that their rooms were no longer being paid for by the SCLC. They packed quickly and left. When asked who told her to deliver the message, the maid told them it was the Reverend Jesse Jackson. In reality, the rooms had already been billed to the SCLC for the night, check-out time for the day being long past. Jackson has denied telling the maid to ask "The Invaders" to leave, claiming he did not even remember "The Invaders" staying at the Lorraine.

Attorney Dr. William Pepper, in *An Act of State*, writes:

> The fact that the order appears to have been given by Jesse Jackson is also curious. Reverend James Orange recently confirmed again that Reverend Jackson had nothing to do with the Invaders and would have had no reason to give such an instruction. In my opinion either Jackson did not give the order and the attribution

---

1 *Walls Came Tumbling Down*, Ralph Abernathy, p. 440.

is wrong, or, he is implicated in the conspiracy.[1]

According to a police report by MPD officer Willie B. Richmond, the Reverend Samuel "Billy" Kyles, a local minister and Memphis Police Department Intel bureau informant, was reported to have been going into various rooms between 5 and 5:50 PM. He was seen going into Room 307, the recently vacated room of Dr. King's assistant, Dorothy Cotton, who had left for the airport. The report stated that the Reverend Kyles knocked on Dr. King's door at 5:50 PM.

Dr. King walked onto the balcony, outside room 306, with the Reverend Ralph Abernathy, and leaned over the balcony railing to speak to his driver for the evening, Solomon Jones, waiting below. Abernathy excused himself and went back into the room to put on cologne because, he told Dr. King, he heard some pretty women were going to be at Reverend Kyle's house for dinner. Solomon Jones suggested to Dr. King that he might need a topcoat as it might turn chilly. Dr. King also spoke to Reverend Jesse Jackson down below. He invited Jackson to dinner as a conciliatory gesture, as the two had been at odds lately. Reverend Kyle, who was standing several feet away from Dr. King, responded that Jackson had already invited himself. Minutes later Reverend Martin Luther King was killed by a gunshot wound which traveled from his lower jaw to his spinal cord, killing him an hour later.

The shot came directly from a brush-covered lot across from the Lorraine Motel room and adjacent to Jim's Café. The lot was buttressed by a 10–15 foot high retaining wall and was slightly higher than the second floor balcony of the Lorraine Motel.

Part-time cab driver Louie Ward was parked on Mulberry Street, close to the Lorraine Motel. He was waiting for a fare to drive to the airport. He claimed he saw a man jump down from the high retaining wall directly across from the Lorraine Motel, run north on Mulberry street, and get into a Memphis Police Department car which was parked across the middle of the intersection of Mulberry and Huling. Louie Ward died later that evening by falling from a speeding car.

A six-year-old boy[2] sitting in a parked car facing south on Mulberry Street claimed he saw a man in the bushes behind the retaining wall opposite the Lorraine Motel. The wall, he indicated, was about ten to fifteen feet high. He described the man as an Arab or Mexican, black moustache, dark hair, medium build, with his left trigger finger on a gun pointed at the Lorraine Motel. The gun, he said, hardly made a sound when fired. He also saw a big-bellied man with a white Tee shirt kneeling next to him, a short distance from the kitchen door of Jim's Grill. His description of the shooter matched that of Raoul as described by Ray. His description of the other man matched that of Lloyd Jowers, owner of Jim's Grill. The boy told his story to Reverend Billy Kyles who told him to keep quiet. Kyles told the boy that the

---

1 *An Act of State*, William Pepper, p. 194.
2 Some accounts identify the boy as being twelve years old.

government killed Dr. King and would kill him too, if he did not keep quiet. The boy also told Reverend Ralph Abernathy.

King's driver, Solomon Jones, on loan from a local funeral home, and a neighbor walking past the motel, both claimed to have seen a man, or several men, in the bushes at the time of the shooting. The back door of the kitchen of Jim's Café, owned by Lloyd Jowers, opened onto those bushes.

Lloyd Jowers, according to attorney and investigator Dr. William Pepper, was a gambler in debt to Frank Liberto, owner of a wholesale produce company Liberto Bros. Frank Liberto was also the local Mafia "capo," working for Carlos Marcello. In March, 1968, an associate of Frank Liberto approached Jowers with a proposition. Jowers' gambling debts would be forgiven; he would receive $100,000 in cash.[1] The cash was later delivered in the bottom of an E.M. Carter Company produce box. The money came from New Orleans, home of Carlos Marcello. In exchange, Jowers would take possession of a rifle from someone. The rifle would be picked up from Jowers at a later time. Jowers was told that the Memphis Police would be nowhere in sight, and, that there would a patsy or decoy.

Sometime later, a Latin or Indian-looking man, 5'9", 145–155 lbs, 35–45 years of age, with dark hair, came to Jowers' café and told him that Jower's assignment was to take possession of a rifle and hold it until someone came to pick it up. On the day of the shooting Jowers received a rifle in a box. Hours before the shooting, Raoul picked up the rifle, then took a nap; and later went into the bushes behind the concrete retaining wall directly in front of the Lorraine Motel. He went through the kitchen door of Jim's Café.

Dexter King, Dr. King's son, and Ambassador Andrew Young interviewed Jowers years later. Jowers told them that planning sessions for the assassination were held in his grill. The sessions were attended by members of the Memphis Police Department, namely Lieutenant Earl Clark, the department's best shot, and Marrell McCollough. McCollough, a black undercover officer, was the first person to reach Dr. King after the shooting. He was photographed as he knelt over the body.

Earl Clark originally testified he was home with his wife, Rebecca, sleeping until they were awakened by the police radio announcing that Dr. King had been shot. Upon hearing the report, Clark told his wife to go to the cleaners to get his uniform. He testified she came back about thirty minutes later. Her alibi for her husband, however, did not hold up, as the cleaners, which closed religiously at five every day, had closed at four on this day. She said she left for the thirty minute round trip to the cleaners around 6 PM.

Betty Spates, a black waitress at Jim's Café, said she saw Jowers run into the kitchen after the shooting. Jowers was carrying a rifle which he broke down into two or three pieces, wrapped in a tablecloth, and hid under the counter. Jowers said to her, "You wouldn't do anything to hurt me, would you, Betty?" The next day, Jowers showed the rifle to a cab driver, a friend,

---

1 Part, or most, of the money may have been for Raoul.

who had come in for lunch. Jowers told Spates to keep quiet about what she had seen. Spates said Jowers' pants legs were wet and muddied.

The lot from which Jowers emerged was muddy from the previous night's rain. Plaster casts of well-formed footprints were made at the scene. The police failed to find a match for the prints.

Renfro Hays, an investigator working for Ray's first lawyer, Art Hanes, claimed to have identified Raoul as "Raoul Esquivel," a Louisiana State Trooper stationed in Baton Rouge. He identified him as a Spanish-looking man[1], 5'9", with salt-and-pepper hair. When arrested, Ray had on him the contact phone number Raoul had given him. The number was traced to the Louisiana State Police barracks.

Ray was never tried after being extradited back to Memphis. His had a brief court appearance after his second attorney, Texan Percy Foreman, convinced Ray to plead guilty to first degree murder to avoid the death penalty. Ray agreed to a plea bargain in court, but refused to agree that there was no conspiracy involved. He was sentenced to ninety-nine years. Three days later, he recanted his guilty plea and asked for a trial. He referred to his attorney, Percy Foreman, as "Percy Foreflusher." Foreman, a Texan from Dallas, was also H.L. Hunt's lawyer. Ray was never given a trial. The judge considering the request for a new trial was found dead of a heart attack, at his desk, slumped over Ray's appeal papers.

In December 1999, thirty-two years after the assassination, the King family brought a wrongful death suit against Lloyd Jowers and "other unknown conspirators." In a three-and-a-half week civil trial attended by very few, and given almost no publicity, Jowers was found guilty as charged and ordered to pay restitution. The King family asked for a token payment of $100.00.

Jowers had essentially confessed, previously, to Sam Donaldson, on "Prime Time Live," that he was an accomplice to the murder. A transcript of this interview was read at Jower's trial (in which he did not testify). The transcript also implicated Frank Liberto as having been the man who recruited Jowers and gave him $100,000 in cash. Liberto was a member of Carlos Marcello's Mafia family. Jowers also claimed that a man named Raoul brought him a rifle in a box the day before the shooting.

After Jower's interview was allowed into the record, witnesses were able to testify about related matters. They testified that two black firefighters, normally stationed at Fire Station 2, adjacent to the Lorraine Motel, were transferred to a firehouse across town, Fire Station 31, the night before the assassination. A black Memphis police officer normally assigned to guard King was escorted home that day because a death threat had been made on his life.

Tactical units of the Memphis Police Department, which consisted of three vehicles and twelve officers for emergency purposes, and which were

1 Raul was from Belize in South America according to one account and Portugal in another.

normally assigned to guard King, were pulled back five blocks sometime before the time of the shooting.

Olivia Catling, who was walking past the Lorraine Motel at the time of the shooting, saw a man running out of the alley of a building across the street from the motel. The man jumped into a green 1965 Chevrolet. A police car pulled up behind the Chevrolet, blocked off the street, and let the Chevrolet go off in the opposite direction. Catling said she heard a shot coming from the bushes behind Jowers Café. She was never interviewed by the Memphis Police Department.

Solomon Jones, King's driver in Memphis that day, also saw a man in the bushes.

It was also brought out at trial that, at 7 AM the next morning, the supervisors and administrators of the Memphis Sanitation Department had cleared away all the bushes from behind Jower's café. An open, vacant lot remained that could no longer be imagined as a possible position from which a shooter could fire unobserved. The Memphis Sanitation Department's supervisors and administrators, who were not on strike, had also cut down a large tree branch outside the second story bathroom window of Brewer's Boarding House. The branch blocked a clear view of the Lorraine Hotel's balcony where Dr. King had been standing. Ray was supposed to have fired from that window the day before.

The judge in the civil suit was Circuit Court Judge Arthur Hanes Jr., who had been Ray's first attorney before Percy Foreman persuaded Ray to change attorneys. He provided what he termed "interesting evidence" to the jury. He told them that as Ray's attorney, he had interviewed Guy Canipe, who had since passed away. Canipe had run Canipe's Amusement Company next door to Jower's café. According to Memphis police, a bundle wrapped in a blanket was found on the sidewalk outside of Canipe's Amusement Company, two minutes after the shooting. It contained a rifle, a radio (on which Ray's prison number was scratched), binoculars, a toiletry bag, two cans of beer, underwear with a laundry marking, and two receipts—all easily traceable to James Earl Ray.

Judge Hanes, however, stated that Guy Canipe had told him that the bundle was dropped in his doorway ten minutes before the shot was fired.

Taxi driver James McCraw gave a deposition in which he claimed he was inside the rooming house where Ray was staying at the time of the shooting. McCraw claimed he had a clear view of the bathroom from which Ray had "admitted"[1] shooting Dr. King. McCraw said the bathroom door was open and the bathroom empty at the time of the shooting. He claimed that the passenger he came to pick up, Charlie Stevens, was so drunk he couldn't get out of bed, and so he left him lying there after hearing the shot.

Charlie Stevens was the state's only witness concerning Ray's presence at the time of the assassination. Stevens swore he saw Ray in the bathroom,

---

1 Ray admitted to the shooting in his plea bargain to avoid the death sentence, on the advice of Percy Foreman.

balancing on the rim of the old cast iron tub, with his finger on the trigger of a high-powered rifle.

Captain Carthel Weeden, in charge of Firehouse No. 2, testified that on the morning of the assassination he escorted two U.S. Army officers to the roof of the firehouse, from which they had a clear view of the Lorraine Motel. The army men carried cameras.

Douglas Valentine, a writer researching a government program called the Phoenix Project (a CIA counterinsurgency program in Vietnam to capture and torture hostile Vietnamese), wrote that members of the 111th Military Intelligence Group photographed the entire assassination of Dr. King as it happened.

Jack Terrell, a former CIA agent, testified that he had been in Memphis on that day as a member of a sniper team. The team was assigned to be on the water tower opposite the Lorraine Motel. The assignment was cancelled without explanation.

Ray's gun, the 30.06 Remington 760 Gamemaster rifle, could not be identified as the murder weapon. The coroner testified the death slug was intact when taken out of King's body. The FBI said it was fragmented and could not be matched to the rifle. The scope on the rifle had never been sighted and could not have been used as is. (Oswald's Mannlicher-Carcano rifle had a similar problem with the scope.)

James Earl Ray, in a plea bargain, confessed and was sentenced without a trial. No one else, including Jowers, has ever been criminally tried in the assassination of Martin Luther King.

Years later, attorney Dr. William Pepper investigated a lead involving Texas oil billionaire H.L Hunt. Atlanta police officer Don Wilson, examining Ray's abandoned Mustang, found an envelope between the seats. He inadvertently put it in his pocket and said nothing for thirty years. He claimed he was afraid he had contaminated the evidence or broken the chain of evidence, and so said nothing. The envelope contained a page ripped out of a Dallas phone directory. The page listed the phone number of the H.L. Hunt family. On the top of the page was handwritten the name "Raoul," the letter "J" and a phone number. The number was traced to the Vegas Club in Dallas, a club belonging to Jack Ruby.

Following up on this lead, attorney Dr. Pepper traveled to Dallas and spoke to Madeleine Duncan Brown, Johnson's mistress; Beverly Oliver, who worked at the Colony Club next door to Ruby's Carousel Club; and Chari Angel, who worked for Ruby. Each identified a photograph of Raoul and claimed they had seen him, Raoul, with Jack Ruby, in 1963, at the Carousel Club. Oliver claimed she once witnessed Raoul give $20,000 in a Piggly Wiggly grocery bag to Ruby.

Doesn't it seem like *déja vu* all over again?

Chapter 18. The Assassination of Robert F. Kennedy and the California Primary

Robert Kennedy was assassinated because Lyndon Johnson, as he crassly put it, "was afraid Bobby would ride his brother's coffin into the White House."

Robert Kennedy was shot in the early morning hours of June 5, 1968, after winning the California primary, and he died the next day. A win in the next primary in Illinois would have given him the nomination for the presidency on the first ballot. Like his brother and Dr. King, Robert Kennedy was publicly executed by a "lone nut" with "no apparent motive."

Sirhan Sirhan, witnessed by dozens of people shooting Senator Kennedy, was convicted of firing eight shots, striking Kennedy three times and wounding five others.[1] He was subdued and disarmed by four of Kennedy's friends who were acting as bodyguards—actor and author George Plimpton, author Pete Hamill, Olympian Rafer Johnson, and former LA Rams linebacker, Roosevelt "Rosie" Grier.

At his trial, Sirhan's behavior in the courtroom was as strange as it was at the scene of the crime, the Ambassador Hotel's kitchen pantry area. Although he had confessed to the shooting in the police car, immediately after being arrested, he was allowed to plead "not guilty" at trial. Upon questioning about his youth, which seemed to bother him enormously, he withdrew his "not guilty" plea and asked to be executed. His defense attorney, Grant Cooper, asked him point blank if he had killed Kennedy and he replied, "Yes, sir." Before the trial concluded, two pieces of evidence and testimony were introduced which muddied the waters of a perfect case for premeditated murder.

First, Judge Walker admitted into evidence three of Sirhan's notebooks. They contained strange scribbling and multiple repetitive phrases, such as "RFK must

---

1 Paul Schrade, William Weisel, Ira Goldstein, Elizabeth Evans, and Irwin Stroll.

die," and "must be assassinated before June 5, 1968." They were writings of an obviously troubled and confused mind.

Then George Plimpton testified that Sirhan, as he was being restrained and disarmed on the night of the shooting, appeared "enormously composed" and "serene," as if in a trance. Roosevelt "Rosie" Grier, a former professional football player with the Los Angeles Rams,[1] remembered he had difficulty restraining and disarming him. Grier had knocked him down and was holding him down over a warming table after Sirhan fired his second or third shot. Grier was being helped by Rafer Johnson and George Plimpton who were also holding him down. Yet, Sirhan was able to fire five more shots while being restrained by a man almost three times his weight, more than a foot taller, and a trained NFL defensive linebacker. It seems obvious Sirhan's mental and physical state was not natural but altered chemically, mentally, or both.

In chambers, Sirhan Bishara Sirhan accepted a plea bargain, allowing him to avoid the death sentence in exchange for a life sentence. Sirhan has since recanted his confession, claiming no memory of the shooting or that evening.

In the 1976–79 HSCA hearings, which reviewed the assassinations of John F. Kennedy and Martin Luther King, the Robert F. Kennedy assassination was ignored for no apparent reason. Or perhaps, it was ignored because the official Robert Kennedy assassination scenario is the most vulnerable to criticism—criticism which appeared almost immediately. As noted earlier, the JFK assassination may have been the sole focus of the re-investigation but the Black Congressional Caucus could have refused to vote for it unless the assassination of Martin Luther King was included.

The next problem that arose concerned the autopsy and the forensic evidence. All eyewitnesses to the shooting claimed Sirhan's gun came no closer to Kennedy than a distance of three feet. The coroner's report, however, was at odds with the eyewitness accounts.

Dr. Thomas Noguchi,[2] Chief Medical Examiner for Los Angeles at the time, performed the autopsy on Robert Kennedy's body over a six-hour period, beginning at 3 AM on June 6th. He took his time because he understood the significance of what he was doing and wanted a perfect autopsy. He concluded, based on "soot" or un-burnt gunpowder residue found in the hair on the back of Kennedy's head, to the left of his right ear, slightly above the level of the ear canal, and the description of the head wound, that the shot that killed Robert Kennedy was fired from a distance of less than three inches and as close as one and one-half inches from the back of Kennedy's head.

Dr. Noguchi was immediately fired.

---

1 Rosie Grier was a member of the Rams' defensive team, called the "Fearsome Foursome." The other three were, Deacon Jones, Merlin Olsen, and Lamar Lundy. He also played for the New York Giants.
2 Dr. Thomas Noguchi was the inspiration for the TV series, *Quincy*, starring Jack Klugman.

The bullet which entered Kennedy's armpit and the one lodged in his spinal column were recovered intact but the bullet which struck Kennedy in the head was shattered, leading to additional controversy and questions.

Was the bullet that struck Kennedy behind his right ear the same type of bullet fired from the front? Was there a second gun, indicating a second gunman?

Nina Rhodes, a Kennedy fundraiser, said she heard twelve to fourteen shots. She was standing six to seven feet from Kennedy. However, Sirhan's gun, a .22 caliber Iver-Johnson Cadet, held eight bullets. He did not have a chance to reload. She told her story to the FBI. After reviewing a transcript of her interview, she said her FBI report contained fifteen errors.

Lisa Urso remembered someone drawing a gun after the first shot and then holstering it.

Eugene Thane Cesar was a last-minute replacement guard from the Ace Security Company. At the time of the shooting he was on duty behind Kennedy's right side. He was holding Kennedy's right elbow with his left hand as they walked through the kitchen pantry area of the Ambassador Hotel. After the shots were fired, Cesar left the pantry area to find his supervisor, Jack Merritt. Merritt claimed Cesar was gone from the kitchen area for about two minutes. When questioned by police, Cesar said he was carrying a .38 caliber revolver in his holster. He said he had owned a .22 caliber revolver, similar to the one used by Sirhan, but had sold it three months earlier, sometime in February, to a co-worker by the name of Jim Yoder.

As well as working part-time as a security guard, Cesar was a plumber who worked the 7 AM to 3:30 PM shift at Lockheed, in Burbank, where the U2 plane was manufactured. He had a high security clearance but, according to fellow workers, no job description. He was twenty-six years old, six feet tall, weighed 210 pounds, had two children, a troubled marriage and was in need of money. He moonlighted for the Ace Security Company for $50.00 per hour.

Years later, a reporter located the man Cesar said had bought the .22 caliber revolver. Jim Yoder produced a copy of the receipt for the .22 caliber revolver he bought from Cesar. The receipt, for $15.00, was for a Harring and Richardson .22 caliber revolver, serial number Y13332. It was dated September 6, 1968, three months after Kennedy was shot. Shortly after speaking to the reporter, Yoder's house was burglarized and the gun was stolen. Cesar, it has been reported, has since moved to the Philippines.

William W. Harper, a retired consulting criminologist, examined the evidence and concluded that there were two firing positions from which Robert Kennedy was shot. One position was directly in front of Senator Kennedy and the other, directly behind.

Another problem that arose after the trial was the account of several witnesses who saw others with Sirhan immediately before the shooting.

Jack Merritt, Cesar's supervisor from the Ace Security Company, said he saw a man and a woman walking away from him, coming out of the kitchen pantry area—smiling. He said the woman was wearing a polka-dot dress.

Sandra Serrano, a young student, was interviewed by LAPD on the night of the shooting. She was sitting on the steps outside the Embassy Ballroom, which was part of the Ambassador Hotel, at around 11:30 PM., when two men and a woman passed by her on the steps and headed into the ballroom. One man was short, Mexican looking, with bushy hair. The other man had long shaggy hair and was slightly taller. He and the woman seemed to be a couple. Later the couple, without the third man, came running down the steps, passed her, and shouted, "We shot him! We shot him!" When Serrano asked the woman who they were talking about, the woman turned to her and said, "We shot Kennedy." The attractive young woman had a pug nose and wore a polka-dot dress.

Serrano was questioned for over an hour by Sergeant Enrique Hernandez, who told her, forcefully and repeatedly, that she was mistaken and that she was dishonoring Kennedy's memory by repeating her story about seeing three people enter and two people exit the ballroom. She stuck by her story that she had seen three people. One of the men she described as a Latin-looking male, 5'5", olive complexion, with long black hair hanging over his forehead. The other male was Mexican-American, 5'3", wore light clothing, and had bushy hair. Both men were in their early twenties. The woman, she said, had an upturned nose and wore a white dress with dark polka-dots. When she saw a picture of Sirhan in the papers, she felt sure he was one of the males who passed her on the steps as they entered the ballroom where Kennedy was speaking.

Vincent DiPierro, a part-time waiter at the Ambassador and son of a maître-d' at the Ambassador, said he saw a man he later identified as Sirhan Sirhan outside the kitchen pantry area with a woman, drinking coffee. Sirhan said something to her and she smiled. She had brown hair, blue eyes and was wearing a white dress with black or purple polka-dots. The police reported that DiPierro later changed his story and admitted he had *not* seen a woman in a polka-dot dress after all.

Police sergeant Paul Sharaga, on duty outside the Ambassador, ran toward the excited crowd outside the ballroom and saw a giggling couple pass by him. He said they were shouting "We shot Kennedy!" The young lady was wearing a polka-dot dress. Sharaga immediately put out an APB for a woman in a polka-dot dress. And no sooner had he issued the APB, when all police communications went dead for twenty minutes. The LAPD later recanted his story for him, saying he must have heard the words, "They shot him," instead.

Additional evidence of LAPD complicity in the cover-up was also obvious and disturbing. Evidence from the crime scene was intentionally destroyed. Shots had been fired into the jamb of the doorway leading out of the pantry as well as into the ceiling tiles. These bullet holes were circled, measured with a ruler, initialed by the crime scene investigator, photographed—and promptly destroyed. The official reason given by Daryl Gates, LAPD Police Chief, and the city attorney, was that, "you can't fit a ceiling tile into a card file."

Thankfully for the prosecution, that evidence never made it to trial. The two holes in the ceiling tile and the three or four holes in the door jamb would have meant a conspiracy, as Sirhan's gun held only eight shots. At least seven of Sirhan's eight shots hit five human targets. Explaining the extra holes would have only confused the jury. Fortunately, the LAPD had help from the Mafia and the CIA.

When the LAPD set up a special task force called "Special Unit Senator (SUS)" to investigate the assassination of Robert Kennedy, it placed two men in charge—Sergeant Enrique Hernandez and former Lieutenant Manual Pena. Hernandez was the same detective who had badgered Sandra Serrano to change her story at the Rampant Division station, a station known for being the most corrupt in the LAPD. Hernandez's resume included police training work in Latin America—for the CIA. Lieutenant Pena was brought out of retirement to head the SUS task force. After retiring a year earlier, he had gone to work for the Agency for International Development (AID) of the State Department. AID was a CIA cover agency which dealt with counterinsurgency and torture in South America.

According to Chicago Mafia boss Sam Giancana's brother and his grandson, Sam Giancana was responsible for the assassination of both Kennedys. He did it because of Kennedy's ingratitude over the Mafia's many favors to the Kennedy family. The favors included John Kennedy's presidential victory by 100,000 votes, mainly from Illinois' Cook County controlled by Giancana's Chicago Mafia Family, and the covering up of John Kennedy's various and numerous sexual escapades. A year before Robert Kennedy's assassination, union boss and Mafia associate Jimmy Hoffa was reported as having told a fellow inmate that if Kennedy got close to being elected, there would be a contract out on his life. Hoffa denied having said this.

In film footage taken the night of the assassination, retired U.S. Army Captain Bradley Ayers identified a certain David Sanches "El Indio" Morales as being in the crowd along with two other CIA agents. Morales, of course, was a member of Brigade 2506 that invaded Cuba as well as a White House operative named by E. Howard Hunt[1] as one of the conspirators in the assassination of John F. Kennedy. Morales has also been identified as a registered guest at the Ambassador Hotel on the night Kennedy was shot, but those records have gone missing. However, David Rabern, a private investigator who was working as a security officer at the Ambassador Hotel, identified a photograph of Morales as the man who was there the night Robert Kennedy was killed.[2]

---

1   E. Howard Hunt has sometimes been cited as the model for the Ethan Hunt character play by Tom Cruise in the *Mission Impossible* movies.
2 Bradley Ayers, *The Zenith Secret*, p. 204.

Setting Up Sirhan

But the real involvement of the CIA was through the MK-ULTRA program that the CIA has admitted was operational at the time. According to Sirhan's last and current attorney, Dr. William Pepper, Sirhan was hypnotized, programmed to believe that Senator Kennedy was a target in a pistol range, programmed to kill Kennedy, and, further, programmed to erase all memory of having been hypnotized.

Sirhan had a love of horses and wanted to be a jockey. He worked for a time at the Santa Anita Racetrack where he "breezed" horses, lightly exercising them in the morning by riding them around the track before the races. One day, he had an accident at the track and fell from a horse, which ended his dream of becoming a jockey. He received compensation of a few thousand dollars which did not last long.

While working at the track Sirhan met an unlikely friend, Jerry Owen, a fundamentalist preacher and an intellectually talented man. Owen had managed to memorize the entire Bible, some thirty thousand passages. He called himself "The Walking Bible." The police called him a con man and they had a long list of arrests to back up their claim. Owen also had a love of horses and, in fact, traded horses on the side. He even gave free pony rides to children who learned a Bible verse. He boarded his horses at Wild Bill's Stables in Santa Ana, which was run by Bill Powers. When Powers needed someone to work at the stables, Owen suggested Sirhan, who was not able to work at the racetrack after his accident.

Owen introduced Sirhan to another friend of his as well. This friend, like Owen, was a preacher and a hypnotist as well. This friend, William Bryan, was a descendant of William Jennings Bryan. William Bryan had gained notoriety in the early 1960s when he was hired by attorney F. Lee Bailey to hypnotize the infamous "Boston Strangler," Albert DeSalvo. Under hypnosis by Bryan, DeSalvo revealed details that could only have been known by the perpetrator of the crime. Bryan was credited with solving the case which was then closed. No other leads in the "Boston Strangler" case were investigated, although some people believed DeSalvo was not working alone.

Bryan billed himself as the leading expert in hypnosis at the time and claimed he consulted on the movie *Manchurian Candidate*, starring Frank Sinatra. The movie is about a hypnotized subject who kills upon hearing an implanted code word or phrase and then remembers nothing about what he did. Bryan also claimed to be a consultant for the CIA on the MK-ULTRA program. He once confessed to prostitutes, the services of which he used on a regular basis, that he was the man who hypnotized Sirhan Sirhan. He claimed to have programmed him to kill Robert Kennedy over a three-month period when Sirhan's whereabouts could not be accounted for by his mother or by the brother (with whom Sirhan lived).

The morning after the assassination, Jerry Owen went to the police station and told the police that he had picked up a hitchhiking Sirhan Sirhan the previous morning. Owen claimed that he had never met Sirhan before that day. Owen told police that Sirhan, after learning that Owen had a horse to sell, said he, by coincidence, was in the market for a horse. They agreed on a price of $300.[1] Owen told Sirhan he would bring the horse in his trailer to the Ambassador Hotel. Later that evening, at around 11 PM, Owen parked the horse trailer on a dimly lit street near the Ambassador Hotel. There is speculation that the horse trailer was a get-away vehicle. But why, or for whom, has never been determined.

After the assassination Owen, who had lived pretty much hand to mouth, came into a large amount of money. So much money that he paid for his own Sunday televangelist show on KCOP, a Los Angeles TV station. The show was called "The Walking Bible." His first guest was Los Angeles Mayor Sam Yorty, a man some accused of having aided the LAPD's destruction of evidence in the murder of Robert F. Kennedy. He introduced Yorty as his good friend. When the station learned of Owen's possible involvement with the Kennedy assassination, they cancelled Owen's program, resulting in a lawsuit.

On November 26, of 2011, attorneys Dr. William Pepper and Laurie Dusek, representing Sirhan Sirhan, filed suit in U.S. District Court in Los Angeles, for Sirhan's release on the basis of new evidence. The petition claimed three main points; (1) that a recently re-discovered and re-analyzed recording, made on the night Kennedy was killed, shows that thirteen shots were fired, proving a conspiracy since Sirhan gun only held eight rounds; (2) that the LAPD criminally destroyed evidence that would have shown a conspiracy; (3) that Sirhan was hypno-hypnotized to shoot Kennedy and programmed to forget anything about his hypnosis and anything connected with the event. The petition further claims that a Harvard professor, a leading expert in the field of hypno-hypnotism, had re-hypno-hypnotized Sirhan over a period of many months, and found that Sirhan believed he was shooting at a target in a pistol range when he shot Kennedy.

The audio evidence referred to by Attorney Pepper in his petition is a tape recording made by a reporter, Stanislaw Pruszynski, who had his Telefunken Model 4001 tape recorder turned on as he was following Kennedy into the pantry area, from a distance of about forty feet. Originally, the poor quality tape seemed to indicate only eight gunshots. More than thirty years later, another reporter, Philip Van Praag, asked for a copy of the recording from the California Archives. He had the tape analyzed professionally and found it contained thirteen shots instead of eight; that two sets of shots, three and four and seven and eight, had come so close together as to make it impossible for them to have come from the same gun. Praag co-authored *An Open & Shut Case*[2] which goes into greater detail.

Sirhan Sirhan continues to claim at parole hearings that he has no memory of shooting Kennedy. Parole has always been denied because he has refused to accept responsibility for his actions, according to the Parole Board.

---

1 When Sirhan was arrested he had four $100 bills in his pocket.
2 Co-authored with Robert Joling.

CHAPTER 19. NIXON—GUARDIAN OF THE TEMPLE SECRETS

"Publicly we say one thing...Actually, we do another."

President Richard Nixon[1]

Nixon was elected President in 1968 with the help of President Lyndon Johnson, for no other reason than to protect the role of Johnson, the CIA, the Joint Chiefs of Staff, and the Mafia in the assassination of John F. Kennedy

Like Woodrow Wilson, Nixon ran for a very specific reason, critically important to the people in power. Nixon had lost to Kennedy in 1960, made an embarrassing exit from politics in 1962 after another defeat in the race for governor of California, and uttered that memorable line to reporters on election night, "You won't have Dick Nixon to kick around anymore because, gentlemen, this is my last press conference."

Nixon moved on into a lucrative but private life, joining a well-connected law firm in New York by the name of Nixon, Mudge, Rose, Guthrie and Alexander. He supported Senator Barry Goldwater in the 1964 election against Johnson and gave Goldwater's nominating speech at the convention, but otherwise worked behind the scenes with the Republican Party. Johnson, likewise, did not support his Vice President, Humphrey, behind the scenes.

But Nixon's background and involvement with the Bay of Pigs and his prior knowledge, if not his participation, in the assassination of John F. Kennedy made him the ideal and necessary choice to guard the secret crimes of the conspirators after Johnson removed himself from the 1968 Presidential race. Johnson knew that the anti-war movement would defeat him in 1968 and refused to run for a second full term. His clinical depression may also have been a factor in his

---

1 Nixon was referring to the secret war in Cambodia.

decision not to run again.

While no official diagnosis of bipolar depression was made, LBJ historian Doris Kearns Goodwin (who was a White House intern in the last months of the Johnson administration) talks about his legendary mood swings and his virtual inability to govern in the closing days of his term. He died five years later a broken, depressed man, according to some historians.

But in 1968 Johnson had to find a successor to preserve his legacy, and more importantly, to continue the cover-up of his part in the assassination of John F. Kennedy. Johnson knew that Nixon had no choice but to continue the cover-up in order to hide his own involvement.

Nixon guarded those secrets with his professional life by resigning from the presidency for what amounted to covering up a "third rate burglary." Impeachment hearings would have been held and, most likely, the vote would have gone against him. Still, he did not even bother to put up a defense, which might have saved his presidency as a vote of impeachment does not automatically mean removal from office. Removal from office requires a separate hearing and a higher level or degree of criminal action. Most likely, the felony offense of conspiracy to obstruct justice would not have been sufficient cause for a Senate vote to remove Nixon from office, which would have required at least a two-thirds majority.

But Nixon was terrified, as were his political allies, that the truth about the assassination of JFK, and the reasons behind the killing, would become public, if the impeachment proceedings continued, especially as the careers and roles of Hunt, Sturgis, Barker, Martinez, and Gonzalez would have been investigated. He fought desperately to obstruct justice in the arrest of the Watergate burglars. He fought desperately to suppress the impeachment proceedings, sacrificing anyone and everyone around him. He resigned without a real fight in Congress, so as to protect those secrets and to keep suppressed the evidence of the conspiracy in the assassinations of JFK, MLK and RFK. So paranoid was Nixon about the Kennedy assassination that he refused to, or couldn't bring himself to, mention the Kennedy assassination by name, and only referred to it as "the Bay of Pigs thing," according to H.R. Haldeman, Nixon's co-Chief-of-Staff. He sent a message to the FBI's L. Patrick Grey, Hoover's successor, that if the investigation of the break-in continued, it could open up the CIA's complicity in the "whole Bay of Pigs thing."

Johnson and Nixon's early lives were somewhat similar. Both grew up in relative poverty which bred in the two men suppressed, conflicted, deep-seated feelings of inadequacy and an unstoppable drive to succeed at any cost. Both men went to small colleges, although Nixon, a true scholar, was offered a full scholarship to Harvard University — but he had to decline it for several reasons. For one, the scholarship covered tuition only and Nixon's family could not afford to pay for his room and board, and, more importantly, he was needed at home to help support the family, after his father, Francis, lost the family's small lemon farm. He attended Whittier

College instead, a small Quaker school. Unlike Johnson, Nixon was popular at school. He was an enthusiastic and dedicated athlete, if not a successful one, sitting out most football games on the bench. He did well in debating, however, as did Johnson. He excelled academically, graduated nearly at the top of his class and received a full scholarship to the newly established Duke Law School. He had become engaged to the daughter of Whittier's police chief, Ola Florence Welsh, but the engagement did not survive much past graduation from Whittier.

After Duke Law School and a short stint with a small local law firm, Wingert & Bewley, Nixon married Thelma Patricia "Pat" Ryan, a high school teacher he had met while performing opposite her in a community theatre production of "The Dark Tower." Nixon claimed it was love at first sight. Pat said she gave up saying "no" after two years. Nixon eventually became a partner at Wingert & Bewley, before moving to Washington, D.C. and working at the Office of Price Administration, a job that quickly bored him.

Nixon joined the Navy even though as a Quaker he could have claimed "conscientious objector" status. He was hoping for something interesting to do, but his naval career was uneventful. After graduating from Officer Candidate School as an ensign, he saw no combat and basically oversaw logistic and cargo operations in the Southwest Pacific during World War II. He left the navy as a Lieutenant Commander, four years later, in 1946. He had managed to save a great deal of money, mainly from his poker winnings. He put this money to good use financing his first Congressional race.

His election to Congress in 1948[1] was equally uneventful until, as a member of the House Un-American Activities Committee (HUAC), he made a name for himself by proving that Alger Hiss, a former State Department official, had lied under oath. Nixon was able to show that Hiss had passed microfilmed, classified documents to Whitaker Chambers, an editor of the Communist newspapers *The Daily Worker* and *The New Masses*. Chambers was also a member of the Communist Party, USA. Hiss had passed classified microfilmed documents to Chambers by hiding them in a hollowed out pumpkin. Hiss was subsequently convicted of perjury.

Nixon's 1950 Senate race, while not as fraudulently won as Johnson's seat was still controversial according to Congresswoman Helen Gahagan Douglas, Nixon's opponent for the U.S. Senate seat.

One of the first women elected to Congress, Helen Gahagan Douglas, had been a Broadway actress and had starred in one movie before entering politics. She was married to movie actor and leading man, Melvyn Douglas.

Nixon painted her as a communist sympathizer because of her liberal voting record, comparing her record to that of New York Congressman Vito Marcantonio, a perceived Communist sympathizer, and, oddly enough, her sympathy for the plight of small growers, like his own father, in California. Nixon said she was "pink right down to her underwear," and put out press

---

1 The same year John F. Kennedy was elected a Congressman.

releases against her on pink paper. Douglas managed to pin the name "Tricky Dick" on Nixon, but Nixon won in a landslide, effectively ending her political career. It was said she couldn't even have won a race for county dogcatcher after Nixon got through with her. She never forgave him and, in his memoirs, Nixon expressed a little remorse for his portrayal of Douglas. In a strange and odd coincidence Douglas was one of Johnson's mistresses in Washington.

As Vice-President under Eisenhower, Nixon was given, and assumed, more authority and responsibility than any Vice-President up until that time. Eisenhower, however, had not known Nixon well before the election.

As mentioned earlier, the Eisenhower–Nixon ticket had been brokered by ex-Senator Prescott Bush, father of George H.W. Bush. Nixon's strong anti-communist stance was welcomed by Eisenhower who, during the campaign, had pledged to give Nixon more responsibility. But Eisenhower's poor health afforded Nixon more opportunities to assume even greater responsibilities than expected. Late in 1955, Eisenhower suffered his first heart attack, during which time Nixon assumed full control of the government for six weeks. The following year Eisenhower suffered a second heart attack and the following year a stroke. The public was only informed about the first heart attack.

Eisenhower was not particularly impressed by Nixon after the election. Nixon did not make many friends as Vice-President, especially with Eisenhower and his staff. By his second run for the Presidency, Eisenhower had decided to drop Nixon as his running mate, offering him a Cabinet position instead. Nixon refused, wisely, knowing it would have destroyed his political career. Still, Eisenhower refused to name him as his running mate, saying the matter should be decided on the convention floor by the convention delegates. Finally, after Eisenhower's poor showing in the primaries without Nixon, Eisenhower named him again as his 1956 running mate.

When Nixon ran for the Presidency against Kennedy, Eisenhower not only did not support him but actually hurt his chances. When a reporter asked Eisenhower what decisions Nixon had been responsible for as Vice-President, Eisenhower said, "Give me a week and I might think of something." Eisenhower tried to explain away the insult later, unsuccessfully.

In a similar political knifing, Johnson did not really support or campaign for his Vice-President, Hubert Humphrey, in 1968 against Nixon. Humphrey, a liberal, was constantly humiliated by Johnson as Kennedy had humiliated Johnson. Although a silent critic of Johnson's war policies, Johnson threatened Humphrey not to speak out against the war or he'd lose Johnson's support for the presidential nomination. Humphrey did not speak out against the war but Johnson still did not support him. He supported Nixon. Johnson needed Nixon, not Humphrey, in the White House.

In the 1968 presidential race, Nixon promised "peace with honor" in Vietnam and an end to the war. He failed to say how he planned to accomplish this, and so the media dubbed it Nixon's "secret plan." The secret was that he had no plan at all—unless you consider the escalation of bombings and the invasion of neighboring Cambodia and Laos a plan to end the war.

Nixon was sworn into office by Chief Justice Earl Warren, no doubt with a wink and a nod. Nixon almost immediately began escalating the war in Vietnam. By March 1969, Nixon had approved OPERATION MENU, a plan initiated under Johnson, calling for massive secret bombings of Cambodia. More bombs were dropped in Cambodia than had been dropped in all of World War II. By the end of the year, Nixon sent out peace feelers to North Vietnam, promising troop withdrawals from Vietnam—all the while sending U.S. combat troops into Laos. At the time, approximately 300 U.S. soldiers and several thousand civilians were dying in Vietnam each week.

When Nixon proposed using tactical nuclear weapons to destroy bridges and dams in Hanoi, which would have resulted in the immediate drowning of 200,000 Vietnamese, Dr. Henry Kissinger, Nixon's Secretary of State and main National Security Advisor, went pale. Nixon told Kissinger to "think big," but did not follow through with the nuclear weapons. Nixon, elected to end the war in 1968, continued the war until he resigned from office in 1974. America lost the war in Vietnam but declared "peace with honor" a year later. If it hadn't been for Watergate, the war might very well have continued for many more years.

Chapter 20. Papergate—The Pentagon Papers Scandal

> "The public is lied to every day by the President, by his spokespeople, by his officers. If you can't handle the thought that the President lies to the public for all kinds of reasons, you couldn't stay in the government at that level..."

> Daniel Ellsberg

Before there was Watergate, there was "Papergate," actually "Pentagon Papergate."

The Pentagon Papers debacle has also been called "Watergate West," because much of it occurred in Los Angeles. The "Pentagon Papers" was the popular name for a classified study, completed in 1969 for Secretary of Defense Robert McNamara, innocuously entitled "Report of the Office of the Secretary of Defense Vietnam Task Force: United States–Vietnam Relations, 1945–1967." It is 7,000 pages long and bound into forty-seven volumes. It was prepared by the Pentagon with the help of thirty-six army historians and analysts from the Rand (Research and Development) Corporation, a global "think-tank" originally founded by the Douglas Aircraft Company to provide research for the U.S. military.

The Rand Corporation was asked by the Pentagon to analyze the situation in Vietnam after the embarrassing Tet Offensive of 1968, a major surprise attack by the National Liberation Front (NLF) Army of North Vietnam against the Republic of South Vietnam. The U.S. and South Vietnamese forces were surprised because the NLF attacked during a two-day cease-fire that had been agreed upon to celebrate the Vietnamese lunar New Year.

The NLF launched an attack with 80,000 troops against more than eighty cities, towns and villages, including provincial capital cities. While the U.S. and

South Vietnamese forces quickly regrouped and managed to rout the "enemy," the attack made headlines in the U.S. and stunned an already war-weary America, setting off even more anti-war demonstrations. It was a major psychological and public relations victory for the North, if not a military one.

The report, which traced the history of U.S. involvement in Vietnam since 1940, stated that Franklin Roosevelt wanted to eliminate French colonialism in Indochina and supported Ho Chi Minh and the Viet Minh, at least in the analysis of historian Bernard Fall, one of the authors of the report.[1] After FDR's death[2] the policy changed.

The Pentagon Papers report also confirmed public suspicions that the Johnson administration had lied repeatedly about the Vietnam War—not only to the American people but to Congress as well. In fact, it was not even called a war but a "conflict," which was intended, somehow, to sound less bloody and deadly.

The report stated that the administrations of Eisenhower, Kennedy, and Johnson knew that the war was unwinnable from the start, and that many more casualties would occur if the war continued. It talked at length about the "secret bombings" in Cambodia. It stated that Johnson had constantly lied about his intentions in Vietnam, sending more and more troops into combat, all the while proclaiming he "sought no wider war." The Pentagon Papers were quickly classified Top Secret.

Daniel Ellsberg, a brilliant scholar, had graduated *magna cum laude* from Harvard with a B.A. in economics and later, after a two year stint in Vietnam as a combat marine captain, a PhD in the same field. At Harvard he met Dr. Henry Kissinger, an ambitious Harvard history professor at the time and later Nixon's secretary of state. Many considered Ellsberg to be Kissinger's protégé.

Ellsberg had worked for a short while under Secretary of Defense McNamara before going to Vietnam for the State Department. In Vietnam, he had worked directly under General Lansdale who was in charge of the war. He returned home after two years and began working for the Rand Corporation where he briefly worked on the Pentagon Papers and had security clearance to access the Rand Corporation's copies of the classified report.

No longer believing the war in Vietnam was a just war, Ellsberg decided to copy the report and bring it to public awareness in hopes of shortening

---

1 This theory that FDR favored Ho Chi Minh at this time lends credence to Col. L. Fletcher Prouty's statement that one half of the armaments from the cancelled invasion of Japan, which had been brought to Okinawa, were sent to North Vietnam and Ho Chi Minh. FDR died on April 12, 1945, before the end of the Battle of Okinawa which ended in July, 1945. It would have been Truman who would have ordered stockpiled arms from Okinawa to be sent to Hanoi and North Korea...or the CIA and the Joint Chiefs of Staff.
2 Stalin once told Roosevelt's son Elliot that he believed FDR was poisoned by Churchill and his gang and this was the reason his representative was not able to view FDR's body because poisoning would have been obvious.

the war. At risk of prosecution under the Espionage Act of 1917, Dr. Daniel Ellsberg together with Anthony Russo, a friend and anti-war activist who had been employed by the Rand Corporation at one time, secretly copied all 7,000 pages over a period of weeks during September 1969. Ellsberg would take home a volume or two in his briefcase, under the nose of the guard, who waved him by without checking his briefcase. Ellsberg would then go the Russo's apartment where Linda Sinay, Russo's girlfriend, would then take them to her offices at an advertising agency where they would copy them on a Xerox machine, usually working through the night.

Ellsberg first tried to give the documents to several anti-war senators, such as Fulbright and McGovern, who had the power to enter them into the Congressional Record without being prosecuted. At first, they were excited, but, when they considered the political ramifications and their careers, they demurred. Next he offered the documents to several newspapers which also declined. However, a reporter, Neil Sheehan, promised Ellsberg confidentiality and publication in the prestigious *New York Times*. Sheehan kept his promise to publish the papers—but not his promise of confidentiality.

In the *New York Times* Sunday Edition of June 13, 1971, the first of a nine part series on the Pentagon Papers was published. As soon as the paper appeared, Ellsberg went underground, staying in various motels in Massachusetts and using pay phones to communicate. The Nixon White House had the Justice Department issue an injunction against further publication after the third part of the series was published. The injunction was quashed by the Supreme Court, which upheld the *Times*' First Amendment right to publish the papers. Publication resumed fifteen days after the injunction had been issued, and a few day before Daniel Ellsberg surrendered to authorities at the federal courthouse in Boston on June 28, 1971. Trial was set for January 3, 1973.

At first, the Nixon White House was not all that upset with the publication of the report because the Pentagon Papers essentially concerned previous administrations and did not directly implicate, or even mention, Nixon. Kissinger, however, said it would jeopardize ongoing secret peace talks. Plus, Kissinger wanted to insure against other leaks by liberals in the government, and so pressed Nixon to make an example of Ellsberg, his former protégé.

Kissinger, reflecting back on his relationship with Ellsberg, now recalled that Ellsberg was "mentally unbalanced." Kissinger urged Nixon to ask the FBI to wiretap possible suspects, without warrants, which was illegal at the time.[1] The wiretaps were later expanded to include Nixon's political enemies, Nixon's so called "enemies list."

A while later, Nixon authorized a special team of investigators to "plug" media leaks, by any means necessary as long as their activities did not lead back to the White House. For that role he chose trusted members of the CIA

---

1 Under the USA Patriot Act of 2001, it may no longer be illegal to wiretap without a warrant.

who had worked with him on the Bay of Pigs planning and other activities. Some of these operatives, such as E. Howard Hunt, were officially retired from the CIA, but, in reality, worked at cover jobs with CIA-affiliated companies. Hunt had been working since "retiring" from the CIA at one such facility, the Mullen Company. Hunt was assigned the task of recruiting a team to plug media leaks. They would work out of the White House under John Ehrlichman, Nixon's co-Chief-of-Staff. Hunt initially recruited his protégé, Bernard "Macho" Barker, plus Eugenio "Musculito" Martinez. Later when the operation was turned over to G. Gordon Liddy, an ex-FBI agent who was working for the Committee to re-elect the President, Virgilio "Villo" Gonzalez, and Frank Sturgis were hired—all of whom, except perhaps Liddy, had also been involved in the Kennedy assassination as well as in the Bay of Pigs with Hunt.

Liddy had been hired by the Committee to re-elect the President, commonly and aptly referred to as CREEP, to infiltrate, bug, disrupt, and harass the Democratic National Committee. At CREEP, Liddy was known as the top "ratf*cker."

Eugenio Martinez, a real estate agent in Miami, was a CIA agent and was involved in anti-Castro activities in Florida. He was recruited by Hunt to take photographs. Some sources claim Martinez was in Dallas on the day of the assassination. He is said, by some researchers, to have been in the Dal-Tex building, acting as a spotter for shooter, Virgilio (Villo) Gonzalez, another of the convicted Watergate burglars, and a member of the newly-formed group. Virgilio Gonzalez was a Miami locksmith, and a CIA agent. Hunt recruited him to ply his lock-picking trade.

After a while, Hunt's group was turned over to CREEP in order to distance itself from the White House. The group was shop-floor managed by G. Gordon Liddy and E. Howard Hunt who took orders from the White House. Liddy seemed to be more in charge and Hunt called him "Daddy," but in a non-complimentary way. On one operation Hunt showed up in black pants with white stripes. Liddy told him, in front of the others, to go to his room and change, because someone could identify such a distinctive pair of pants. The group was supervised from the White House by Nixon's co-Chief-of-Staff, John Ehrlichman, and Nixon advisors Chuck Colson, David Young and Egil "Bud" Krogh. They nicknamed themselves the "Plumbers," because of a sign David Young had placed on his office door located in the basement of the Old Executive Building. The sign read, "Mr. Young, Plumber." The idea for the sign came to him when a relative told Young that Young's grandfather, a plumber, would be proud that he was "fixing leaks" for the White House.

Liddy devised an elaborate master program of "dirty tricks" called "OPERATION GEMSTONE." Liddy's proposals were so blatantly illegal that Attorney General John Mitchell, who was Nixon's campaign manager, twice threw Liddy out of his office. Later, in prison, Mitchell lamented that he should have thrown him out permanently.

OPERATION GEMSTONE was a derivative of OPERATION

SANDWEDGE, which had been put together by Haldeman and Ehrlichman, Nixon's dual Chiefs-of-Staff, sometimes referred to as the "Berlin Wall," because they were so tough to get past. But to distance the White House from the illegal activities, it was handed off to G. (George) Gordon Liddy.

OPERATION SANDWEDGE was child's play compared to Liddy's grand scheme. OPERATION SANDWEDGE sought merely to disrupt the Democratic Party and anti-Vietnam War demonstrations with hired thugs. OPERATION GEMSTONE was a much grander, sinister scheme consisting of eight parts, each with its own code name—Coal, Ruby, Sapphire, Emerald, Opal, Topaz, Garnet, and Turquoise. Besides the normal dirty campaign tricks, it included planes flying around to bug radiophone transmissions; saboteurs at the Democratic Convention in Miami; sham pro-Democratic rallies intended to anger voters into switching their votes; payoffs to Democratic politicians for covert support; kidnappings of anti-war leaders and relocating them to a foreign country; hiring sophisticated prostitutes and housing them on floating bordellos on the Potomac in order to blackmail opponents, plus other "black bag" operations, all clearly and knowingly illegal.

Liddy asked for a budget of one million dollars before General Attorney John Mitchell, Nixon's former law partner and head of the CREEP, told him to leave. Mitchell, after pressure from the White House, agreed but scaled down the budget to $250,000.

The "Plumbers' " first assignment, under OPERATION GEMSTONE, was to "smear" Daniel Ellsberg by discrediting him publicly and, later, to physically incapacitate him, possibly permanently, by hiring thugs to attack him at an anti-war rally. Nixon wanted Ellsberg tried and convicted in the press before being tried in a court of law. Nixon had done this successfully before, in the case of Whittaker Chambers.

The smear campaign began with a break-in and burglary of the Beverly Hills offices of Ellsberg's psychiatrist, Dr. Lewis Fielding. There they hoped to find embarrassing, personal evidence in Ellsberg's confidential files. This break-in at Dr. Fielding's office was the first "black bag" operation conducted by the "Plumbers." The last was Watergate.

Liddy turned out to be a better thinker than doer. According to some of the "Plumbers," it was not a well-thought out, coordinated, or rehearsed operation such as they had been used to in previous CIA operations.

This operation, around April, involved just three men besides Hunt and Liddy—Barker, Martinez, and one of Martinez's partners in his real estate business in Miami, Felipe de Diego. Diego was a CIA man and had been at the Bay of Pigs and so was trusted by the others.

Barker, Martinez, and Diego were told to meet the next day at the Miami Airport and bring clothes for two or three days. Only at the airport were they told they were going to Los Angeles. They were put up at the Beverly Hills Hotel. They had one quick briefing before the break-in—definitely not what they had been used to.

Hunt, who gave the briefing in his room at the Beverly Hills Hotel, had no written plan. He just sat around and talked about what they were going to do, namely, break into a psychiatrist's office, photograph psychiatric records of a "traitor" called "Ellsberg," and leave, making it look like the burglary had been done by addicts looking for drugs.

The next day, Martinez, Barker, and Diego were sent to the local Sears to buy two cameras (a Polaroid and a 35 mm camera), photo lights, delivery men type uniforms, phony glasses, and beards.

The plan was to deliver the cameras inside the offices, leave a back door open, and go back at night to photograph the files. Barker and Diego, looking foolish and amateurish in their disguises, went to deliver the package to Dr. Fielding's offices and unlock a back door. The men returned after office hours.

Not knowing when the cleaning lady would finish, they waited outside for hours until a cab came and picked up the cleaning lady. Barker, Martinez and Diego went to the back door that they had unlatched earlier, but it was locked. Barker called Liddy, because Hunt was watching Fielding's house to make sure he did not return to the offices unexpectedly. Liddy appeared and told them to cut a hole in the glass window with the cutter Hunt had given them earlier. The glass cutter was so dull it wouldn't cut the glass, so they broke the window, reached in and unlocked the door. The offices were on the 2nd floor and the three had been given a thin rope to climb out the window, in the event of a surprise, except, according to Martinez, the rope was so thin and cheap, it would not have supported anyone.

Martinez covered the windows, set up his photographic equipment and took a Polaroid of the office before they started—so they could put everything back the way it was originally. Their search turned up no files on Ellsberg. The only mention of Ellsberg was a listing in Fielding's phone book, which Martinez photographed so the break-in would not be a complete waste and he would have something to show Liddy and Hunt. Martinez then spilled some pills, probably vitamin C, on the floor before leaving the building.

Unexpectedly, they found Hunt nervously waiting for them downstairs. Hunt was supposed to be watching Dr. Fielding at his home. Dr. Fielding, however, had gotten back into his car and driven off. Hunt followed him but lost Dr. Fielding in traffic. Therefore, Hunt went to the offices and parked downstairs in case Dr. Fielding showed up.

At the Beverly Hills Hotel, Hunt was strangely exuberant over what the men considered a botched operation. Hunt opened a bottle of champagne and thanked the men for a successful job.

Not finding any files on Ellsberg, Liddy requested permission to break into Fielding's home to look for Ellsberg's file there, but permission was denied by Ehrlichman. The men returned to Miami.

The second operation the "Plumbers" undertook was in late May and required additional manpower. Barker, on orders from Hunt, recruited four more men—Frank Sturgis, James McCord, Reinaldo Pico, and Virgilio Gonzalez, all CIA operatives. McCord, an electronics expert, was recruited to plant listening devices. Gonzalez was recruited because he was a professional locksmith, and Sturgis and Pico were to be lookouts. They were told to check into the Manger Hay-Adams Hotel in Washington, D.C. on May 22, and attend another of Hunt's briefings.

Hunt told the men they were going to break into the McGovern campaign headquarters with the help of a young fellow who had infiltrated McGovern's campaign for the CIA. He told them they were going in to find evidence of Castro giving money to McGovern. The break-in was aborted three days later, probably because the boy got scared or proved unreliable.

Next, Hunt told the men to check into the Watergate Hotel and pretend to be executives for a fictitious company, the Ameritus Company of Miami. They bought business suits and briefcases in order to look the part and went to Hunt's room for a brief briefing for another poorly planned and ultimately unsuccessful operation.

Hunt's plan, or perhaps Liddy's plan, was to rent a private banquet room in the Watergate Complex under the Ameritus name. The banquet room had elevator access to the offices of the Democratic National Committee on the 6th floor. After dinner, Hunt was to play a film while the others went up to the 6th floor to break in after the campaign workers left. But no one had checked to see when the campaign offices usually closed. At 2:30 AM the lights in the offices were still on and the hotel guard asked them to leave the banquet room so he could lock up. Hunt, improvising quickly, grabbed Gonzalez, the locksmith, and hid in a closet, telling the others he would let them back in after the guard left. But Gonzalez was unable to open the door, and Hunt and Gonzalez ended up spending the night in the closet.

At the next day's briefing, Hunt said that this time they would wait downstairs until all the lights went out on the 6th floor before knocking on the front door. When the guard let them in, they would tell him they were doing work on the 8th floor, which housed the Federal Reserve. McCord had previously done some electronics work for the Federal Reserve and knew some of the guards on the 8th floor. Then they would walk down the steps to the 6th.

At midnight, they knocked on the door and the guard let them in. They signed the register and took the elevator to the 8th floor and then walked down to the 6th. The plan worked flawlessly up until they tried to open the door to the Democratic National Committee offices—and couldn't. The locksmith, Virgilio Gonzales, said he didn't have the right tools with him. Finally, briefcases in hand and heads held high, they marched out the front door shortly after 2 PM.

Hunt, furious at Gonzales, sent him back to Miami for the right tools. He threatened to make him pay for the round trip to Miami out of his own pocket, which annoyed the others. The next day, Gonzalez brought back every lock-picking tool in his shop. The others said they had never seen so many tools to pick locks.

Later that night, Sturgis and Gonzales picked the lock in the garage exit door, announced over the Walkie-Talkies that "The horse is in the house," and let the rest of the group inside. Barker handed Martinez pages of lists of democratic contributors, which he photographed while McCord planted three eavesdropping devices. If there was evidence of Castro's funneling money to McGovern, it was not found or photographed. Martinez claimed he photographed thirty or forty pages of lists of contributors. He gave the film to Hunt. The burglars left the Watergate complex about 5 AM, and, except for Liddy and Hunt, returned once again to Miami.

Several weeks later, Hunt went to Miami and gave Barker two rolls of unexposed film to have developed, but did not explain what was on the film. Barker took the film to a neighborhood lab, Rich's Camera shop, to be developed. Later, Hunt told Barker the film was from the Watergate break-in. Barker, in a panic, took Martinez and Sturgis to Rich's Camera shop and asked for the film. Martinez and Sturgis covered the front and back doors in case the police came.

The developer had enlarged the prints and noticed the documents in the prints were being held by a gloved hand as they were being photographed. Barker tipped him $30.00, which evidently was too much or not enough, as the man called the FBI soon after Barker, Sturgis, and Martinez left. Martinez decided he had had enough of Liddy and Hunt's Mickey Mouse operations and decided to quit the group. He told them he would do one last job. Prophetically, it was his last job for a long while. He would serve eighteen months in prison.

CHAPTER 21. THE TRIAL OF DANIEL ELLSBERG

> "Only we, the public, can force our representatives to re-
> verse their abdication of the war powers that the Constitution
> gives exclusively to the Congress."

Daniel Ellsberg

Dr. Daniel Ellsberg faced a maximum of 115 years[1] in prison, even though the Supreme Court had upheld the First Amendment right of the *New York Times* to publish the Pentagon Papers. Nixon was determined to prosecute Ellsberg lest it "happen all over the government."

Anthony Russo refused to testify before a grand jury in Los Angeles, citing his 5th Amendment rights. He refused to testify even after being granted immunity from prosecution. He was sentenced to six weeks in jail. After his release he was indicted, along with Ellsberg, on fifteen counts of theft and espionage. Linda Sinay, Russo's girlfriend, was named an unindicted co-conspirator.

Ellsberg and Russo's first trial ended in a mistrial when it was discovered that the prosecution team had taped a conversation between the defendants and their attorney. A new trial was ordered and a new jury empaneled.

David Nissen, prosecutor in the case, presented his case essentially proving that: the Pentagon Papers were classified Top Secret; Daniel Ellsberg had signed a non-disclosure agreement with Rand; Linda Sinay had observed Ellsberg and Russo copying the documents; Ellsberg had requested, and was granted, special permission to access the Pentagon Papers; Ellsberg and Russo's fingerprints were found on the Pentagon Papers.

Anthony Russo admitted, under oath, that he had helped photocopy the Top

---

1 Some accounts claim 105 years.

Secret material, and that Ellsberg did not have the authority to show it to him. But he also testified about his previous work at Rand, which shocked the jury.

His assignment from Rand had been to go to Vietnam in the late 1960s and write a report on the effectiveness of the anti-personnel weapons which the military was using at the time: shiny little bombs with a delayed fuse. They were strategically placed to be found by children. Attracted to these shiny objects, young kids would bring them home. They were timed and intended to kill the child's family as well.

Russo also testified that the Vietnamese were not fanatics, but honest, committed people fighting for their homeland. His reports, he later found out, were being rewritten to glorify the military. He left the Rand Corporation and became an anti-war activist, and when Ellsberg asked him to help bring the Pentagon Papers to light, he agreed.

Ellsberg testified under oath that what he observed in Vietnam was not what was being reported to the generals and Pentagon officials back home. He agreed with Russo that lying and deception about Vietnam seemed to be the norm rather than the exception. He also said he did not believe that anything he copied would hurt the national defense or he would not have copied it. He hoped that by making the information available to Congress, Congress might act to end the war. When the people he approached in Congress to introduce the Pentagon Papers into the Congressional Record failed to act, he was forced to give the Pentagon Papers to the press.

Ellsberg and Russo might well have been convicted had not Judge Byrne introduced into evidence a memo from Watergate prosecutor Earl Silbert to Assistant Attorney General Henry Peterson. The memo detailed the break-in of the offices of Ellsberg's psychiatrist, Dr. Fielding, by G. Gordon Liddy and E. Howard Hunt, working on behalf of the White House.

Secretly, the White House, twice, offered Judge Byrne the directorship of the FBI. He refused to consider it while the case was in progress.

Three days after the memo was introduced in open court, Nixon fired John Ehrlichman and H. R. Haldeman, Nixon's co-Chiefs-of-Staff. He also fired Richard Kleindeinst, acting Attorney General, and John Dean, White House senior advisor and, according to the FBI, "master manipulator of the Watergate cover-up."

Six weeks later, Judge Byrne granted the defense's motion for dismissal of all charges based on the government's "gross misconduct." He was not offered the directorship of the FBI again.

Chapter 22. Watergate—The "Whole Bay of Pigs Thing"

> "I will never leave this jail alive if what we discussed about Watergate does not remain a secret between us."
>
> Frank Sturgis

> "The reason we burglarized the Watergate was because Nixon was interested in stopping news leaking relating to the photos of our role in the assassination of President John Kennedy."[1]
>
> Frank Sturgis

According to my cousin's account, the Watergate break-in was a one-act farce that quickly turned into full blown Shakespearean tragedy, toppling a sitting president, sending an acting Attorney General to jail, and resulting in the firing and criminal conviction of dozens of high government officials. It also brought about a Congressional investigation that turned into a scandalous "Saturday Night Massacre" involving Nixon's firing of the Special Prosecutor, Archibald Cox, who had been appointed to investigate the break-in, and prison terms for dozens of White House and government officials. And most tragically, it buried the real secrets of Watergate, perhaps forever.

I nearly fell off the bed when my cousin told me about the hours before the final Watergate break-in. He was enjoying my amusement as I tried to fit the pieces of the puzzle into a finished tableau that made sense.

"Frank used to run a bar," he said, "somewhere in Virginia, I think. Frank and the guys had some time to kill before breaking into the Watergate offices and

---

1 *San Francisco Chronicle*, May 7, 1977.

were doing a little drinking in the Watergate bar, a little before midnight. "Anyway, they're all drinking and Burt Lancaster, the actor...he comes in...and Frank calls him over. Frank knew everybody...probably from when he was running Lansky's casino in Havana. He even knew Errol Flynn. Anyhow, Burt, Frank tells me, was a 'wanna-be wise guy.' He liked to hang out with 'Mafia types'."

"Maybe he was researching for the tough guy parts he used to play...he was pretty good," I said.

"Maybe."

"Anyway, Frank gave Barker five dollars to go out and buy batteries for the Walkie-Talkies they were using that night... Barker, probably drunk, pocketed the money and never bought the batteries!"

The burglars were using army-issue Walkie-Talkies, but the batteries were weak. I did read one account that said the Walkie-Talkies used rechargeable batteries but I haven't been able to verify this or whether they even had rechargeable batteries back then. The earliest commercial rechargeable batteries did not come into existence until the late 1980s.

It is funny when you think of it. It's always the little things that come back to bite you. A lousy little battery and Nixon is forced to resign the most powerful office in the world.

According to Martinez's written account of his activities with the "Plumbers," called *Mission Impossible*, McCord went to the Watergate early in the evening, signed in at the desk, and went up to the 8th floor. On his way down, he taped all the doors from the 8th floor to the basement and exited out the garage.

Then they all waited until everyone had left the offices of the DNC. After a while Hunt went to check that the tapes were still there before they went in, and they were. But, just before going in, Virgilio and Sturgis discovered the tape on the garage entry door had been removed. They wanted to abort the mission, but McCord, after discussing it privately with Hunt and Liddy, said no. So Virgilio picked the lock and they entered and headed for the 6th floor. McCord said he had to go somewhere first, and would join them later, so they re-taped the door for him so he could get in. When McCord caught up with them five minutes later, they asked him if he had removed the tape on the door, and he replied he had—although he hadn't.

The Watergate guard, Frank Wills, who had discovered and removed the tapes earlier, had come back and discovered the door had been re-taped and called the police. When the police arrived downstairs, the look-out tried to call up to the DNC offices, but the batteries were too weak to carry the signal. Martinez claimed they didn't hear the warning because the "gain" or volume on the Walkie-Talkies was turned down since it was producing too much static, but this was probably not the case.

Instead of neatly slipping out of the offices, they were taken by surprise by three plainclothes detectives, Sergeant Paul Leeper, and Officers John Barrett and Carl Shoffler, of the Metro Police Department, who shouted,

"Come out with your hands up or we'll shoot." They answered, "Don't shoot, we give up!"

Earlier, when they had met in one of the two rooms Hunt and McCord had taken for the evening in the hotel area of the Watergate Complex, Hunt had taken everyone's ID. He had put the IDs into one of the six suitcases they had taken into the rooms, and gave everyone fake ID's. He gave Sturgis his old CIA fake ID in the name of Edward J. Hamilton. He also told everyone to keep the keys to the rooms with them so that, in the event the mission was aborted, they could get into the rooms and hide out. Hunt also handed out $200 in cash to everyone to use for a bribe, if needed. Later, the room keys led the detectives to Hunt and Liddy. Liddy and Hunt led to the White House.

When they were arrested, wearing business suits and rubber gloves, they had forty unexposed rolls of 36 exposure film, two cameras, three pen-size tear gas guns, Walkie-Talkies, listening devices, and $2300 in cash.

What they were really doing there has been the subject of much debate and deliberate disinformation. Three possible motives have been mentioned for the Watergate break-in. The first concerns Senator George McGovern, a liberal democrat from South Dakota who had run for the presidency in 1968 and 1972. It was rumored that he was accepting campaign funds from Fidel Castro and documentation of that was at the DNC at the Watergate. This rumor seems to have been spread by Sturgis, who had been trying to connect Castro to the JFK assassination, possibly as a way to force the US to invade Cuba again. He had also claimed earlier that Ruby was an agent of Castro. This version is not entirely credible.

A second reason has been elaborated on in several works and this one also may stem from Sturgis (although there may be other sources). According to Detective Rothstein, during the interrogation of Sturgis at Marita Lorenz's apartment in 1977, "Sturgis said the break-in was to get the 'book' that had the names of clients who used the prostitution and pedophilia ring operating out of the Democratic National Headquarters. This information was to be used to compromise both Republican and Democratic clients who used the ring."

While this is very credible, it does not address the issue of Nixon's paranoia about the JFK assassination and his desire and need to win the 1972 election. Nixon's connection to the assassination and to Hunt and Sturgis would have been extremely embarrassing and destructive to his re-election chances. And this connection would have been obvious if the "tramp" photos of Hunt and Sturgis were publicized, because of Nixon's close connections with both men—both in OPERATION 40 and the Bay of Pigs invasion which Nixon had originally planned, under Eisenhower.

In Frank Sturgis' own words quoted at the beginning of this chapter, they were there to get rid of the photos relating to E. Howard Hunt and his own role in the assassination of Kennedy, which Nixon was afraid would be leaked to the press in a classic "October Surprise." That's what Watergate was really all about—covering the role of Nixon, Hunt, and Sturgis in the conspiracy to assassinate Kennedy.

Chapter 23. The Tapestry

> "If the American people knew the truth about Dallas, there'd be blood in the streets."[1]

Robert F. Kennedy

A tapestry is a story woven from threads that run vertically, called wefts, and threads that run horizontally, called warps. A tapestry differs from normally-woven cloth in that a tapestry is a weft based weaving, meaning the warp threads are not obvious in the finished work. This is well-known to textile artists, and, oddly enough, to conspirators from time immemorial.

The Emperor Nero, if he did not burn Rome, at least saw an opportunity and used it to build a new Rome. No successful leader or politician (leaders-in-waiting) would ever let a disaster or crisis like that pass without considering the opportunity it presents to advance his own agenda.

In modern times, the sinking of the battleship USS *Maine* in Havana Harbor in 1898 led to the Spanish–American War, with the United States taking over Spanish-controlled Cuba and becoming a world power. The "yellow press" at the time concluded that the *Maine* had been mined. "Remember the *Maine*" was the battle cry and the excuse for war. The ship's captain thought the explosion was the result of a coal-bin fire, which then ignited the gunpowder on board. The United States wanted control of Cuba from Spain—why waste an opportunity?

Since the winners invariably write the history books, the warp threads of an historical tapestry are easy to hide in the hands of a skilled weaver—or an official historian.

The warp threads running through the tapestry of the Bay of Pigs, the

---

1 Found in *LBJ*, Nelson, p. 540, originally from *Brothers*, David Talbot, 2007, *New York Free Press*, p. 268.

JFK assassination, the MLK assassination, the RFK assassination, Chappaquiddick, and Watergate are difficult to see, at times, because of all the disinformation and suppression of the facts. But enough of them should be painfully obvious to most observers.

How is it possible not to see the sinister hands of the major conspirators, when the conspirators have appeared so often at the exact moment when these historic crimes have unfolded? Could it really be mere coincidence that E. Howard Hunt, Bernard Barker, and Frank Sturgis, among others, would all be at the Bay of Pigs, in Dealey Plaza, in Los Angeles, on Chappaquiddick Island, and at the Watergate Complex at the critical, historic moments history was being made? Were they psychic or prescient—or were they involved? If the same people kept showing up repeatedly at the scene of the crime, can there not be a causal connection? This is not guilt by association or coincidence—this is guilt, pure and simple, of foreknowledge of and participation in a series of crimes.

And what of the common scenario surrounding these events? The storyline is repeated over and over again with only minor variations. A public execution blamed on a lone gunman, with no motivation, obvious or otherwise; immediate, almost instantaneous, identification of the pathetic patsy; exculpatory evidence destroyed or hidden; eye witnesses dismissed, threatened, or killed; no trial or no real trial; official investigations conducted in secret, in Washington, outside of the legal state jurisdiction in some cases and by persons or groups with a vested interest in concealing the truth; evidence destroyed, altered, or fabricated; evidence hidden away from public scrutiny for upwards of seventy-five years; mainstream media coverage denied, distorted, or blocked by overt design and calculated programs of disinformation; acknowledged payments, in reality bribes, to mainline journalists; the institutionalizing of critics in military prisons, without trials or hearings; the intellectually insulting conclusions reported by official investigatory bodies; the dissemination of works put out by CIA-paid writers to deliberately mislead and obfuscate; and the branding by government officials and government-sanctioned media spokespeople of critics of the official explanations as "conspiracy theorists."

Warp Thread I—The Body Snatchers

At the instant John F. Kennedy was pronounced dead, the hydra-headed, meticulously-conceived and plotted conspiracy to cover up evidence of the overthrow of the United States government was activated and executed with military precision.

Immediately, Johnson pretended to be in fear for his life and the life of the nation. In front of Parkland Hospital, he claimed the government was under attack and the leaders, especially its new president, were in danger of being killed. When Acting[1] White House Press Secretary Malcolm Kilduff was told of Kennedy's death, he went to Johnson.

"Mr. President, I have to announce the death of President Kennedy. Is it OK with you that the announcement be made now?"

Johnson told him, "I think I had better get out of here...before you announce it. We don't know whether this is a worldwide conspiracy, whether they are after me as well as they were after President Kennedy, or whether they are after Speaker [John] McCormack or Senator [Carl] Hayden. We just don't know."[2]

He quickly surrounded himself with Secret Service Agents and Police Chief Jesse Curry and was driven, crouched down between the seats, to Love Field Airport with a large complement of motorcycle escorts. When they arrived at Air Force Two, the Vice-Presidential plane, Johnson insisted on being driven to Air Force One parked nearby, claiming he had been advised by Kennedy people at Parkland that he needed the more sophisticated communication and security features of Air Force One. Johnson knew full well that the two Boeing 707 planes, Air Force One and Two were identical in every way except for the tail number designation and that whichever plane the President was riding in was automatically called Air Force One regardless of the tail number. He also knew that it was crucial to the preconceived master plan to remove as much of the crime-scene evidence as possible from Dallas to Washington immediately, especially the body and the limo. Within twenty-four hours almost all of the evidence would be moved to Washington under the tight control of J. Edgar Hoover.

Once on board Air Force One, Johnson, no longer in fear of his life, became abusive and impossibly rude to everyone but especially the Kennedy people who had slighted him in the past. He was upset that the Kennedy people were not paying him the same respect and deference that they had paid Kennedy hours before. The Kennedy and Johnson people split into hostile camps, communicating only by written notes and hurried messengers.

Johnson had ordered the limo cleaned (even before Kennedy was pronounced dead), covered with the bubble top which was in the truck[3], and driven back to the cargo plane that had accompanied Air Force One and that was parked nearby. He ordered Kennedy's body to be brought to the plane, by force of arms if necessary. He ordered his luggage and that of his staff transferred from Air Force Two to Air Force One and threw off half of the Kennedy people to make room for his entourage. He took special delight in kicking off liberal Senator Yarborough, whom he no longer had to tolerate now that Kennedy was no longer around. He had argued vehemently with Kennedy that morning in Kennedy's suite about Yarborough's seating in

---

1 Pierre Salinger, White House Press Secretary, was overseas with members of Kennedy's cabinet.
2 *The Johnson Treatment*, Jack Bell, 1965 as quoted in Wikipedia, *Timeline of the John F. Kennedy assassination*.
3 Some reports claim it was on Air Force One.

the motorcade. Johnson had wanted Yarborough to sit with Kennedy and Connally to sit with Johnson, hoping a stray bullet would hit Yarborough.

Johnson took over Kennedy's stateroom and he and his aides Cliff Carter, Bill Moyer, and Jack Valenti began making phone calls. They did not even move when Mrs. Kennedy came into the stateroom, surprised at seeing Johnson, in shirtsleeves[1], sprawled on her bed. The calls[2] were not recorded because calls on Air Force One were only recorded when the plane was airborne. (Some of the calls made during the flight to Washington, however, would later be erased.)

Johnson had been telling everyone moments before that the country was under attack from Cuba or Russia—everyone except the Secretary of Defense, the Joint Chiefs of Staff, the National Command Center, the White House Situation Room, or the rest of the Cabinet. Somehow he had neglected to inform them that the country was under attack.

When Kennedy's bronze casket arrived at the plane, the captain started the engines. Johnson had the engines shut down. He told everyone, including Jacqueline Kennedy, it would be well over an hour before the plane would take off for the two-hour plus flight to Andrews Air Force Base—barely enough time for one of the most critical operations of the cover-up—kidnapping and removing Kennedy's body from the bronze casket it had been placed in at Parkland Hospital.

In a carefully conceived, macabre operation, Kennedy's body was callously removed from the heavy, ornate casket, stuffed unceremoniously into a standard military body bag, dumped into an ordinary looking shipping crate, and carried to Air Force Two as part of the luggage transfer between the two planes needlessly ordered by Johnson. All this was taking place while Johnson was being sworn in as President by Judge Sarah Hughes, in a purely symbolic ceremony, with Jacqueline Kennedy by *his* side instead of her husband's.

Navy photographer John T. Stringer testified years later at his deposition for the Assassination Records Review Board that before X-rays of Kennedy were taken in the morgue, he witnessed Kennedy's body being taken out of a "brownish" metal casket and that the body "was wrapped in two sheets; one around the head and one around the body."[3]

But Stringer's assistant, Floyd Riebe, testified a year later before the ARRB and attorney Gunn and described the casket as "gun metal gray...It wasn't a ceremonial casket. It was a very plain, inexpensive type casket." When asked by Gunn how Kennedy was dressed or wrapped or covered,

---

1 The air-conditioning was not on, as the electricity required only came on when the engines were running.
2 According to J.W. Bullion, LBJ's stockbroker, Johnson called him to inquire about his stock portfolio. He also called his attorney, Abe Fortas, to check on the Senate Rules' Committee investigation of his misconduct with Billy Sol Estes. This was around 2 PM, Eastern Standard Time.
3 ARRB, Deposition of John T. Stringer, 7/16/1996, p. 67, lines 19-20.

he answered: "He was in a rubberized-type body bag."[1] Riebe also claimed morgue technician Paul O'Connor and two others removed Kennedy's body from the zippered body bag and placed it on the autopsy table; that during the autopsy Dr. Finck probed Kennedy's back wound but he "didn't go in very far"; saw Kennedy's brain being removed "what little bit there was left… it was less than half a brain"; that the right side of the back of Kennedy's head was gone in the "occipital area"; that he had to take a "secrecy oath" and sign a statement to the effect that if he talked about any of this he could be court martialed. After being shown photographs of the head wound showing a gaping hole not in the occipital area but the temporal-parietal area, he admitted he may not have remembered the wound properly.

Navy Aide Sandra Kay Spencer, working at the Naval Photographic Center, also testified around this time before Mr. Gunn. She said the pictures she developed showed a two-inch hole at the back of Kennedy's head; that the wound on the throat was about one-half inch, the size of a finger; and that the photos she was shown were not on the same paper used at the Naval Photographic Center at the time—she brought with her a sample photo done around the same time showing it was not the same paper.

"Q: So, based upon your experience, would it be safe to say that it is your best recollection, best understanding, that the print of the autopsy that is in the Archives does not correspond with the paper that you were using in November 1963 at NPC?"

"A: Correct."[2]

And most unbelievably, she testified that she believed the photographs she was shown and the ones she developed were taken at different times and "between those photographs and the ones that we did, there had to be some massive cosmetic things done to the President's body."[3]

Navy X-ray technician Jerrol Francis Custer, appearing before the ARRB, swore under oath that after he took the first round of X-rays of Kennedy's head in the basement morgue, he took the elevator to the 1st floor on his way to another set of elevators to go to the film processing lab on the 4th floor. He was stopped by Secret Service agents before he could enter the rotunda because Jackie and Robert Kennedy were coming in. He also testified that the last time he saw Kennedy's body it was "literally butchered"; that he was told by the duty officer that the corpse was first taken to Walter Reed Army Hospital; that there was a chief with a deformed hand taking movies[4]; that during the autopsy they would remove organs and cut them up like little

---

1 ARRB, Deposition of Floyd Albert Riebe, 5/7/1997, p. 20, lines 11-12 & p.30, line 9.

2 ARRB, Deposition of Sandra Kay Spencer, 6/7/97, p. 45, lines 17-22, p. 46, line 1.

3 ARRB, Deposition of Sandra Kay Spencer, 6/5/97, p. 58, lines, 8-9, 18-21.

4 Custer also testified this chief (perhaps a man named Pitzer) committed suicide. The gun was found in his deformed hand. There is no other record of a film of Kennedy's body.

---

pieces of meat looking for bullet shells:

A: "They would pull out an organ—a big organ, and be up there cutting it up like a piece of meat."

Q: "This is on November 22nd?"

A: "Right; November 22nd. And then—Their basic thing was, 'We're looking for shells, bullets, fragments.' They weren't looking to, what caused it? How was it done? What was the tracing—what was the path of the bullet?"[1]

Equally compelling is Custer's testimony about a four-star general[2] who directed the autopsy from the gallery and was giving orders to Commander Ebersole, M.D., who conveyed the general's instructions to Commander Humes, M.D., who was conducting the autopsy. Instructions such as "Stop that. Don't do that anymore. The Kennedy family would not allow...like you to pursue that path any further. We do not want you to go any more in this direction."

Custer, too, mentioned the presence of a second casket, a gray shipping casket brought by a black Cadillac hearse to the back of the hospital, plus the bronze casket Jacqueline Kennedy had in her entourage.

In his testimony regarding Kennedy's wounds, Custer stated that the neck wound was the size of his little finger.[3] Regarding the back wound he testified:

Q: "Did you ever see a wound on the back of President Kennedy?"

A: "That's when I picked him up, and the bullet dropped out of there. There was a small wound."[4]

When Mr. Gunn read Dr. Ebersole's testimony to Mr. Custer regarding Ebersole's trip past the rotunda and observing Mrs. Kennedy—("He [Dr. Ebersole] personally carried the cassettes containing the X-rays to the X-ray department, which was on the fourth floor.")[5], Custer replied: "Baloney."

Johnson need not have used Kennedy's plane.

Johnson need not have been sworn in. The Vice-President automatically becomes President on the death of the President.

Johnson need not have transferred his luggage since both planes arrive almost simultaneously at the same place.

Johnson needed the delaying maneuver of the swearing-in ceremony;

---

1 ARRB, Deposition of Jerrold Francis Custer, 10/28/97, p. 46, lines 12-20.
2 The general has been identified as Air Force General Curtis LeMay, a four star general.
3 The tracheotomy done at Parkland was a clean incision through the neck wound. When the tracheotomy tube was removed the wound closed up showing the entry wound.
4 ARRB, Deposition of Jerrol Francis Custer, 10/28/97, p. 90, lines 21-22, p. 91, line 1.
5 Ibid. p. 190, lines 21-22, p. 191, line 1.

Jacqueline Kennedy's presence away from her husband's casket; the ruse of transferring luggage—all to cover up the medical evidence of a conspiracy to kill Kennedy and to hide the role of the conspirators.

Air Force Two always landed first although it took off second. This was, and probably still is, a standard protocol maneuver called "leap-frogging." Air Force Two passes Air Force One in flight to land earlier— fifteen minutes earlier—so the Vice-President can be at the bottom of the stairs to greet the President as the President walks down the steps of the aircraft to the tarmac.

Air Force Two landed around 6 PM, or slightly sooner. Kennedy's body, now housed in a metal-jacketed, military-style casket, was taken by helicopter to Walter Reed Army Hospital, only minutes away, for a brief preliminary examination. At Walter Reed bullets and fragments were removed from the body. It was then flown to Bethesda Naval Hospital by helicopter around 7 PM for a "pre-autopsy." From the helicopter the gray casket was loaded into a black Cadillac hearse and driven to the Bethesda Hospital morgue. But before Kennedy's body could be autopsied the caskets had to be switched again so that Kennedy's body could be removed from the bronze casket rather than the gray metal casket it had been transferred to on Air Force One.

The casket snatch-and-switch was successfully, if comically, executed with the use of three hearses, two gray, Navy, Pontiac hearses and a black Cadillac hearse.

First a gray hearse picked up the empty bronze casket from the front of Air Force One while Kennedy's body, now in a plain gray metal shipping casket, was flown to Walter Reed Army Hospital, where the body was inspected for bullets and replaced in the gray metal casket.

From Walter Reed Army Hospital (which was walking distance to Bethesda Naval Hospital) a black hearse drove Kennedy's body in a gray navy metal casket to the morgue located in the back of Bethesda Naval Hospital in the basement where a quick pre-autopsy was performed. At the pre-autopsy, naval technician Jerrol Custer took X-Rays and proceeded to the processing lab which was on the 4th floor. This required a change of elevators and a walk past the main rotunda.

At approximately the same time, another gray hearse pulled up to the front of Bethesda Hospital. This one contained the bronze casket (along with Jacqueline and Robert Kennedy, who had met the plane when it landed) that had earlier been taken off Air Force One. This hearse waited for about fifteen minutes before Jacqueline and Robert Kennedy exited the hearse and accompanied the empty bronze casket into the rotunda of the hospital, at which point Jacqueline and Robert Kennedy were escorted to the V.I.P. lounge. The casket remained in the rotunda for a while. Jacqueline and Robert Kennedy passed Jerrol Custer who was on his way to develop the recently taken X-Rays of Kennedy's body in the morgue.

The bronze casket was then returned to the gray hearse outside to be taken to the morgue in the back. At the same time an honor guard that had been helicoptered in from Fort Bragg, NC, arrived and parked next to the gray hearse with the bronze casket. Instead of a solemn procession to the morgue, the gray hearse suddenly accelerated to speeds of over fifty miles per hour, losing the honor guard which was confused by a second gray hearse which suddenly appeared between the first gray hearse and the honor guard.

The first gray hearse carrying the bronze coffin now arrived at the morgue without the honor guard which mistakenly followed the second gray hearse. The first gray hearse then unloaded the bronze casket and placed it in the hallway outside the morgue.

As soon as the bronze casket appeared, the Secret Service ordered everyone out of the autopsy room, wheeled in the bronze casket, placed Kennedy's body in a body bag, placed the body bag in the bronze casket, and returned it to the gray hearse which drove back to the front of the hospital.

Shortly after this the honor guard arrived at the morgue and, not seeing the hearse, the honor guard then returned to the front of the hospital at which time they saw the first gray hearse—now driven by Admiral Calvin B. Galloway, head of Bethesda Naval Base.

The gray hearse, with Kennedy's body now back in the bronze casket, was then driven again to the morgue at the rear of the hospital in solemn procession.

Kennedy's body, now in a body bag inside the bronze casket, was unloaded from the bronze casket and placed on autopsy table for a second time to begin the official autopsy.

The Secret Service explained away the presence of the gray casket in the corner, saying it contained a sailor awaiting an autopsy.

Kennedy's body was removed from the body bag in the bronze casket by 1st Class Petty Officer Dennis David and Corpsman Paul O'Connor, according to their testimony. According to O'Neil Funeral Director Aubrey Reich, the man who placed a rubber liner in the bronze casket, a white sheet around Kennedy's head, and closed the casket in Dallas, there was no body bag in the bronze casket. A YouTube video of Reich's version of placing a plastic sheet in the coffin and wrapping Kennedy's head in a sheet may still be available.

According to Bill O'Reilly in *Killing Kennedy*:

> Meanwhile, Vernon O'Neal [owner of O'Neal's Funeral Home, not funeral director Aubrey Reich] places a sheet of plastic down on the inside of the coffin, lining the bottom. He then carefully swaddles the body of John Kennedy in seven layers of rubber bags and one more of plastic. Finally, the president's body is laid inside.[1]

Before beginning the autopsy, Dr. Humes asked who was in charge. According to one account, Air Force Chief of Staff Major General Curtis

---

1 Bill O'Reilly and Martin Dugard, *Killing Kennedy*, p. 284.

LeMay[1] put his cigar in his mouth and said, "I am." None of the ranking admirals questioned his authority to assume command on a naval base. It was now nearly 8 PM, almost two hours since Air force Two had landed with Kennedy's body and Air Force One with his empty bronze casket.

After the autopsy was completed, Gawler Funeral Home sent over four embalmers to prepare the body for public viewing before burial[2] in Arlington National Cemetery.

Warp Threads II—Of Bullets and Ballistics

Among the many, many strange, unusual, impossible and incredible discrepancies the public has been asked to believe is the failure of forensic investigators to match any of the bullets that killed JFK, MLK, and RFK to the weapons with which they were supposedly killed. The bullets which killed Officer J.D. Tippit in Dallas could not be matched to Oswald's pistol. The bullet taken from Dr. King was intact according to the coroner but fragmented according to the FBI; the bullets to the back of Robert Kennedy's head could not be matched to Sirhan's gun; the bullets to the throat and head of John Kennedy could not be found, let alone matched to the Mannlicher-Carcano rifle supposedly used by Oswald.

Warp Thread III—Patsies and Reverse Patsies

In all three murders, the "killer" is immediately identified and immediately sought and/or captured. All turn out to be loners—men outside of mainstream society with a problem past of some sort—men without means, formal education, strong community attachments, or initially, good attorneys. All are quickly silenced without a real trial, without their day in court. They all have "friends" that suddenly appear and guide the last months of their lives. Friends like Ruth and Michael Paine, George DeMohrenschildt, Jerry Owen, and Raoul—friends who seem to have ties to the CIA or the Mafia or someone high up in the government. All had been carefully, deliberately, and maliciously chosen to be the scapegoats of the rich and powerful. They are the patsies.

In the case of Ted Kennedy, the role of the patsy is reversed. The killing of Ted Kennedy by another lone assassin would have been impossible to

---

1 General Curtis Le May was widely known for his attempts to provoke World War III and his call for a first strike against Russia. In the movie, *Dr. Strangelove*, he was characterized as the trigger happy General Jack D. Ripper. He argued with Kennedy during the Cuban Missile Crisis and called for total annihilation of Cuba. He called the Cuban Missile Crisis the greatest defeat in American history.

2 Kennedy's body was buried in a mahogany casket. The bronze casket, claimed to be damaged, was drilled full of holes, weighed down with three eighty pound sacks of sand, was dumped into the Atlantic at the request of Robert Kennedy.

dismiss as another coincidence, even by a compliant media and a gullible public. Besides, the death of Ted Kennedy was not necessary—just the death of his potential presidential ambition. So he was made the scapegoat or patsy in the clever, morbid murder of an innocent young woman, Mary Jo Kopechne—a young woman who did not drown in the back of Ted Kennedy's car as reported but who was shot in the head with a .25 caliber pistol and placed in the back of Kennedy's car.

Warp Threads IV—Altered, Planted, And Hidden Evidence

Why does the Zapruder film conflict with immediate eyewitness testimony and show irreproducible rapid human movements? Why do exhibits and testimony in the Warren Commission contradict the conclusions? Why is John Kennedy's brain missing? Why were all the investigations of the assassinations conducted in secret and the evidence gathered hidden from public scrutiny for decades and decades? Why were all the investigators chosen primarily from people with a vested interest in the outcome? Why are so many eyewitnesses to these events silenced through threats, intimidation or death? How many innocent people have to die to cover up the truth of these events? Why is anyone who criticizes the "official" version of these events ridiculed, ostracized, and branded a lunatic, communist or unpatriotic?

Warp Thread V—The Warren Commission, LBJ, and J. Edgar Hoover

The Warren Commission was controlled from the inside by the CIA through fired ex-CIA Director Allen Dulles. It was controlled from the outside by FBI Director J. Edgar Hoover, who supplied the Commissioners with reports of its investigations, pre-witness interviews and the testing of the physical evidence. The Warren Commission had no source or means of investigating—other than J. Edgar Hoover, who filtered all eyewitnesses, exhibits, and forensic evidence.

Not only were Hoover and Johnson neighbors and business partners, but they also shared a mutual and intense hatred of both John and Robert Kennedy dating from their first encounters. Johnson saw JFK as an impotent senator and an oversexed playboy who accomplished nothing in the Congress or the Senate and did not deserve to be president. Johnson thought of RFK as a dog's chew toy that he enjoyed teasing and embarrassing. The first meeting in the Senate cafeteria between Johnson and Robert Kennedy has been characterized as the meeting of two hostile dogs. Robert Kennedy, at the time a staffer for Senator Joe McCarthy, refused to stand up and shake hands with the powerful Senate Majority Leader when Johnson made his way through the cafeteria. Johnson, not one to suffer slights of this kind, planted himself in front of Kennedy until Kennedy was forced to stand and shake hands. Johnson would laugh about Kennedy's discomfort with his cronies and took every opportunity thereafter to confront Kennedy and force him to shake hands knowing it annoyed Robert Kennedy no end.

When Robert Kennedy became Attorney General he repaid Johnson by shunning him at every opportunity and deliberately leaving him out of the decision-making loop, especially the Bay of Pigs and the Cuban Missile Crisis. Robert Kennedy's hostility for Johnson spilled over to J. Edgar Hoover, who was ordered to keep a dedicated phone on his desk with which the Attorney General, his superior, could call at any time without having to go through Hoover's secretary, Mrs. Gandy. Within minutes of John Kennedy's assassination, Hoover called Robert Kennedy on the dedicated line, told him "The President's dead," hung up without waiting for a reply or reaction or expressing any sympathy, and ordered the dedicated phone removed to Mrs. Gandy's desk.

In less than twelve hours almost all the physical evidence of a crime— the body, the limo, the rifle, the Zapruder and other films and photographs, the autopsy X-Rays and photographs—had been placed in Hoover's control. Within hours, Johnson aide Cliff Carter had been on the phone telling Dallas District Attorney to charge Lee Harvey Oswald only with simple murder— not a conspiracy. The Police and Sheriff's Department had been told by Carter to shut down their investigations, as they already had their man.

James Earl Ray had been identified as the killer of Dr. King within the hour in an all too familiar script.

Exculpatory evidence in the murder of Robert Kennedy had been destroyed by the LAPD shortly after the murder.

Evidence of the premeditated murder of Mary Jo Kopechne by gunshot has been hidden.

Warp Thread VI—A Compliant Media

Within days, if not hours, the media was proclaiming Oswald's guilt in the papers and on the air. The murders of JFK, MLK, and RFK have never really been covered by the media, which is reluctant to even bring up the matter except in biased documentaries prepared by government sources. The autopsy of Mary Jo Kopechne was not allowed by the family.

How long will it be before the Internet is censored, no doubt in the name of protecting the constitutional rights of all Americans? Why are journalists paid by the CIA? Why are operations like PAPERCLIP, ZR/RIFLE, SANDWEDGE, GEMSTONE, COINTELPRO, MOCKINGBIRD, NORTHWOODS, ARTICHOKE, MK-ULTRA and others we have not heard about, allowed to continue, let alone start in the first place?

The fact that the assassinations of John F. Kennedy, Martin Luther King Jr., and Robert F. Kennedy have never been openly and honestly investigated shows unmistakably the impotence of the American people and the god-like powers of those running our government and most of the world.

IMAGES

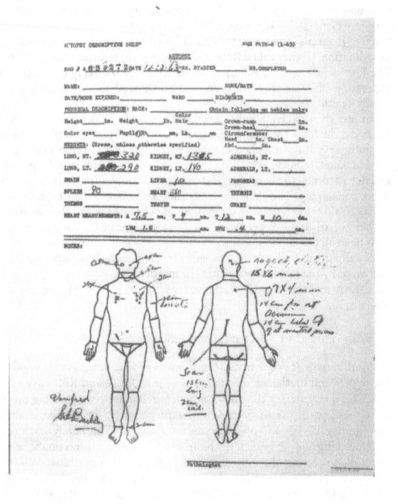

Figure 1: JFK autopsy descriptive sheet signed by Kennedy's personal physician, Admiral Burkley.

Thomas Evan Robinson

ADDRESS AND PHONE INFORMATION DELETED
FOR MR. ROBINSON'S PRIVACY

lay 26, 1942 (phone)

    Wounds :

- large gaping hole in back of head. patched by stretching piece of rubber .... over it. Thinks skull full of Plaster of Paris
- smaller wound in right temple. crescent shape, flapped down (3")
- (approx 2) small shrapnel wounds in face. packed with wax.
- wound in back (5 to six inches) below shoulder. to the right of back bone.
- Adrenlin gland and brain removed.
- other organs removed and then put back.
- No swelling or discalaration to face. (died instantly)

Dr. Berkley (family Physician) came in and ask....
    "How much longer ???
    He was told (Funeral Director)"Take your time"

Is in favor of Exuming Body ... to settle once and ... for all ."Good Pathologists would know exactly "

Figure 2. Autopsy notes. Transcription on following page.

Thomas Evan Robinson
Personal contact info deleted to protect Mr. Robinson's privacy

May 26, 1992 (Phone)

Wounds:

Large gaping hole in back of head.
patched by placing piece of rubber.....over it.
Thinks skull full of Plaster of Paris.

Smaller wound in right temple.
Crescent shped, flapped down (3")

(approx 2) Small sharpnel wounds in face.
Packed with wax.

Wound in back (5 to six inches) below shoulder.
To the right of the back bone.

Adrenlin gland and brain removed.

Other organs removed and then put back.

No swelling or discoloration to face.
(Died instantly)

Dr. Berkley (family physician) came in an ask.....
"How much longer???"
He (Robinson) was told (funeral director)
"Take your time."

Is in favor of exhuming body.....to settle once and....for all.
(Robinson quote) "Good pathologists would know exactly"

Figure 3. Transcription of autopsy notes.

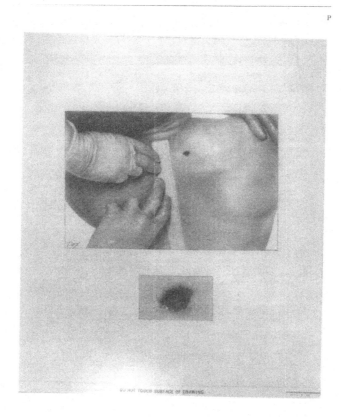

Figure 4. Image of JFK's wounded back.

All autopsy-related images reprinted with the gracious permission of the Mary Ferrell Foundation.

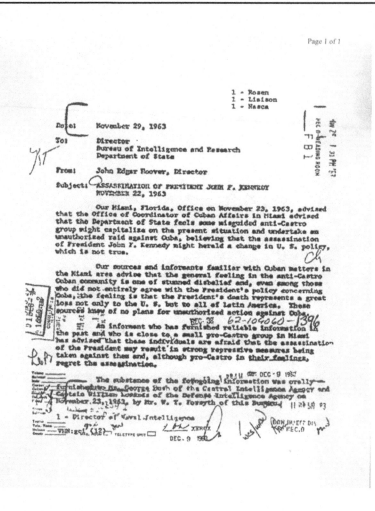

Figure 5. Letter from J. Edgar Hoover referencing George H.W. Bush's briefing about JFK assassination and Bush's membership in the CIA at the time.

UNITED STATES GOVERNMENT

Memorandum

TO : SAC, HOUSTON   DATE: 11-22-63

FROM : SA GRAHAM W. KITCHEL

SUBJECT: UNKNOWN SUBJECT;
ASSASSINATION OF PRESIDENT
JOHN F. KENNEDY

At 1:45 p.m. Mr. GEORGE H. W. BUSH, President
of the Zapata Off-shore Drilling Company, Houston, Texas,
residence 5525 Briar, Houston, telephonically furnished
the following information to writer by long distance
telephone call from Tyler, Texas.

BUSH stated that he wanted to be kept confidential
but wanted to furnish hearsay that he recalled hearing in
recent weeks, the day and source unknown. He stated that
one JAMES PARROTT has been talking of killing the President
when he comes to Houston.

BUSH stated that PARROTT is possibly a student
at the University of Houston and is active in political
matters in this area. He stated that he felt Mrs. FAWLEY,
telephone number SU 2-5239, or ARLINE SMITH, telephone
number JA 9-9194 of the Harris County Republican Party
Headquarters would be able to furnish additional information regarding the identity of PARROTT.

BUSH stated that he was proceeding to Dallas, Texas,
would remain in the Sheraton-Dallas Hotel and return to his
residence on 11-23-63. His office telephone number is
CA 2-0395.

ALL INFORMATION CONTAINED
HEREIN IS UNCLASSIFIED
DATE 10-15-93 BY 9803 AJO/KSR

GWK:djw
(2)

Figure 6: Letter referencing Bush's phone call and presence in Dallas at time of
the assassination

A conversation with Frank Sturgis

Watergate figure Frank Sturgis with Journal's Ed Lang
...interview took place at home of North Miami Beach friends of Sturgis

By ED LANG
Journal Staff Writer

Figure 7: First interview given by Frank Sturgis after release from prison, in the living room of Ben and Hazel Fazzino.

APPENDIX: Ben Fazzino—Unsung Marine Hero of Okinawa

Figure 8: Ben Fazzino as a young marine

Although I requested Ben's military records many years ago, and receipt of the request and proper paperwork was acknowledged, I never received the documents. Thus, I am not positive about my cousin's exact classification or military assignment during Okinawa; but on August 19, 1946, he is listed as being with the 1st Battalion, Marine Regiment, 1st Marine Division (Reinf) FMF. To this day the Marine Corps and the Navy have not released the military records of Benjamin Fazzino.

His career in the Marines was eventful to say the least.

From Boxer to Soldier to Hero

By the time Biaggio was old enough to join the Marines on November 28, 1944, he was already a champion amateur boxer. He won a few amateur titles and one day a promoter asked him to fight the contender for the title in a pre-title fight. He won easily. However, he was supposed to lose. The contender, it seems, was backed by a Mafia figure who was more than upset. Ben's trainer drove him to the Marine Corps recruiter as soon as Ben was dressed.

After basic training he was sent to the Pacific Area from April 14, 1945, to January 22, 1947. First he went to Guadalcanal and then to Okinawa to join the First Marine Division, First Brigade, 5th Marine regiment, which had been fighting on Okinawa since April 1, 1945. He was in Okinawa until the Japanese surrendered on June 21, 1945.

The Battle of Okinawa requires a little background to put it in perspective and context as it differed so dramatically from other Pacific battles such as Luzon, Leyte, and Iwo Jima at which the Japanese fought using offensive as opposed to defensive tactics. It was also where Benjamin Fazzino showed his heroism under fire risking his life behind enemy lines.

This last and bloodiest battle of the Pacific lasted just over eighty days and ended less than two months before Hiroshima and Nagasaki. Combined casualties of both Hiroshima and Nagasaki were *less* than the combined casualties of the Battle of Okinawa. It was that horrific.

Nine months before the invasion of Okinawa, General Dwight D. Eisenhower had led the largest invasion fleet ever assembled for the D-Day invasion of Normandy which led directly to the Allied victory in Europe. The invasion fleet which attacked Okinawa on April 1, 1945, was, in reality, *far larger* in many respects, than that assembled for Normandy. But L-Day, for "Landing Day," lacked a key element—the element of surprise of D-Day. The Japanese were waiting. In fact, they had been waiting and preparing for a year.

The Japanese understood that after the U.S. air strikes on Truk Lagoon (part of the Caroline Island group in the central part of the Pacific), in February, 1944, an invasion of Okinawa was inevitable and imminent. It was to be the precursor of an invasion of "mainland" Japan, that is, its four primary islands, some 340 miles from Okinawa.

Realizing this, the Imperial General Headquarters (IGHQ) set out to prepare itself for the attack by garrisoning the island with the newly formed 32nd Army of the Imperial Japanese Army (IJA) headed by Japan's finest general—Lieutenant General Mitsuru Arikawa Ushijima, and three key officers. Ushijima's Chief of Staff was Lieutenant General Isamu Cho, whose chief subordinate was Colonel Hiromichi Yahara. Yahara requested and was granted from IGHQ the services of Japan's most respected and leading artillery specialist, Major General Kosuke Wada. Wada's 5th Artillery Command had control of all heavy artillery on the island.

Mere hours before the final surrender of Okinawa, Colonel Hiromichi Yahara was ordered by his superiors, Ushijima and Cho, *not* to commit *Seppuku*, or *Harakiri*, literally "stomach cutting," as they were about to do, in order to rescue the honor they had lost in battle, before meeting their ancestors. Yahara was ordered to escape to Japan to tell the Japanese version of the battle of Okinawa to the emperor. He attempted to escape, dressed as an Okinawan school teacher, but he was captured and interrogated.[1]

The fate of Major General Kosuke Wada is known only to high Japanese officials and only to a few Americans whom my cousin chose to tell. Most Japanese sources list Kosuke Wada as Lieutenant General (three star) Wada instead of Major General (two star) Kosuke Wada. I assume he was awarded the third star posthumously because at the time of his death around the 15th of June, 1945, on Okinawa, *he was wearing the two star insignia of a Major General.* He did not commit *seppuku* in Japan after the war as is reported in some Japanese history books, although some accounts do say he was killed in battle in Okinawa. What follows is the real story of Major General Wada's last minutes.

The U.S. 10th Army, which was put in charge of taking Okinawa, was divided into the III Amphibious Corps, consisting of three marine Divisions—the 1st, 6th, and the 2nd which was held in reserve and used as a diversion before the first landing,[2] and the XXIV Corps, consisting of the 7th, 96th, 77th, and 27th Infantry Divisions.

Approximately 130 large naval vessels, including 17 aircraft carriers, mainly British, and hundreds and hundreds of smaller ones, completed the nearly 200,000-man, 7-division army and marine task force.

The Japanese 32nd Army consisted of approximately 70,000 army, 9,000 navy, and approximately 40,000 locals, called *Boeitai*, hastily impressed into service without uniforms or guns to perform non-combat roles such as enlarging caves and moving supplies.

The shrunken Imperial Japanese Navy (IJN) was no match either for the Allied navy. Japan's prize ship, the Yamamoto, which represented the world's largest battleship and featuring the world's largest naval guns at 18.2 inches, was sunk as it made its way to Okinawa. This was a desperate move in any case, as the Yamamoto had set sail with only enough fuel to reach Okinawa—unaccompanied by sufficient support ships and no aircraft. The strategy was to beach the Yamamoto on Okinawa and use its guns as a battle station against the overwhelming superiority of the American armada.

The Japanese did have some 7500 Kamikaze aircraft available, by some accounts, versus an assortment of roughly 2000 Allied craft. The year before the battle of Okinawa the Japanese had developed a new strategy called the "*Kamikaze,*" or "*Divine Wind*" strategy, by which they hoped to overcome the

---

1 Many years later Yahara would write a volume called *The Battle for Okinawa* which would be translated into English.
2 They were also used in the closing days of the invasion.

overwhelming superiority of the US Navy and Army task force by crashing into its vessels. Though somewhat successful and highly destructive when they hit their targets, the majority of Kamikaze planes and pilots were ill equipped to do so with no instruments and limited training, so that the majority of planes missed their targets when they did manage to find them. There were also Kamikaze boats, but they too were only marginally effective. The strategy of the Kamikaze was embodied in a slogan composed by Colonel Yahara—one plane for one warship, one boat for one ship, one man for every ten of the enemy or one tank.

From the beginning, the Imperial Japanese Army (IJA) realized it would be fighting a defensive war. To that end it began a massive cave-excavating program consisting mainly of manual labor. Proper earth moving and cutting equipment, although requested from Japan, was not available. Multiple airport runways were built in clusters so that in the event one might be destroyed by bombs, another would be nearby. This plan was in vain as the Japanese were running out of everything including planes at the time. Later, Colonel Yahara, who had been in charge of planning the defenses of Okinawa, lamented that they had built the airfields for the benefit of the Allies.

The island of Okinawa is approximately sixty miles long running north and south, and anywhere from three to eighteen miles wide on the east and west, with dozens of jutties. The southern third of the island is the most habitable, the north being more mountainous and rugged and least populated. General Ushijima decided to concentrate and cluster artillery power under Major General Kosuke Wada in the south, that being the most natural landing site. The north was basically forfeited to the Americans.

The Japanese strategy was to hide the entire defense force of over 100,000 men in caves; allow the Allies to come ashore unchallenged; and then attack from all sides on land and sea. As anticipated the Allies landed on the beaches at Hagushi. The Americans expected *Bonzai* charges—the normal Japanese strategy—but landed unopposed.

Although there were natural caves in the south—some even capable of housing 1,000 men—most had to be enlarged and interconnected with a series of tunnels for communication and covert movement. Toiling through the thirty to sixty feet of concrete-like coral which covered most of the island, the Japanese managed to build sixty miles of tunnels and cavernous spaces to house their entire army. The caves were dug out in a method called "reverse sloping." The caves were ingeniously designed in L-shaped patterns with entrances/exits on the sides. The front opening was only big enough to allow large guns to be rolled into position, as needed, on railroad tracks or sometimes on stout lumber.

After the April 1, 1945, (landing on April Fool's Day and Easter Sunday) the 1st and 6th marine divisions traveled north to secure that sparsely inhabited, mountainous terrain. They accomplished this in short order as there was no real defense. They returned south to join up with the army as they literally rooted out the 32nd Army of Lieutenant General Ushijima, man by man, cave by cave, yard by yard—some days advancing only 100 yards.

Knowing they had no chance of winning but only of delaying the inevitable takeover of Okinawa, in hopes of giving the mainland more time to husband resources, the Japanese clung on to Okinawan soil in a death grip. The Allied forces would eventually equip tanks with flame throwers to force the Japanese out of the caves. The American soldiers called these tanks "Zippos" and "Ronsons."

Only once did the Japanese attempt a significant counter attack. Around the 4th or 5th of May, the Allies moved on the 32nd Army's main concentration of forces located under Shuri Castle in the south. The Japanese counterattacked in force before being forced to retreat back into their caves. It was a disaster resulting in the needless loss of 5,000 Japanese soldiers. In his memoirs about the war, Colonel Yahara wrote that, against his advice, Lieutenant General Cho convinced Lieutenant General Ushijima to mount the counteroffensive. After the defeat, Lieutenant General Ushijima promised to listen only to Yahara's advice—a hollow promise as the war, everyone realized, was only weeks from being lost.

The marines were also taking heavy losses, for the first time, on Okinawa. Major General Wada's main artillery weapons were kept deep in the caves of Sugar Loaf Hill (Hill 52), Tomari Hill, Makabe, and Asato, among others. They fired and then receded out of sight of the Allies.

One of Major General Wada's powerful guns, buried deep in the bowels of one of the larger cave formations, hindered the marine advance and was keeping some ships from approaching the coast with reinforcements. Wada's guns took a deadly toll. In one marine company there were 250 casualties and only 8 survivors.

Arriving at Okinawa on June 10, 1945, Ben Fazzino's ship was prevented from approaching the coast by inland shelling from one of General Wada's large guns that the Japanese rolled in and out of a reverse slope cave—a maneuver making it nearly impossible to destroy by airpower. Private Benjamin Fazzino volunteered as the point man on a three man squad to take out the big gun. He and the others were given a crude hand-drawn map, two 25-pound satchel bombs, a carbine, and a bayonet.

Transported ashore by submarine and rubber raft, Ben crawled behind enemy lines and traveled at night, reaching the artillery cannon more by chance than navigational skill. Reaching the enormous cave, Ben realized that a rope would be needed to lower someone down to set the satchel charges.

Remembering a cargo dump he had seen the night before, Ben left the two other marines and set out for the rope. He found a cargo net, cut it apart and took what he needed, and headed back to the cave. On his way back he was met with gunfire, which he quickly returned with his own. After a few rounds, he crawled to the other side, within a few yards of the enemy, surprising him. The enemy soldier, obviously an elderly officer, from this close a distance, turned to fire. The Japanese officer's carbine jammed.

Throwing it away in disgust, he drew an enormous samurai, held it over his head and prepared to attack, Bonzai style, his nemesis.

Ben said the samurai sword was as big as the officer. He told me that he felt the soldier was "calling him out," and challenging him to duel. It was a flawed strategy.

Knowing that a carbine, the worst military weapon in the American arsenal, could not stop a charging enemy a few yards away, Ben threw down his carbine, too, and drew his bayonet. He told me that if he had been issued a .45 automatic sidearm,[1] it would have been no contest—but a questionable carbine against a samurai-bearing warrior was another matter and he was not about to take the chance.

Ben knew he was more than a match for the ancient warrior who wielded an unsteady samurai on a hilly terrain. He was eighteen and in top physical condition, a trained boxer—plus he was ten feet tall and bulletproof, like all eighteen-year-olds, especially marines.

Ben skipped the goriest details but he told me it was over in a matter of minutes. He said he feinted left as if he were jabbing at a boxing opponent then turned and slashed the Japanese soldier's left leg behind the knee, bringing him instantly to his knees. The rest was instinct—a knee in the small of the back and a quick thrust in the back—at heart level.

Having dispatched the soldier to his ancestors, Ben stopped only long enough to cut off the soldier's insignias of rank and grab a few personal papers from the officer's helmet as a souvenir. Had he not been carrying the satchel bombs, he told me, he would have taken the sword, too.

Barely recovering from the adrenaline rush of a bloody fresh kill, he was confronted by another enemy soldier, slightly younger and more agile, but still no match for Ben. He performed another unscheduled and premature *Harakiri* ritual in short order, although it took a little more time and effort than the first. This time at least there was no samurai drawn. Several quick cuts to the stomach and one through the heart, and another Japanese soldier's career was ended. Ben quickly stripped him of his insignia, personal papers, payroll records, and a regimental flag—a prized possession which the Japanese warrior carried in his helmet.

Ben returned to his two comrades and was lowered down by his ankles into the cave, where he set the satchel bombs with twenty-second fuses. He was pulled up safely, but not before suffering a concussion. Ben and his two companions crawled back to American-held territory. Days later, on June 21, 1945, the Japanese surrendered Okinawa.

The battle for Okinawa ended. Truman dropped atomic bombs on Hiroshima and Nagasaki; the Japanese surrendered a few weeks later, thereby ending the war in the Pacific. Private Benjamin Fazzino's heroic deeds behind enemy lines were written up in a letter of commendation for the Congressional

---

1 The marines would later issue .45 automatic side-arms, technically known as M1911 Colt .45 automatic pistols.

Medal of Honor by his commanding officer. The commendation got as far as General MacArthur's desk before being denied for two reasons.

The first reason given was that the cave, which housed the big gun that Ben and his two fellow marines had neutralized, was also being used as a hospital and non-combatants were killed—evidently a rare occurrence in the experience of General MacArthur, who apparently read only official government casualty reports that do not mention civilian casualties.

Second, and obviously more important, the two men that eighteen-year-old Private Benjamin had killed along the way were senior staff officers of the 32nd Imperial Japanese Army—Major General Kosuke Wada and his aide Colonel Konpo—and Ben had the insignia and personal papers and regimental flag to prove it.[1]

This was a major embarrassment for the Japanese—or would have been, had it become known. MacArthur closed the file on Ben's Medal of Honor and, most likely, returned the bodies to the Japanese in diplomatic pouches, so that a virtual ceremonial Harakiri could be performed and a promotion to the rank of Lieutenant General given to Major General Kosuke Wada, head of the 5th Artillery—posthumously, and preposterously, of course.[2]

Today, some Japanese historical accounts claim that General Wada died honorably by committing seppuku in Japan, after the war. Since there is no account of anyone escaping to Japan from Okinawa, it is difficult to see how General Wada could have escaped or why he would leave his post and not commit seppuku with Ushijima and Cho. The ceremonial suicide of Ushijima and Cho was observed by their staff and reported by Colonel Yahara in his memoirs after his capture, interrogation and imprisonment by US forces as he tried to escape. No records of Wada and Konpo exist after the 14th or 15th of June, 1945. Most official versions of the Battle of Okinawa barely mention General Wada, if they mention him at all. If he was killed honorably, in action, why would he be ignored by historians—both Japanese and American?

MacArthur, in fact, went so far in his deference to Hirohito to blatantly aid in the exoneration of Hirohito and all members of the Imperial family implicated in war crimes.[3] It has been suggested that MacArthur had presidential ambitions and expected financial support from the Japanese government and the Hirohito family for a presidential bid.

MacArthur's prosecution team at the Japanese War Trials functioned as a *de facto* defense team for the royal family, according to many observers. At

---

1 Plates of the regimental flag and payroll records are displayed in the back of this book.
2 While a few of the accounts of the Battle of Okinawa mention General Wada briefly without mentioning his outcome, the definitive account by four American military historians who observed the battle firsthand (*Okinawa: The Last Battle*, by Roy Appleton, et al.), make no mention at all of General Wada—even though they mention the other major Japanese generals and colonels.
3 *Hirohito and the Making of Modern Japan*, Kumao Toyoda.

the Japanese War Crimes Trials, many officers of the Imperial Japanese Army and Navy were convicted of the most horrific crimes against humanity—more brutal and unconscionable than the Nazi army—namely cannibalism; vivisection and amputation of live American and other captives *without the use of anesthesia*—which the Japanese claimed would distort the scientific data; rape; torture and beheading of prisoners for sport. (Japanese officers sometimes competed to see who could behead the most number of people in record time.)

MacArthur freed or commuted the death sentences of many of these criminals after their conviction at the Japanese War Crimes Trials in exchange for the data on the 'scientific' experiments on live, un-anesthetized, vivisected prisoners of war. One of the most blatant examples was the case of Dr. Shiro Ishii who headed the Ishii Corps Unit 731. He was responsible for infecting thousands of POWs with deadly germs for test purposes. MacArthur traded his death sentence and those of Unit 731 for the test results of his deadly experiments.

> In 1950, the military governor of Japan, General Douglas MacArthur, commuted all of the death sentences and significantly reduced most of the prison terms. All of those convicted in relation to the university vivisections were free after 1958.[1] In addition, many participants who were responsible for these vivisections were never charged by the Americans or their allies in exchange for the information on the experiments.[2][3]

It's not difficult to see why MacArthur denied my cousin the Medal of Honor.

As a gesture, of sorts, to acknowledge his bravery, however, Private Benjamin Fazzino was assigned as personal bodyguard to General George Marshall, a five-star general who was responsible for the Marshall Plan to patch up post-war Europe. In that capacity he was in China, mainly Beijing, from October 7, 1945, to January 3, 1947. As personal bodyguard to General George Marshall during negotiations with Generalissimo Chiang Kai-shek, Ben once again showed his courage, if not the medal he should have worn.

Chinese Torture of a Heroic Marine

Private Ben Fazzino's stint in Beijing, China, after Okinawa, proved to be exhilarating. The young marine even had time for sight-seeing and for absorbing the culture and the language. In post-war China, he was paid $90 per month, and he was able to rent a huge villa for $22 per month outside the

---

1 *The Fallen: A True Story of American POW's and Japanese Wartime Atrocities*, Marc Landas, 2004, Hoboken: John Wiley.
2 *Unit 731 Testimony*, Hal Gold, 2004.
3 The above sources are re-quoted from a Wikipedia article entitled, *Japanese War Crimes*.

city. Befriending two out-of-work and homeless Italian ex-embassy workers from the vacated and shuttered Italian Embassy,[1] Ben exchanged services for room and board. One of the services was to teach him a speaking and writing knowledge of Chinese—a blessing and a curse.

The blessing was that it endeared him to Madam Chiang Kai-shek, for whom he occasionally acted as chauffeur. She helped him choose a silk chrysanthemum-patterned kimono for his future wife, Hazel Williams, a Navy WAVE on Admiral Forrestal's staff. His rudimentary Chinese also served him well in the Korean War, when he would holler Chinese expressions to ferret out the location of enemy troops, like a deadly game of whack-a-mole.

However, knowing the language definitely did not serve him well later during his time in China, because as personal bodyguard to General Marshall he was privy to the negotiations between Generalissimo Chiang Kai-shek and Chou En Lai, who represented Mao Zedong. The negotiations centered around the Chinese presence in North Vietnam and France's desire to reclaim its former colonies, Vietnam, Laos and Cambodia.

Desperately desiring to know what he knew about the ongoing negotiations, the Red Chinese army tore up the railroad tracks of a train in which he was riding, halted the train, and took him captive.

For nearly a month Ben was kept in a deep pit. The pit was covered with a bamboo grill which allowed the rains, urine and feces from Chinese soldiers to insult his body on a regular basis. Stripped naked except for his shoes, he killed huge flesh-eating rats, thrown down randomly by his captors for sport. What food he was given consisted of raw fish heads and, on occasion, a little rice. His well-toned 130-pound frame quickly shrunk to 70 pounds.

Almost daily he was subjected to interrogations, beaten, burned with cigarettes, and hit in the side of the head with the butt of a rifle—never breaking, never talking, never forgetting he was a marine. He spared me the more gruesome aspects of his time in captivity but told me that just before despairing, he heard an American voice call out from the heavens, "Is that you down there, marine?"

Taken to a Chinese hospital, he recovered quickly. He consulted Chinese doctors for the remainder of his life because he was so impressed with their skill. He recovered so well that he returned to duty with General Marshall, and when he encountered two of his captors on a street one day, it was their last encounter with anyone ever again.

When General Marshall's mission ended, Admiral Forrestal, later Secretary of the Navy, requested Ben Fazzino's services as his personal bodyguard. And that was all the honor he publicly received. His comrades, however, showed their respect to the end of his days.

[1] Italy, originally a member of the Axis, closed their embassy in China after Hitler's defeat.

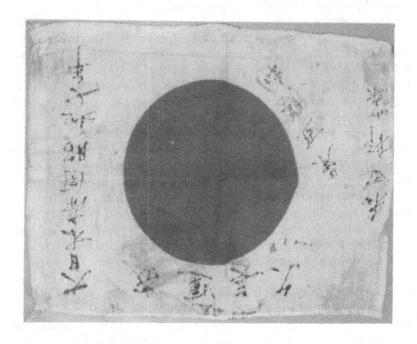

Figure 9: Picture of regimental flag given to Colonel Konpo by Major General Kosuke Wada

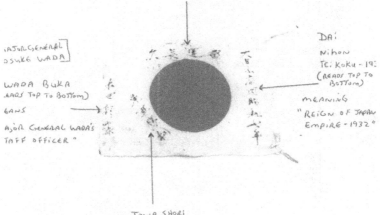

Kiun Chokyū (READS RIGHT TO LEFT)
MEANING: "Lucky opportunity for Glory!"

MAJOR GENERAL
OSUKE WADA

WADA BUKA
(READS TOP TO BOTTOM)
GANS

MAJOR GENERAL WADA'S
STAFF OFFICER"

DAI
Nihon
Te: Koku - 19:
(READS TOP TO
BOTTOM)

MEANING
"REIGN OF JAPAN
EMPIRE - 1932"

TOWA SHORI
(READS LEFT TO RIGHT)
MEANS "JAPANESE VICTORY"

THIS FLAG WAS PRESENTED TO HIGH RANKING STAFF OFFICER'S
BY MAJOR GENERAL WADA AFTER SEIZING CONTROL OF NANKING.
THE ATTACHED PHOTO IS THE OWNER OF THE FLAG BEHEADING
A CHINESE BOY. HE IS THE COLONEL NAMED IN THE PAYROLL
CONTROL DOCUMENT. HIS NAME WAS COLONEL TARUYOSHI KONPO.
HE PERSONALLY BEHEADED OVER 100 CHINESE MEN, WOMEN & CHILDREN
AND CUT UNBORN BABIES OUT OF THE LIVING WOMBS!

Figure 10: Translation of Colonel Konpo's regimental flag

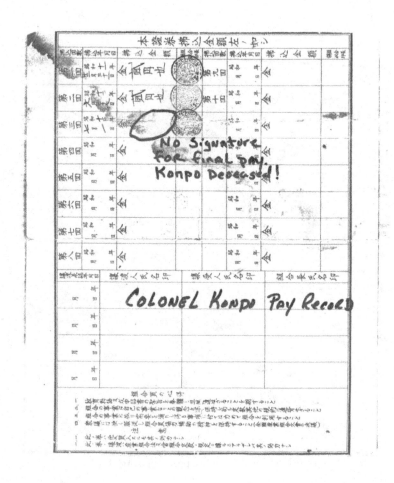

Figure 11: Payroll record of Colonel Konpo taken from his helmet showing his last payment

BIBLIOGRAPHY

Ayers, Bradley, *The Zenith Secret*, 2006, Vox Pop/Dench Kiss Media Corporation

Baker, Judyth Vary, *Me & Lee: How I Came to Know, Love, and Lose Lee Harvey Oswald*, 2010, Trine Day, LLC

Bowen, General Russell S., *The Immaculate Deception: The Bush Crime Family Exposed*, 2000, American West Publishers

Brown, Madeleine Duncan, *Texas in the Morning: The Love Story of Madeleine Duncan Brown and Lyndon Baines Johnson*, 1997, Conservatory Press

Connelly, Michael, *The President's Team*, 2009, MVP Books

Cova, Antonio Rafael de la, *The Moncada Attack: Birth of the Cuban Revolution*, University of South Carolina Press, 2002.

Craig, John R. & Rogers, Philip A., *The Man on the Grassy Knoll*, 1992, Avon Books

Crenshaw, Dr. Charles, *Conspiracy of Silence*, 1992, Penguin Books

Crenshaw, Dr. Charles, *Trauma Room One: The JFK Medical Cover-up Exposed*, 2001, Paraview Press

Crowley, Monica, *Nixon in Winter*, 1998, Crawley & Baron, Inc.

Damore, Leo, *Senatorial Privilege: The Chappaquiddick Cover-up*, 1988, Regnery Gateway

Ellsberg, Dr. Daniel, *Secrets: A Memoir of Vietnam and The Pentagon Papers*, 2003, Penguin Group (USA)

Farrell, Joseph P., *LBJ and the Conspiracy to Kill Kennedy: A Coalescence of Interest*, 2011, Adventures Unlimited Press

Fetzer, James, (Edited by) *The Great Zapruder Film Hoax: Deceit And Deception In The*

Death of JFK, 2003, Open Court

Fetzer, James, *Murder In Dealey Plaza: What We Know Now That We Didn't Know Then*, 2000, Open Court

Fonzi, Gaeton, *The Last Investigation*, 1993, Thunder's Mouth

Frank, Gerald, *An American Death*, 1972, Doubleday

Garrison, Jim, *On the Trail of the Assassins*, 1991, Warner Books

Giancana, Sam and Chuck, *Double Cross*, 1992, Warner Books

Giancana, Sam, *Family Affair: Treachery, Greed, and Betrayal in the Chicago Mafia*, 2010, Berkley Books.

Groden, Robert J., *The Search for Lee Harvey Oswald*, Viking Penguin, 1995

Haldeman, H.R., *The Ends of Power*, 1978, Times Books

Haslam, Edward T., *Dr. Mary's Monkey*, 2007, Skyhorse Publishers

Hill, Jean with Bill Sloan, *JFK: The Last Dissenting Witness*, 1992, Pelican Publishing

Hunt, E. Howard, *American Spy*, 2007, John Wiley & Sons

Hunt, E. Howard, *Compulsive Spy: The Strange Career of E. Howard Hunt*, 1974, Viking Press

Hunt, E. Howard, *Give Us This Day*, 1973, Arlington House

Janney, Peter, *Mary's Mosaic: The CIA Conspiracy to Murder John F. Kennedy, Mary Pinchot Meyer, and their Vision for World Peace*, 2012, Skyhorse Press

Kaiser, Robert Blair, *RFK Must Die: The Assassination of Robert Kennedy*, 2008, Overlook Press

Lane, Mark, *Last Word*, 2011, Skyhorse Press

Lane, Mark, *Plausible Denial*, 1991, Publisher's Group West

Lane, Mark, *Rush to Judgment*, 1966, Holt, Rinehardt and Winston

Lecke, Robert, *Okinawa: The Last Battle of WWII*, 1995, Penguin Group

Mailer, Norman, *Oswald's Tale: An American Mystery*, 2007, Random House Trade Paperbacks

Marrs, Jim, *Crossfire: The Plot that Killed Kennedy*, 1993, Basic Books

Marrs, Jim, *The Trillion Dollar Conspiracy: How The New World Order, Man-Made Diseases, and Zombie Banks are Destroying America*, 2010, Harper-Collins

McClellan, Barr, *Blood, Money, & Power: How LJB Killed JFK*, 2004, Hanover House

McCoy, Alfred, *The Politics of Heroin in Southeast Asia*, 1973, Harper & Row

McCoy, Alfred, *The Politics of Heroin: CIA Complicity in the Global Drug Trade*, 1991, Lawrence

Morrow, Robert D., *Betrayal*, 1976, Henry Regnery Company

Morrow, Robert D., *First Hand Knowledge: How I Participated in the CIA-Mafia Murder of JFK*, 1992, S.P.I. Books

Nelson, Philip F., *LBJ: The Mastermind of JFK's Assassination*, 2010, Skyhorse Publishing

O'Reilly, Bill, *Killing Kennedy: The End of Camelot*, 2012, Henry Holt & Co.

Pepper, William, *An Act of State: The Execution of MLK*, 2003, Verso Press

Pepper, William, *Orders To Kill: The Truth Behind the Murder of Martin Luther King*, 1995, Carroll & Graf, Inc.

Posner, Gerald, *Case Closed*, 2005, Anchor Press

Prouty, Colonel L. Fletcher, *JFK: The CIA, Vietnam, and The Plot to Assassinate John F. Kennedy*, 1992, Birch Lane Press Book, Carol Publishing Group

Rasenberger, Jim, *The Brilliant Disaster*, 2011, Scribner, sold by Simon and Schuster

Ray, John, *Truth at Last*, 2008, Lyon Press

Sheim, David, *Contract on America: The Mafia Murder of John F. Kennedy*, 1989, Zebra

Uschan, Michael V., *Watergate*, 2009, American History Series, Lucent Books

Waldren, Lamar, *Legacy of Secrecy*, 2009, Counterpoint

Waldren, *Ultimate Sacrifice*, 2005, Carroll & Graf

Wrone, David R., *The Zapruder Film*, 2003, University of Kansas Press.

Wyden, Peter, *The Bay of Pigs: The Untold Story*, 1979, Simon & Schuster

Yahara, Colonel Hiromichi, *Battle for Okinawa*, 1995, Pacific Basin Books, John Wiley & Sons

Zirbel, Craig, *The Texas Connection: The Assassination of John F. Kennedy*, 1991, The Texas Connection Publishers

Web Books

Alexander, Colonel Joseph H, USMC (Ret.) *The Final Campaign: Marines in the Victory on Okinawa*, www.ibiblio.org/hyperwar/USMC/USMC-C-Okinawa/index.html

Huber, Thomas M., *Japan's Battle Of Okinawa, April-June, 1945*, www. Leavenworth/ Papers, usacac.army.mil/cac2/cgsc/carl/csi/Huber/Huber.asp

Mullins, Eustace, *Secrets of the Federal Reserve*, 2011, www.org/apfn/reserve.htm

Nichols, Major Charles S., Jr. USMC, *Okinawa: Victory in the Pacific*, www. ibilio.org/hyperwar/usmc/-m-okinawa-fwd.html

Torbitt, William, *Nomenclature of an Assassination Cabal*, www. newsmakingnews.com/Torbitt.htm

Reference Works

Final Report of the Assassination Records Review Board, 1998

Final Report of the Select Committee on Assassinations of the United States House of Representatives, 1979,

Report of the Department of Justice Task Force to Review the FBI–Martin Luther King, Jr. Security and Assassination Investigations, 1977, United States Department of Justice

Report of the President's Commission on the Assassination of President Kennedy, (Warren Commission Report), 1964

Articles & Speeches

Eisenhower, Dwight D., *Farewell Address to the Nation*, January 17, 1961

Griffin, G. Edward, *Federal Reserve — The Enemy of America*

King, Martin Luther, Jr., *Beyond Vietnam*, April 4, 1967

King, Martin Luther, Jr., *I See the Promised Land* (aka Mountaintop), April 3, 1968

Lorenz, Alice, *Confidential Magazine, Fidel Castro Raped My Teenage Daughter*, May 1960

Orchard, William, *The Shots in Dealey Plaza: A Scenario of the shots in Dealey Plaza*, 2010, 2011 www.theshotsinDealeyplaza.com/?page_id=12; www.apfn. org/APFN/reserve2/htm

Internet Verification

Nearly every historical person, event, or subject mentioned here has been researched on Wikipedia, Spartacus Educational, New World Encyclopedia, and the Mary Farrell Foundation.

Videos

Howard Hunt's Last Confession, Youtube

Secret Service Standdown, Youtube.

Turner, Nigel, "The Men Who Killed Kennedy," History Channel